CASEBOOK SERIES

Three Contemporary Poets
Thom Gunn
Ted Hughes
&
R. S. Thomas

A CASEBOOK

EDITED BY

A. E. DYSON

M

MACMILLAN

First published 1990
Reprinted 1991

Published by
MACMILLAN EDUCATION LTD
Houndmills, Basingstoke, Hampshire RG21 2XS
and London
Companies and representatives
throughout the world

Typeset by Wessex Typesetters
(Division of The Eastern Press Ltd)
Frome, Somerset

Printed in Hong Kong

British Library Cataloguing in Publication Data
Three Contemporary poets: Thom Gunn, Ted Hughes & R. S.
Thomas: a casebook.
1. Poetry in English. Gunn. Thom, Hughes, Ted, 1930–, &
Thomas, R. S. (Ronald Stuart), 1913–, Critical Studies
I. Dyson, A. E. (Anthony Edward, *1928*–
821'.914'09

ISBN 0–333–31942–7
ISBN 0–333–31943–5 pbk

CONTENTS

Part Three   *R. S. Thomas*

System of Titling: here and in the Selection, exterior quotemarks are used for editorially devised captions. In other cases, the caption employs the original title of the writer's book, chapter or section of a book, article of essay (in some instances abbreviated from that), and it is displayed without exterior quotemarks.

GENERAL EDITOR'S PREFACE

The Casebook series, launched in 1968, has become a well-regarded library of critical studies. The central concern of the series remains the 'single-author' volume, but suggestions from the academic community have led to an extension of the original plan, to include occasional volumes on such general themes as literary 'schools' and genres.

Each volume in the central category deals either with one well-known and influential work by an individual author, or with closely related works by one writer. The main section consists of critical readings, mostly modern, collected from books and journals. A selection of reviews and comments from the author himself. The Editor's Introduction charts the reputation of the work or works from the first appearance to the present time.

Volumes in the 'general themes' category are variable in structure but follow the basic purpose of the series in presenting an integrated selection of readings, with an Introduction which explores the theme and discusses the literary and critical issues involved.

A single volume can represent no more than a small selection of critical opinions. Some critics are excluded for reasons of space, and it is hoped that readers will pursue the suggestions for further reading in the Select Bibliography. Other contributions are severed from their original context, to which some readers may wish to turn. Indeed, if they take a hint from the critics represented here, they certainly will.

A. E. DYSON

INTRODUCTION

The generations of poetry in our time seem to cover a span of about twenty years. I do not mean that the best work of any poet is limited to twenty years: I mean that it is about that length of time before a new style of poetry appears. By the time, that is to say, that a man is fifty, he has behind him a kind of poetry written by men of seventy, and before him a kind written by men of thirty. That is my position at present, and if I live another twenty years I shall expect to see another younger school of poetry.

(From: T. S. Eliot: 'Yeats', a lecture delivered in 1940)

Fortunately, Eliot's essay improves, when he reaches Yeats. These opening generalisations, male-centred, vague ('style', 'kind', 'school'), and based on Europe in the past few centuries, seem handmade to offend virtually anyone who reads them today.

When I was young, they were in the air, and deterred many would-be poets. The lack of A. N. Other's *Collected Poems*, or one slender volume even, could be laid at their door.

Still: such notions did not deter real poets, and were never likely to, however fiercely their champions raged. While F. R. Leavis struck me (for instance) as 'the ogre of Downing', a view I still hold to, Thom Gunn has a different story to tell:

I went to lectures of F. R. Leavis, then in his prime, whose emphasis on the 'realised' in imagery and on the way in which verse movement is an essential part of the poet's exploration were all-important to me.

(Thom Gunn: 'My Life Up To Now', 1977)

To cap this, Gunn chose next to study under Yvor Winters – the one critic who makes Leavis look indulgently soft. This time, he took what he could, but fed on Elvis's songs, James Dean's and Marlon Brando's films also, and backed off Winters, when the astringency was felt as a threat:

Back at Stanford Winters encouraged me to attend his workshops regularly, but I went to them less and less, from something of an instinct for self-preservation. . . . (*Ibid.*)

Even so: one of Gunn's finest early poems is 'To Yvor Winters, 1955' (*The Sense of Movement*, 1957), and is not to be missed by admirers of either man, or of both. Gunn pays homage of course to a fellow poet, and to a man he admired for heroic qualities in his life. The whole poem is too long to quote here, but the final lines seem appropriate to all three poets yoked together in this Casebook, so here they are:*

> You keep both Rule and Energy in view,
> Much power in each, most in the balanced two:
> Ferocity existing in the fence
> Built by an exercised intelligence.
> Though night is always close, complete negation
> Ready to drop on wisdom and emotion,
> Night from the air or the carnivorous breath,
> Still it is right to know the force of death,
> And, as you do, persistent, tough in will,
> Raise from the excellent the better still.

Well. Today we encourage creativity, which is excellent; it can be a formative, exploratory, healing part of many young lives. My one caveat is that 'creativity' is not art *per se* and should not be confused with art, however valid its content, deep its emotion, or honest its thought. Far more is needed before genuine creativity becomes also poetry for the mainstream: mastery of language (a tough battle; no easy victories; no let-up ever): more, the rare power to fuse thought and emotion in image and symbol; which, in turn, release power both precise and memorable in sensitive minds.

And, since we need great art for our general social healing and richness and for human civility, critics like Leavis and Winters still have their rightful place, in the literary arc. As R. S. Thomas puts it:

> Ah, but a rare bird is
> rare. It is when one is not looking
> at times one is not there
>   that it comes.
> you must wear your eyes out,
> as others their knees . . .
>   ('Sea-Watching', *Laboratories of the Spirit*, 1975)

If an ideal critic keeps a generous spirit towards young writers new to creation, doing all he can to encourage them, he must also sea-watch with Thomas. This is his long, testing rôle, the rule of his own art; the only possible *raison d'être* for a life's chosen career.

It so happens that when Brian Cox and myself started *Critical Quarterly* in 1959, four British poets of note were first making their mark. We had the good fortune to publish new work by all of them –

---

* For Yvor Winters' brief comment on Gunn's early poems, see p. 23 below.

R. S. Thomas, Philip Larkin, Thom Gunn, Ted Hughes – along with poems by that extraordinary American genius, Sylvia Plath, who also emerged then. So Eliot's expectations for a new crop of poets twenty years on proved fruitful for us; even though, *pace* 'The Movement', they did not come in the guise of a 'style', or a 'kind', or a 'school'. *Critical Quarterly* had the great good fortune to put poetry first, criticism second on its agenda, as the 60s dawned.

When I planned this Casebook, I wanted to include Larkin with the others; but the word-count defeated me. As material piled up inexorably, one poet had to be excluded. So the choice fell to the three who personally mean most to me. Their work has been part of my life for thirty years, and by now, it seems part of myself. They pass the one lasting test I know for art. They belong with the composers and writers, past and present, whose sounds haunt my mind; shape my sense of the real.

Have Gunn, Hughes and Thomas much in common? Not on the face of it; but then major writers seldom do, from their own view of things. Donne would be amazed to know he is a 'metaphysical'; particularly, since his putative 'school' had mostly still to grow beyond childhood at the time when he died. Wordsworth and Coleridge were friends, and interacted as poets; but how come they in one boat with Blake, Byron, Keats, Shelley (and how many more?). The word 'romantic' has a fatal lure, and does less harm than most labels: but only because it means so many, often opposite, things. Luckily, most readers still feel akin to some or most of these poets; and the word 'romantic' still, on the whole, sounds good.

No one word applies to my three poets here, though I will risk 'symbolist'. Their work is all to a high degree resonant like (say) Berlioz and Mahler; and 'symbolist' is the word that sounds good to *me*. Further, they are all 'elemental' poets, and all distinctively 'modern': best reach, at this point, for 'Burnt Norton', to replace labels with art:

> Footfalls echo in the memory
> Down the passage which we did not take
> Towards the door we never opened
> Into the rose-garden. My words echo
> Thus, in your mind.
> But to what purpose,
> Disturbing the dust on a bowl of rose-leaves,
> I do not know . . .

Now (to shift ground, slightly): they are all loners, by lifestyle and temperament, steering well clear of London (in Gunn's case, literary London only); avoiding literary cliques, or disciples, like the plague. Ted Hughes is a Yorkshireman, now farming in Devon; R. S. Thomas is a Welshman, most at home on the Lleyn Peninsula or on Bardsey Isle. Gunn is an urban poet, a lover of New York, London (but for their cosmopolitan boisterousness, their anonymity, their nightside incipience) and at home now in San Francisco (the unfashionable side).

More: they are prophets, men on the sidelines of their century by choice but in touch with its centre. In the future – if there is one – their poems will belong with the music of Britten and Shostakovich, for anyone wanting the 'feel' of the third quarter of the twentieth century and the ambiance surrounding it (our major changes in 1945; then 1979, I would think). To open out from here, slightly: they will belong with Tennyson, Blake, Pope, Shakespeare for those seeking the 'inside' of a period. Maybe, this quest is an illusion; maybe, men will give up the effort. But for those who still try it, whatever the problems, it is artists like these who will offer the entrée beyond all other data – whether journals, Memoirs, Diaries, even snapshots and films.

The differences between Gunn, Hughes and Thomas are more important than the links, to the men themselves certainly: if, that is, one omits the major link, which is poetry itself.

Because so much has been written on them already, and they are still happily with us, I have not offered the usual division of 'first reviews' and 'general critical debate'. Instead, the material for this Casebook is taken from the earliest serious criticism to about 1980 – the period when their stature emerged to the full, and each had a substantial body of published work. I also excuse myself the usual editorial comments in this Introduction, since these are placed in the text, where they better belong. My piece on Hughes was a review of *Hawk In The Rain*, his first major volume, and is therefore the earliest (1959). The R. S. Thomas section is extracted from *Yeats, Eliot and R. S. Thomas: Riding The Echo* (1981), choosing material which I hope best supplements the other critics here. The Thom Gunn piece results from a haunting through the 80s by all Gunn's poetry, and by *The Passages of Joy* (1982) most of all. It is, therefore, recent; finished at midsummer 1989, with this volume in mind.

A. E. DYSON

PART ONE

Thom Gunn

1. GUNN ON HIMSELF AND POETRY

. . . Obsession is another name for passion, perhaps. But you do have to be obsessed about something to write well about it. I'm often asked about the genesis of poems, and my answer is that I might begin just with an idea, really rather a general one – it might even be a concept, but you don't just sit down and write about a concept unless you're in the eighteenth century. The thing you want to write about – whether a specific scene, incident or idea – gestates, and the process of writing becomes an exploration. You discover things about yourself and about your insight into your subject matter that you often didn't guess at. The surprises that occur on the way are often the most exciting things about writing. Sometimes when a poem is going flat I realise it's because the poem has become an exposition of my original idea and no more. It is the discoveries that make the poem. I agree to that extent with writers like Robert Duncan who believe so much in the improvisation of the moment. But my point is that the subject of a poem can only gestate if you are obsessed by it in the first place. . . .

Reading Donne . . . at about the age of 21 . . . was a tremendous explosion for me, and I think a lot of . . . *Fighting Terms* [1954; revised 1958] shows it. There are certainly worse influences, and I don't regret it: in fact I learned everything from it. I think one thing Donne taught me was what Frank Kermode calls the relationship between Image and Discourse, and to be able to accept discourse as a proper part of the poem in the twentieth century, as opposed to those (both in England and in America) who thought that poetry was entirely image. . . . Right now so much of the young American poetry seems to be enormously influenced by Robert Bly. I think Bly was a very fresh and vital influence at first, but now I see so many young poets publishing books of Bly-influenced surrealistic imagery and little else. Like Sylvia Plath, Bly has had an influence that has been the origin of an awful lot of bad poetry. . . . I'm slightly bored with poets' personalities. Berryman is an exception in that he has an interesting personality. Quite frankly I get bored by, let's say, Anne Sexton's personality, though she was far from untalented. . . . I remember one of her poems which treats a visit to the dentist as a major tragedy. . . .

The process of becoming a better artist lies in opening up more and more areas that you can speak about. One of the limitations of my first books is that I had been reading so much Shakespeare, Donne and Stendhal, and I was writing about the heroic. I wasn't able to bring in too much of my experience because so little of it fitted in with this vague idea of the heroic. I remember G. S. Fraser, in an otherwise very nice review, said that one thing Thom Gunn lacks is a sense of humour, and indeed I wasn't able to bring humour into poems until quite a bit later. The breakthroughs in my poetry have all been into new areas, new kinds of experiences. . . .

A poem I've loved since I first read it is Williams's 'Spring and All', and what's so terrific is the way it simply consists of description, and yet it is making statements about what it is like to be born. . . . Getting outside oneself was one of the things I learned from Williams, who's been very important to me for a long time. . . . I think of myself as a writer about experience modified by ideas; those ideas in turn are modified by experience, and so on endlessly. . . . A poem is obviously an artefact, but it's also part of my experience of living. Poetry is an action, one of many different kinds of action such as taking a walk, eating a meal, or making love. When I first started writing I would have emphasised the idea of poem as artefact. . . .

'Confessions of a Life Artist' in . . . *Touch* [1967] . . . is perhaps one of the last of my self-conscious poems. The man is a Life Artist in that he thinks he can control his life like a work of art. He's not me, he's somebody who's got fucked up by his consciousness. Everything is rather too perfectly as he'd intended it to be, but at the same time, he's missed out. I suppose, now I think about it, it's a little like Henry James's 'The Beast in the Jungle'. . . . I was aiming for something like that. At the end he realises that what he's missed is nothing tangible. In a sense, that fictional character is one side of any human being. As a pimp he possesses all these beautiful girls, he possesses them but he can never be them. . . . I find that ex-Catholics have far more feeling against their religion than those who have given up other faiths. I'm just glad I didn't have that additional confusion on top of all my other confusions when I was growing up. I suppose that makes me rather an unspiritual person. I'm not a dogmatic materialist, I'm aware that there are many possible communications in existence that I don't know about. In fact it often strikes me that just as animals are colour-blind we may be blind to other sense. I'm just grateful that I wasn't brought up with any dogma. It does seem possible that there might be some kind of life after death. James Merrill's recent work, which is about séances, is extraordinarily interesting. Merrill says quite honestly that he doesn't know whether it is all self-projection, but even if it's complete delusion *Mirabel* is still a wonderful book to read. . . .

Moly [1971] . . . is my favourite book by myself, partly because it's the neglected child. I also think that there I extended my range a great deal and I'm not sure I've got very far beyond it yet. It's a phase of my writing that I'm probably still in. Not that it is only about drugs. Poems like 'From the Wave' were in some way answering an earlier poem like 'On the Move', and I hope a poem like 'Being Born' can be understood purely in metaphorical terms. The theme of the book as a whole, if you like to speak in those terms, is of metamorphosis, as in the second poem, where the man is actually being turned into a pig. Taking LSD and writing *Moly* was an answer to the tentativeness of *Touch*. . . .

During the most exalted days of taking LSD I remember thinking that it's different from Christian's experience in *Pilgrim's Progress* in that while Christian drops his burden of sin I think we don't drop our burden. I don't call it sin, I just call it past experience. You carry the burden of everything you know on your back: it's a very interesting burden. I don't regret it, I like it. I don't want to drop it into the river that comes before the Heavenly City. . . . It's all past experience, sensual joys, mistakes, everything. I think that just as in 'The Idea of Trust' – as somebody pointed out to me last night – it could be seen that I understand the character Jim's predicament so well that I sympathise with him . . . that's how I like the whole book [*Jack Straw's Castle* – Ed.] to be taken, as facing both ways. What I want to get across is that one can learn from the ecstasy just as well as one can learn from the mistakes and unhappiness. They modify each other. . . . The poem called 'Yoko' is about a colossal Newfoundland dog owned by a friend of mine in New York. I wanted to write a poem that is completely doggy, since so many poems about animals – by Lawrence, Marianne Moore or Ted Hughes – are marvellous, but the subjects are dealt with from a

human point of view. There's a wonderful line in Hughes's 'Pike' –
'stunned by his own grandeur' – but it's not really true. I don't
criticise that kind of poem for a moment, but I wanted to write a
poem that is all dog. Then I read Gertrude Stein's *Three Lives* and I
found the enthusiastic but naive voice I could use, and I was
delighted that I could even find a Jamesian phrase at one point
when the dog is sniffing a turd – 'I can place it finely' – but of
course James was one of Gertrude Stein's masters. Once I'd got the
key I enjoyed writing the poem. . . .

[In answer to a question about his being so long yoked, in the
public mind, with Ted Hughes – Ed.] . . . Yes, and we have almost
nothing in common. I find myself working on my own. I was
reading a book of short stories by Scott Fitzgerald the other day –
Taps at Reveille – and I realised that he and I have something like
the same strategies in common. He's a big old romantic, and you
can tell from his first books just how awful and slushy that
romanticism could be, but then he suddenly became more artistic
and aware. Like Stendhal, as he gets older he gets more intelligent,
but his intelligence doesn't destroy the romantic figures; it abets
them; it helps them to come alive. . . . Fitzgerald's terrific at
describing the wonderful girls and he comes to life in a way that
you can't deny them, but he's retaining his irony and criticism.
The irony, as with Stendhal, doesn't undercut the romanticism, it
actually reinforces it, and I think this is what I've been doing
throughout. I've had my romantic notions, which have varied
somewhat, but I've been trying to make them intelligible and to
bring them to life other than by simply celebrating them in a kind
of dumb way. I am romantic, and I try to make the object of my
romanticism credible. It's romantic subject matter rather than
romantic techniques.

I'm trying to make what might often seem to be untenable
emotions or unadmirable subjects – feelings which I find attractive –
credible. In a poem such as 'On the Move' I'm treating a subject
which at that time I found heroic in my own terms, since that kind
of heroism is my early subject. That's the way I see myself as
Fitzgerald, so there's a kinship. I learned an awful lot from
associating as a friend with Robert Duncan, who taught me a great
deal without knowing it. . . . But no . . . I don't know anybody

who's trying to do the kind of thing I'm trying to do most of the time. . . .

Source: extracts from 'Experience and Ideas: An Interview with Thom Gunn' conducted by John Haffenden, first published in *Quarto* (July 1980), edited by Craig Raine and Richard Boston; reproduced in Haffenden's *Interviews with Poets* (London, 1981). The interview took place early in 1980 in a basement flat in Hampstead which Gunn had occupied for some years during his teens.

II   A Comment   (1979)

. . . I do not either like or dislike myself inordinately. I have just had *Jack Straw's Castle and Other Poems* published. I cannot guess what my next book will be like.

Source: conclusion of 'My Life up to Now', an autobiographical piece written for Jack W. C. Sagstrom and George Bixby, *Thom Gunn: A Bibliography, 1940–1978* (London, 1979); reproduced in Gunn's *The Occasions of Poetry: Essays in Criticism and Autobiography* (London, 1982).

2. CRITICAL STUDIES

G. S. Fraser   On the Move   (1961)

. . . His are poems without a Muse, or the Muse rather is a male Muse, village Edmunds, warriors in byrnies, black-jacketed James Dean characters roaring through small American towns on motor-cycles. But a fine intellectual discipline can make something universal out of this, as it might seem in itself, somewhat dubious material.

Let me take, as an example of what seems to me a very notable success on Gunn's part, the first poem in his 1957 volume, *The Sense of Movement*. This is called 'On the Move', and these young men on motor-cycles are vividly the topic but, savingly in the end, not the theme of the poem. The theme, rather, is Sartrean existential humanism. I want to examine in turn the last three lines of each of the five eight-line stanzas. In these last three lines, in each stanza, Gunn presses from particulars towards a persuasive generality, which becomes progressively more firmly defined; he presses towards the stating of a moral. In the first stanza, the poet vividly observes birds on the edge of a dusty American road, birds which 'follow some hidden purpose', while the poet himself is vainly 'seeking their instinct, or their poise, or both'. He sums it up:

> One moves with an uncertain violence
> Under the dust thrown by a baffled sense
> Or the dull thunder of approximate words.

'Baffled sense' is not there, or only partly, what it might be in Keats, sensuous apprehension baffled by trying to reach beyond itself, but baffled intellectual apprehension; the baffled sense of what it is all about.

In the second stanza, the boys on motor-cycles, anticipated already in the first stanza in the dust and the scariness of the birds, roar by. And we are told of them in the last three lines:

> In gleaming jackets trophied with the dust,
> They strap in doubt – by hiding it, robust –
> And almost hear a meaning in their noise.

The baffling dust here becomes a trophy, a prize, of pointless speed; and the noise of the motor-cycles (in communication theory *noise* is contrasted with *sound*, and means any interference with the transmission of the message) becomes paradoxically for them a kind of communication. Very often in Gunn apparently simple and ordinary words like 'meaning' and 'noise' can, in their juxtaposition, carry in this way a lucid paradox.

In the third stanza, Gunn points out that the motor-cyclists are not riding towards any known goal but as fast as possible away from a known and frustrating background. It is they who scare the birds across the fields but it is inevitable that even a right natural order should yield to even a subrational human will. And there is this to be said for the motor-cyclists, that they are emblems of a larger human condition:

> Men manufacture both machine and soul,
> And use what they imperfectly control
> To dare a future from the taken routes.

The idea behind these admirably compact lines is Sartre's that man creates himself, creates his 'soul', by arbitrary but important choices. His choices cannot be made in complete foreknowledge of their consequences ('use what they imperfectly control'). But what is even more worrying is that the *general* consequences of all possible choices might be thought to be boringly worked out already. This abstract philosophical idea is beautifully translated into properly poetic language. The 'taken' routes are at once the routes daringly taken, or undertaken, by the young motor-cyclists to create a future and they are also the routes, the roads there on the map, which would not be there at all if they had not been 'taken' dully by generations of men already. Again, very plain, apparently obvious words produce a paradox.

The fourth stanza justifies the choice of the motor-cyclists as at least a partial solution of the human problem. Man is not necessarily at odds with the world because he is not purely an animal. Nor is he damned because, half but only half an animal, he has to rely not on 'direct instinct' but on movements – say, movements of history or politics – which carry him on part of the way, even though in the end movement 'divides and breaks':

> One joins the movement in a valueless world,
> Choosing it, till, both hurler and the hurled,
> One moves as well, always toward, toward.

What one moves 'toward' is not to be abstractly defined, but one is moving away from that which one has found valueless (but there is also the Sartrean idea that value is imposed by choice, not there in the world to compel choice). One may be moving towards value.

   In the fifth and last stanza, the cyclists vanished, the 'self-defined, astride the created will'. (Again notice how a philosophical concept is beautifully translated into a poetical conceit, the 'manufactured' soul finding its emblem, or symbol, in the 'manufactured' motorcycle.) The cyclists are right, for Gunn, to burst through and away from towns which are no homes either for the naturalness of birds or the stillness of saints who, like birds, 'complete their purposes'. The justification of these 'rebels without a cause' is that our civilised world, the world, say, which Larkin sadly accepts, has in its frustrating complication no home for either naturalness or holiness. And when one is, however restlessly and violently, 'on the move',

> At worst one is in motion; and at best,
> Reaching no absolute, in which to rest,
> One is always nearer by not keeping still.

Gunn is not in any ordinary sense of the word a religious poet, but he is (both in the ordinary and to some degree in the literary sense of the word) a metaphysical poet. The kinds of metaphysics that interest him are very different from those that interest Eliot, . . . yet there are obvious broad affinities between the pattern of argument in this poem and some of the patterns of argument in *Four Quartets*.

   I have thought it better . . . to examine what one might call the broad human interest of Gunn's poetry, taking . . . sample poems as pegs to drape my exposition round, rather than to . . . re-review his volumes in detail, or to go in detail into the verbal texture of his work. Swiftness, directness, lucidity, beautifully exact dramatic or logical construction in a poem, mark his work much more than richness of imagery or any sort of lyrical cry; the kind of technical-appreciative words one would use about his verse are supple, muscular, 'on the move'. But his deep authenticity comes from range of curiosity, an undefeatedness of spirit, and a swift readiness to make choices, without any hesitant bother about how the choices will be socially taken. If Larkin is a fine poet born, in a sense, middle-aged, Gunn is a poet who should have a peculiarly direct appeal not for angry, but for fierce, young men.

SOURCE: extract from 'On the Move', article in *Critical Quarterly*, 3, no. 4 (1961), pp. 364–6.

Yvor Winters   Early Gunn   (1967)

. . . The number of interesting poems [from *The Sense of Movement* and *My Sad Captains*] is too large for a list here; I will name only a few: 'Autumn Chapter in a Novel', 'The Corridor', 'Vox Humana', 'In Santa Maria del Popolo', 'The Annihilation of Nothing', 'From the Highest Camp'. The best of these is probably 'In Santa Maria del Popolo'. . . . The poem is remarkably vigorous; it is far better than anything by half-a-dozen poets of this century who are commonly called great. The fragmentary but vivid description of Saul beneath the horse, and the rhetorical effectiveness of the explanation in line 12 and four lines following; the unpleasant or pathetic people in the third and fourth stanzas – these things are effective. The command of grammar and syntax is admirable; the rhythm is vigorous without being very subtle. . . . But like Donne at his best, Gunn seems merely to make his peace with the metre; the metre is not a medium in which he lives. . . . [It] is a distinguished poem, and misses being a great poem by very little. Like many of Gunn's poems, it exists on the narrow line between great writing and skilful journalism. . . .

SOURCE: extracts from section on 'Early Gunn' in *Forms of Discovery* (Denver, Colorado, 1967), pp. 344–5

Martin Dodsworth   Poetry as Action and Submission   (1970)

. . . Like Byron, Gunn thinks of the poet as *one who acts*; he does not think like a philosopher, because his thoughts take the form of action, of a doing something – they are immediately expressed as deeds. To be sure, these deeds are of a special kind; they are poems. They differ from the poems of other men in this way: the reader feels that in writing them the poet has committed himself to what he has to say in such a manner that he is irrevocably changed by it. The poem is an action, because it represents an attempt to form or to transform the poet's identity.

'He writes as habitually as others talk or think – and whether we have the inspiration of the Muse or not, we always find the spirit of the man of genius breathing from his verse.' Hazlitt's description of Byron is useful to us not in its emphasis on the *habitual* nature of his writing verse, but in the suggestion that it was a natural activity, like talking or thinking, only secondarily self-expressive. It is for this reason, one supposes, that the author's spirit is displayed whether his poem succeeds or not – something that is certainly true of Gunn too, although, like Byron again, he is often shamelessly imitative in style. Both poets exercise over us a command of personality, a force which Hazlitt describes as 'genius'. We would not; we have misgivings about that word which are surely justified. Yet Gunn's poetry, by contrast with Byron's, reminds us that poetry can usefully serve to realise for us the idea of a character made strong by the candour with which its conditions of life are regarded. Byron's adversities are largely self-willed, and strike us as though he had in the first place brought them into being, yet is now only half-conscious of the fact; Gunn's really do exist, not only for him, but for all of us, though we are not necessarily continuously aware of them. This marks a very large difference between the two poets. What we feel to be a fine phrase when applied to Byron – 'he grapples with his subject, moves, penetrates and animates it with the electric force of his own feelings' – is seen simply to be true when applied to Gunn. In the one case, the active imagination drove Byron further and further into a world of animated fantasy; on the other, it has brought Gunn further and further into the world of all of us, where there really are substantial powers to be grappled with.

Like Byron and unlike: of course. Any account of Gunn's work must deal with the movement away from fantasy in his verse which distinguishes him so clearly from the author of *Childe Harold* or *Don Juan*. Nevertheless, it seems good to begin with an account of the personality felt to underlie all the poems, that is, with the part of Gunn which we may imagine to have set his poetry in one direction

rather than another, and to have made of his poems more than
receptacles of thought – to have made them that kind of poetic act
of which a description has already been attempted. The conviction
is strong that the valuable quality in Gunn's work lies in the *whole*
of it rather than in those moments of success that we often believe it
is a critic's first duty to sort out. A good deal of Gunn's excellence,
that is, has to do with his general aim in writing poetry, and this
quality, whilst not blinding us to his defects, can lead us to see merit
in those very defects. . . .

. . . in and through most of Gunn's poems a change of some kind
takes place . . . we will find it . . . in a poem like 'Touch', one of
Gunn's more recent poems. It is about getting into bed in the dark,
where a lover is already lying in the warm, about the thawing-out
of the body and consciousness in the embrace of the sleeping lover,
and, finally, about the commitment of our own natures that seems
to be inextricably involved in our experience of love. Here are the
last lines of the poem:

> What I, now loosened,
> sink into is an old
> big place, it is
> there already, for
> you are already
> there, and the cat
> got there before you, yet
> it is hard to locate.
> What is more, the place is
> not found but seeps
> from our touch in
> continuous creation, dark
> enclosing cocoon round
> ourselves alone, dark
> wide realm where we
> walk with everyone.

This is very hard kind of verse for someone to grasp who has been
brought up to think largely in terms of fixed metrical feet. Here
there is nothing fixed; on the contrary, everything flows. The lines
are irregular, but they may have one thing in common, that each
one leads into the next, either from a verb to its complement, or
from a subject to its predicate, from an adjective to its noun or from
a conjunction to the clause it introduces. The full stop in the middle
of the passage is only a pause, and is immediately seen to be so,
since the next line begins by emphasising its own continuity: 'What

is more . . .' The shortness of the lines plays its part in working on us, too; it makes it difficult for a rhythmical norm to be set up, so that the reader's efforts to discern or to impose an order of some conventional kind are defeated. He is compelled to read the lines in a groping way, uncertain where the emphasis may fall as each sentence develops, and given no hints by the arrangement of the lines themselves. Their continuity is hesitant, the continuity of exploration and discovery.

Gunn takes advantage of this at the very end of the poem, where he allows new meanings to explode on us in a process of 'continuous creation'. The 'dark / enclosing cocoon' changes to a 'dark / *wide* realm', from the exclusiveness of 'ourselves alone' to the inclusiveness of walking 'with everyone'. The change is a change in consciousness, from one way of looking at 'the place' to another; there is a suggestion that what we have in common with each other is our very aloneness. But that is represented not as an 'enclosing', imprisoning condition, but as one in which we may walk – that is, one which permits us continuing free action.

It is consistent with this poet's emphasis on *doing* that there is a subdued and unostentatious quality about the language of 'Touch'. This may at first seem surprising; we might expect the verbal equivalent of action to lie in the field of the extraordinary, to constitute a verbal assault on the sensibility. There is no such attack in 'Touch'; instead, the minimum of artifice required to make a complete and expressive statement is used. One cannot say that the poem uses entirely the speech of common life, but when it deviates from that language it is to make emphases that are at least not in conflict with the view that poetry should be subservient to the common life. In language and syntax, the poem seeks to persuade us that life can be lived as a process of 'continuous creation', and that the process can be as simple and natural as walking. Its persuasiveness is not that of logic but that of experience; the poem is persuasive if at all by its own nature, and not by the cogency of what is said. It wants to work on us directly and immediately, by contact – to induce in us the sense of being 'in touch' in the metaphorical sense underlying the whole poem.

'Touch', is a poem that acts on us, but it does not do so by means of verbal aggression . . . . The poem's own movement is a seeping from line to line, which we must follow in a careful, groping movement of the mind. In a sense we are *seduced* by the poem, which acts by refusing us a point of rest until we have reached its end. Its beginning is designedly simple, so as to make one ask what the point of it is at all. If one is in the slightest interested (and of course the poet risks that one will not be) then one is held. It is difficult to *stop* reading (or quoting):

> You are already
> asleep. I lower
> myself in next to
> you, my skin slightly
> numb with the restraint
> of habits . . .

And so on. There is no obscurity to repel one: only a continuous creation of suspense in the passage from one line to another, a sufficient stimulus to curiosity to reach the end, and, all the way through, an evocation of the sort of situation which is or will be part of the life of almost all of us. Like touch, it seduces us into an awareness of what it is we share with everyone – what we all have in common.

As the 'patina of self' gives way to consciousness of the other person's living, physical presence, so the speaker's world opens up to include the domain of others. It has already been suggested that this is a characteristic move in Gunn's poetry, particularly in the books succeeding *The Sense of Movement* [1957]. It is worth drawing attention to the fact also that here, as in many other poems, 'real' life is imagined as a place. Gunn does not evoke an *object* like the bird in Yeats's 'Byzantium', nor is his place enclosed, as Eliot's rose-garden; it is wide open, a place for infinite meetings. (It cannot be said that Yeats's Byzantium gives us that sense either.)

Consequently, the 'real' world into which the poem opens, to which it leads us, is notably unspecific. It evades precise definition. It 'seeps from our touch'; one might almost say that it flies from our touch, that because it exists only in immediate experience it cannot be defined; we are only aware of it when it *has been*. The same mysterious quality is implied in the phrase 'continuous creation'; to be continuous, creation can never be complete, and so, in a sense, is never properly creation. The paradox is familiar, but the form of Gunn's poem realises it afresh for us. And this is his task: to help us realise our lives, and our worlds, as giving us space in which to encounter imaginatively, among others, the poet himself. It is a task performed by his making the poem the act by which he himself realises the world as a place of shared possibilities.

The same movement and the same paradox appear, for example, in 'The Goddess', in which a life-force is imagined travelling upward from the earth's centre to men and women:

> Goddess,
> Proserpina: it is we,
> vulnerable, quivering,
> who stay you to abundance.

The force is *stayed* by us, but *abundance* gives the lie to this temporary halt. We *stay* her, because both *we* and *she abound*, and so exist in a relationship never truly halted. (It is a pity that this poem is spoilt by what I feel to be a dreadful wrong note – the line 'her dress tight across her ass', which just does not fit in with the language of the rest.)

'Flying Above California', from an earlier volume (*My Sad Captains*) depends on this kind of contradiction too. It is a poem about the 'richness' of the Californian landscape, a richness which includes the 'cold hard light' of fogless days, 'that reveals merely what is'.

> That limiting candour,

> that accuracy of the beaches,
> is part of the ultimate richness.

To see the point of the poem you have to feel a conflict between *limiting* and *richness*. *Ultimate richness* should be a richness without limit: here, the limit, which should mark the outward bound of a thing, is mysteriously included inside the thing itself, and is *part* of the ultimate richness. It is as though Gunn were saying that he knew there were things that we called limits and that we respected as such, but that ultimately, though real and existent, they ceased to count. We experience the circular and limited world as limitless (particularly, of course, when flying above it). . . .

The relevance of existentialist thought to an understanding of Gunn's poetry has often enough been remarked on – by John Mander, for example, in his interesting essay on the poet in *The Writer and Commitment*. The positive influence on Gunn is best illustrated by 'The Corridor' in *The Sense of Movement* which depends directly on a passage in Sartre's *L'Etre et le Néant* (the section on 'le regard'). Existentialist theory is obviously relevant to the subject-matter of 'Flying Above California' and 'In the Tank'. The poems present contrary points of view, the physical situation (plane, cell) figuring as a metaphor for the mental. The question is: how is the transition made from one point of view to another? The answer would seem to lie in the realm of the act of faith, the existentialist leap, another version of the 'quick illogical motions' which proved to be beyond the reach of Merlin in the cave.

In existentialist philosophy the idea of personal freedom figures largely. It is felt to be implicit in the self's ability to project itself in time and to be conscious of its own potentiality. Emmanuel Mounier in his *Introduction aux Existentialismes* puts the matter in this way:

. . . the human existent is always more than what he is (at a given moment), although he may not yet be what he will become. He is, according to Sartre, the 'being who is not what he is, and who is what he is not'. This conception of existence as forward-looking is opposed by Heidegger to inertia, to the totally determined nature of classical *existentia*, of substance, or at least of the degraded image which is often offered in its place.[1]

The quotation is useful to us, incidentally, because it points to another influence than that of Yeats at work in 'Jesus and his Mother', but it is here principally because it introduces an important pair of contraries, Heidegger's inertia and the projection into possibility which is its complement. The prisoner of 'In the Tank' could well exemplify inertia, just as the air-traveller of 'Flying Above California' could be said to look at the world from a point of view of projection.

There seems to be an ambiguity in existentialist thought about the extent to which the self's consciousness of its own potentiality or freedom is voluntary or not. On the one hand, human conscious-ness may be viewed as determined by the polarity of inertia and its opposite, and in this case the sense of freedom seems to be something more or less involuntary, something inherent in the human situation; on the other, since the consciousness of potentiality is actually threatened by the dead weight of inertia, it would seem necessary that it be kept alive by an effort of the will. This ambiguity is present in the idea of *risk* which crops up frequently in existentialist thought. A risk involves calculation and choice, the assent of the will, and also a submission to its consequences which must overrule the will. Mounier here describes Kierkegaard's notion of risk, but much the same sort of thing is to be found in other thinkers in this tradition. Man is free, rises above inertia, in the act of risking to choose:

The constitution of a man made in order that he should choose can only be that of a being who takes *risks*. Am I sure, you say, when I engage in such and such a course of action, that such and such a reward in eternity, or even in history, awaits me? If you were sure, replies Kierkegaard, you would not be exactly engaged in an action of an eternal order, you would be making a profitable speculation.[2]

The essence of a risk is that it is a voluntary commitment to the irrational.

Gunn's poetry is centred on the irrational. In his early work there is an emphasis on the will and consequently on the act of choosing risk, like the motor-cyclists in 'On the Move'; this gives way to the less intimidating view that the world of freedom and possibility remains in a sense perpetually available, with a consequent reduction of anguish. Although life is still most fully lived at moments only, it does not lapse into the kind of non-being posited by such a poem as 'Wind in the Street': 'The same faces, and then the same scandals . . .' Now, life outside the moments of fullness is sustained by a faith in the availability of that fullness.

Faith is not certainty, is not rational. The leap from the imprisoning self is a mysterious and irrational act, like the one by which the central character of 'Misanthropos' rejoins the world of others. He has believed himself the sole survivor of some universal catastrophe for some long period of time, until a party of other survivors appears. He hides: but when one of the others is scratched by a briar and bleeds:

> he performs an action next
> So unconsidered that he is perplexed,
> Even in performing it, by what it means –
> He walks around to where the creature leans.

The risk is not consciously taken, as it would have been by the speaker of almost any poem in *The Sense of Movement*. Gunn's existentialism now draws on the view of life as *necessarily* (that is, *naturally*) dependent on the polarity between inertia and choice, the leap out into the world where possibilities are realised.

The poetry of *Fighting Terms* and *The Sense of Movement* is just as irrational in principle as the rest. A poem like 'Lazarus Not Raised' is set out in an ostentatiously lucid manner; it is orderly, but what it describes is nevertheless mysterious and impervious to reason. This seems the expressive function of what would otherwise be an unnecessary complication in the following lines: the repetition of the

word *rest* at so close an interval with opposite meanings which all
the same coincide is quite as puzzling as the decision by Lazarus
not to be raised:

> He chose to spend his thoughts like this at first
> And disregard the nag of offered grace,
> Then chose to spend the rest of them in rest.

As Gunn rewrites the Bible story, Lazarus so perfectly exemplifies
the force of inertia that he is not even raised from the grave in order
to return to it. Although he is said by the poet to choose, he is not
seen to choose on a rational basis. The *rest* of his thoughts are spent
in *rest*: they seem to exemplify a natural, necessary and inexplicable
relationship to inertia, which is in ironic contrast to the orderly form
of verse used throughout the book in which the poem appears.

The complementary figure to that of Lazarus in *Fighting Terms* is
the soldier in 'Incident on a Journey', whose commitment to a life
of action is no more rational than the choice of Lazarus not to be
raised:

> And always when a living impulse came
> I acted, and my action made me wise.

There is nothing in the early style quite like the 'seductiveness' of
'Touch' and its companions. In some ways the early style is more
complex in intention and effect than the later. Partly it works as an
ironic counterpart to the highly subjective nature of the experiences
recorded in the poems; but partly, too, it stands for an orderliness
to which the speaker in the poems would often aspire. It is the
imposed order of a victorious army. In this way the style reflects
Gunn's interest in the anti-self of Yeats – it is an aesthetic reflection
of Yeats's general observation that 'if we cannot imagine ourselves
as different from what we are, and try to assume that second self,
we cannot impose a discipline upon ourselves though we may accept
one from others'. . . .

However, it seems to me that the main effect of the early style is
felt neither as an achieved irony of tone nor as the successful or
unsuccessful attempt to don a mask of complete control over
a subjective and irrational content, but rather as an agonized
consciousness of the gap between what is said and the manner of
saying it. A poem like 'Carnal Knowledge' works by giving a sense
of the difference between the polish of manner and the extremity of

the situation discussed. It is not enough to describe the poem as ingenious; the play on words is more emotionally exhausting than intellectually dazzling:

> Even in bed I pose: desire may grow
> More circumstantial and less circumspect
> Each night, but an acute girl would suspect
> My thoughts might not be, like my body, bare.
> I wonder if you know, or knowing, care?
> You know I know you know I know you know.

Surely one is struck in this poem by the incongruity of its style; the situation demands a cry from the speaker, and not the deliberation of speech which Gunn supplies and which, I think, we may legitimately describe as a stifled or inhibited cry. Precisely what seems not quite polished enough to be consistent with the rest is here the most potent part of what is said – the pairing of *More circumstantial and less circumspect*, which seems pointless, is especially effective for that very reason: it emphasises the total pointlessness of the attempt at 'poise' in such a situation (which, incidentally, bears a clear relation to Sartre's account of the psychology of love in *L'Être et Le Néant*).

This point is worth labouring because it brings us back to . . . the element of submissiveness in Gunn's poetic character. In the early poems one is most acutely aware of a tendency to think in terms of a divided self, illustrated by 'The Secret Sharer', 'Lofty in the Palais de Danse' or, a poem excluded from the revised *Fighting Terms*, 'A Village Edmund'. The duality in the protagonist's nature in these poems seems to correspond to that between subject-matter and style in 'Carnal Knowledge', and to that between submissiveness and self-willed, self-justifying action in the poetic character of this poet. What has been said of 'Lines for a Book' would also make it possible to phrase the duality in terms of stasis and action, or in Heidegger's way, in terms of inertia and projection.

What seems to happen in the development of Gunn as a poet is that the stifled cry of 'Carnal Knowledge' becomes progressively apparent in poems like 'The Beaters', 'Julian the Apostate' and 'Jesus and his Mother', culminating in the 'one convulsion' of 'Saul becoming Paul' in the beautiful poem 'In Santa Maria del Popolo'. From this point on, the poetry becomes increasingly *persuasive* in intention, and the semblance of reasonableness ('I circle because I have found/That tracing circles is a useful spell/Against contentment' and so on) becomes less and less significant. In this way the books so far written describe one single action.

Many poets regard their art as lying in an ordering of significance, a making sense of what we find in everyday life intractable for one reason or another. I don't think that this is true of Thom Gunn, whose poems ask rather for an act of faith on our part. They do not help us to understand experience, they help us to believe in certain kinds of experience – the ultimate richness of 'Flying Above California', the spiritual poverty of 'In the Tank' (which is analogous to that of 'Carnal Knowledge'), and the gaps between them. The poems exist primarily to be experienced, secondarily to be understood; and what there is to be understood is not necessarily new in the context of Gunn's poetry, or conceptually very astonishing. 'Lights Among Redwood', for example, is not a poem that makes any extraordinary statement; it simply calls the reader into the experience described, so that the experience becomes his own. One might say that the poet's aim is to make his reader feel 'This is beautiful' rather than 'This is true', except that 'beautiful' suggests static perfection of a work of art whilst his poem is above a movement, and is movement, action, itself:

> Calm shadow! Then we at last
> remember to look upward . . .

'Lights Among Redwood' like 'Touch' depends for its success on a syntactic movement across lines:

> And the streams here, ledge to ledge,
> take care of light. Only to
> the pale green ribs of young fern
> tangling above the creek's edge
> it may sometimes escape, though
> in quick diffusing patterns.

Ledge to ledge describes the sinuous course of the literal sense as it trickles here from line to line. 'Quick diffusing patterns' describes the minimal effect of the rhymes, whose impact is diffused because neither rhythm nor meaning permits that they should be dwelt on. 'Elsewhere it has become tone,/pure and rarified', we are told, concerning the light; but up to the moment when we look upward with the speaker the poem is entirely an illustration of 'tone', particularly in its avoidance of a personal pronoun. This delayed entry of the personal element ('we at last/remember to look

upward . . .') works by contrast with the indefiniteness of mere
'tone'; *we* are not *pure and rarified* but stand embodied in the shadowy
forest scene and in contrast to it. Furthermore, the oblique course
by which the reader is made, first to enter the tonal *dimness* of
the poem and then to encounter the pronoun, encourages his
identification with it. *We* refers not simply to 'I speaking in the poem
and my companion', or to 'anyone happening to be in the same
situation as I speaking in the poem', but also to 'I speaking in the
poem and you reading it'. The place described is like that in 'Touch',
a place where imaginative encounter is possible in a given experience:

> constant, to laws of size and
> age the thick forms hold, though gashed
> through with Indian fires. At once
> tone is forgotten: we stand
> and stare – mindless, diminished –
> at their rosy immanence.

This is the experience towards which the rest of the poem leads
us: our sense of diminishment before the actually defined and other.
The trees distinguish themselves from mere tone; they are permanent
and substantial. *Hold* is a word felt to relate to *laws of size and age*,
but is also felt absolutely: the trees hold, where everything else
tangles or is muted. They are *thick* forms, not Platonically ideal. But
why are we diminished, made mindless by them? Their very size
makes us feel small, but also, and especially, their *immanence*. The
word is used by Kierkegaard, who took it, in his turn from Hegel,
in order to disagree with him. Outside a specific philosophical
context, the word is therefore ambiguous, as it is here. The word
implies a paradox of the kind we have already seen in 'Touch'; it
means firstly the actual existence of these trees in this world shared
by the speaker and the reader of the poem, and in this sense a
supernatural quality is implied but not stated – the trees are like
God, who is immanent in the universe, not apart from it. At the
same time the word has a meaning in conflict with this first one.
Their *immanence* is then the trees' quality of fulfilling or having
fulfilled intrinsic purposes which do not connect with our world at
all. This is the N.E.D.'s sense 2 for *immanent*: 'Immanent act (action):
an act which is performed entirely within the mind of the subject,
and produces no external effect: opposed to a *transient* or *transitive*
act.'

In this sense the trees' *immanence* is completely unobservable: it is something we intuit, that the trees exist in total indifference to us. And so we are made to feel two different things at once, *diminished* both because we recognise something marvellous, akin to religious feeling, in the discovery of the substantial reality of the world in which we live (we are then *mindless* because no longer prisoners of our own minds, no longer in the situation of, let us say, the speaker in 'Carnal Knowledge'), and also because we are apart from and less than the world outside us, which continues whether we like it or not, and according to its own *laws* (we are then *mindless* because our sense of the trees' indifference to us temporarily extinguishes our consciousness of ourselves).[3]

One thing more: it is a *rosy* immanence. It has the health of rosy cheeks, the promise of rosyfingered dawn. Contradictory though the experience is, it is also salutary: it puts us where we have to begin again, to give ourselves again a mind, a consciousness. This sense of promise as inherent in our condition of life is what Gunn wishes to give us – to give us, not to prove.

The poem illustrates how Gunn has brought the two sides of his poetic character into harmony; the submissiveness is present in the way the experience is recorded, in which the charm of 'tone' is expressed equally with the overpowering definition of the trees' 'immanence', and yet so is the quality of action, of guiding, of swaying, the reader.

One activity in particular requires a willingness to submit to experience in equal proportion to be the ability to shape it, and that is the explorer's. Gunn's poetry seems truly to be exploratory, with an exactitude of meaning one can rarely achieve.

That is what, ultimately, distinguishes him from Byron:

> His touch
> Was masterful to water, audience
> To which he could react until an end.
> Strong swimmers, fishermen, explorers: such
> Dignify death by thriftless violence –
> Squandering with so little left to spend.   ('Lerici')

Byron 'squandered with so little left to spend'; he was, like the speaker in Gunn's early poems, a *poseur*. The paradox which applies to him is obvious and strained, and calls on no qualities held in common with the reader. By contrast, Gunn's later poems proceed with a sinuous and plastic grace, far from the rigidity of *pose*, and suggests not a death dignified by violence, but a life that manifests, like his best poetry, a sense of inexhaustible vitality, of what Mounier calls 'cet être qui jaillit de l'être', 'that being which wells up out of being'. The notion of an energy not to be defeated, figured by the persistence of some deep well, a continual bubbling forth, is perhaps too facile as a description of the various action of Gunn's poetry; but in its general emphasis it is also, perhaps, the necessary one.

SOURCE: extracts from 'Thom Gunn: Poetry as Action and Submission' in Dodsworth's edited volume of essays by various writers, *The Survival of Poetry* (London, 1970), pp. 193–4, 199–204, 206–15.

NOTES

1. Emmanuel Mounier, *Introduction aux Existentialismes* (Paris, 1947), p. 40. (Martin Dodsworth's translation.)

2. Ibid., p. 46.

3. What the poem seems to be getting at in this use of the word 'immanence' could be well expressed in Heidegger's account of the dual aspect of 'being': '"Being" meant for the Greeks: permanence in a twofold sense:

(a) standing-in-itself (In-sich-stehen) in the sense of arising (Ent-stehen, standing-out-of) (*physis*),

(b) but, as such "permanent" (ständig), i.e. enduring (*ousia*).' – Martin Heidegger, *An Introduction to Metaphysics*, translated by Ralph Manheim (New York, 1961), p. 52.

Colin Falck   Uncertain Violence
(1976)

In his note acknowledging the selection of *Jack Straw's Castle* as a Poetry Book Society Choice,[1] Thom Gunn remarked that

There was a journalistic cliché a few years ago about 'voice'. So and so has at last found his voice or, conversely, so and so has failed to find a distinctive voice. I have never felt easy about the kind of stress implied. Distinctiveness can look after itself, what I want is the kind of voice that can speak about anything at all, that can deal with the perceptions and concerns as they come up. I do not court impersonality so much as try to avoid personality, which I'd prefer to leave to the newspapers. . . .

One might suspect Gunn of extracting a virtue rather prematurely from a private necessity here, but it's a respectable enough critical doctrine and the sheer assurance he offers it with could give us confidence in his poetic intentions whatever the actual waywardness of some of his verse. Gunn has been accused of lacking poetic personality – 'Gunn has not enough of a poetic personality (or maybe of course he has renounced it) to be parodied, even by himself' – John Bayley,[2] but we are really so sure what poetic personality means, or why it matters? – what Shakespeare's poetic personality was (or Tolstoy's?), and whether the work we admire 'him' for was good because of it, in spite of it, or quite independently of it? A poem should strike us as a wording of our own highest thoughts, Keats said – which (if he was right) would seem to preclude its merely striking us as a wording of someone else's. The poet who has given us the lines of most near-to-Shakespearian power in twentieth-century English or American verse could well be Thom Gunn in 'The Wound' (*Fighting Terms*, 1954):

> The huge wound in my head began to heal
> About the beginning of the seventh week.
> Its valleys darkened, its villages became still:
> For joy I did not move and dared not speak,
> Not doctors would cure it, but time, its patient skill.

The Trojan War fill-in of the centre section of the poem was an exercise in the kind of extended metaphor (in this case seemingly an encoding of the poem's occasion) which Gunn went in for at that time – and which, with the blunt personal address of his 'love' poems, earned him not wholly irrelevant comparisons with Donne – but the poem finally resolves itself back into the compelling and metaphorically structural imagery it started out from:

> . . . and turning I could feel
> My wound break open wide. Over again
> I had to let those storm-lit valleys heal.

With the game set up like this it's not surprising if Gunn sometimes disappoints the critics who require an identifiable 'voice' or 'personality' in what they read.

But of course there's something in the criticism. What there is in it probably depends on the differences between the poetic conditions of the sixteenth and seventeenth centuries and those of the twentieth. In his early verse Gunn tended to lean on Elizabethan, Jacobean and other pre-Romantic poetic devices – the allegorically worked-out or cerebrally worked-up metaphor, the clinching generality ('I saw that lack of love contaminates' etc.) – and these tendencies helped to get him bracketed with the British 'Movement' poets of the 1950s (Amis, Davie, Holloway Wain & Co.) whose pre-Romantic – and anti-romantic – affiliations he shared. Gunn's speciality of using ceremonious forms in an insolently ill-made way and with a flat modern content fitted in well with the anti-literary postures of that period:

> You are not random picked. I tell you you
> Are much like one I knew before, that died.
> Shall we sit down, and drink and munch a while
> – I want to see if you will really do:
> If not we'll get it over now outside.

This playing off of content against form was a way of embodying the rebelliousness and social deviance which Gunn went on to explore more thematically in *The Sense of Movement* and his other later verse. The shift to thematic treatment was an advance, because the critics were surely right who suspected that this sabotaging of traditional forms from within ('The Wound' is the great exception in Gunn's early verse, the only poem where he commits himself straight out to poetic intensity) could only be a temporary expedient and that it threatened to collapse a potentially ambitious poetry into burlesque or pastiche (others among the 'Movement' poets followed Empson into a related type of unmodernity); who saw that Gunn's reliance on pre-Romantic poetic devices might prevent him from getting his own emotions properly into poetry at all ('The Wound', again, is exceptional in that it manages the rare feat – almost impossible for the modern poet – of attaining the grand manner whilst leaving the personal foreground largely unoccupied) – and that what Gunn needed to do was to use the stuff of the modern world not merely as illustration for ideas and opinions he had come by elsewhere but as the focus and growing-point for his own poetic intuitions. To do this would mean generating personal rhythms (something Gunn has always found it hard, or not seen the need, to do – but which could very well be a way in which personality may have to get itself into modern verse) and an experiential feel in the handling of the material. Gunn edged perceptibly in this direction in *The Sense of Movement*, where the pop stars, motorcycles and other fifties-existentialist hero-figures are introduced with some kind of apparently serious intention of exploring, rather than merely prejudging, their significance. It was these anarchistic concerns which got Gunn his early following and which separated him from the academicism and emotionally aridity of the more typical 'Movement' poets.

The circumstantial detail of Gunn's early poems has – predictably – dated, but their underlying themes have persisted into his later work. The sense of solipsistic isolation within human relationships – a kind of Dostoevskyan hypertrophying of will and self-consciousness – which must have led Gunn to put 'Carnal Knowledge' ('I know you know I know you know I know' etc.) at the front of *Fighting Terms* provides the central theme of *Jack Straw's Castle* twenty-two years later. The first poem of *The Sense of Movement* 'On the Move', states what is really the deepest concern of all Gunn's writing either before or since (the unerringness with which he selects either the best or else the most thematically significant poems for the start and finish of his books is always reassuring):

> The blue jay scuffling in the bushes follows
> Some hidden purpose, and the gust of birds
> That spurts across the field, the wheeling swallows,
> Have nested in the trees and undergrowth.
> Seeking their instinct, or their poise, or both,
> One moves with an uncertain violence
> Under the dust thrown by a baffled sense
> Or the dull thunder of approximate words.
>
> On motorcycles, up the road, they come . . .

Humanity, the motorcyclists remind us, is necessarily alienated from the comforting thought-precluding necessities of the natural world of birds and animals. The poem's linked propositions – 'They strap in doubt – by hiding it, robust'; 'Much that is natural, to the will must yield'; 'Men manufacture both machine and soul' etc. – sketch out some kind of a response to a genuine philosophical anxiety, and nearly all of Gunn's later poems have an aspect of the same anxiety somewhere about them. 'Human Condition', in the same volume, contains the explicit lines 'I am condemned to be / An individual', and it would probably be fair to say that Gunn was always conscious of the ambivalence, as both blessing and curse, of his early-Sartrian conception of freedom. The end of 'On the Move' ('One is always nearer by not keeping still') seems to be as much a projection of the motorcyclists' conviction as a flat statement of the poet's own, though the two are in close enough sympathy while the poem lasts. Gunn occasionally pushes his futuristic open-roadism towards a personal affirmation, for example in 'In Praise of Cities' –

> She presses you with her hard ornaments,
> Arcades, late movie shows, the piled lit windows
> Of surplus stores. Here she is loveliest;
> Extreme, material, and the work of man

– but the lyricism here seems itself to have a slightly willed quality and the 'she' to be faintly suspect; the beauty, though part-genuine (Gunn is one of our few real poets to have responded authentically to the beauty of machines or cities) seems also partly borrowed. What one mostly registers in these early poems is wilful assertion in the face of doubt or bafflement: a rational celebration of will or energy but with *kamikaze* overtones. Uprootedness from nature comes over as a doubtful liberation (commenting on 'On the Move' Martin Dodsworth remarked that it seemed too reminiscent of the Flying Dutchman[3]) and although the idea of travel as a curse is familiar enough – Wordsworth made a good deal of it – the unavailability of a settled at-one-ness with God or nature as a possible alternative means that the weight of the curse is harder to evaluate as well as simply harder to lift; in his second well-known motorcycle piece, 'The Unsettled Motorcyclist's Vision of his Death', Gunn's dying motorcyclist asserts his will perversely against 'the mere embodiment' and sees, as he sinks into the marsh, 'gigantic order in the rim / Of each flat leaf', of a nature which is not only perfect but also perfectly alien.

Gunn's philosophising is worth taking seriously even if it tends to pre-empt the operation of any very delicate concrete imagination – many of his best moments owe their power to the fact that they happen towards the abstract end of the poetic spectrum – and to leave much of his verse on a level of approximate words and with an uncertain basis in experience. It reminds us, for one thing, that there is a way open for the modern poet between didacticism, however engagingly or ironically carried off, and a merely imagistic kind of concreteness ('Go in fear of abstractions' etc.). Gunn gives us hints at least of how contemporary poetry can sustain an honest dialectic between experience and generality, and his answers to the questions he entertains are satisfying up to a point in so far as they nearly always spring from defiantly honest responses. One can say up to a point, because an advantage of Gunn's readiness to be philosophically explicit is that it makes it easier for us to see when his ideas themselves have gone awry and have perhaps helped to trap him in confused perceptions. When he writes

> I circle because I have found
> That tracing circles is a useful spell
> Against contentment, which comes on by stealth

– movement, this time, with no kind of direction or progress in it at all – one realises that his objection is not to particular (say bourgeois) forms of contentment but to any contentment whatsoever. . . .

The connections between problems of content and problems of style in Gunn's verse becomes clearest in *My Sad Captains*, where in the second part of the book he abandons the traditional metrics – mostly the iambic pentameter [in favour of syllabics – Ed.] . . . The actual amount of rhythmically vital verse in Gunn's syllabics is about the same as it was before, and his best achievements – inevitably – come when the inner movement of what he is expressing manages to coincide or co-exist with the mechanical demands of the syllable-count (so that the syllable-count itself simply drops out of consideration as irrelevant). This happens in one way in 'The Feel of Hands', where the delicately slipping line-breaks of the first lines perfectly embody the tentativeness that the poem starts out from:

> The hands explore tentatively,
> two small live entities whose shapes
> I have to guess at. They touch me
> all, with the light of fingertips
> testing each surface of each thing
> found . . .

It happens in a different way in some of the lines of the title poem 'My Sad Captains', where the avoidance of a full-bodied metre allows the poem to take on some of the emotion of ordinary understated speech (which makes it finely heightened conclusion correspondingly more effective), and where the syllable-counting . . . doesn't interfere with the poem's coming over as properly organised free verse:

> They remind me, distant now.
> True, they are not at rest yet,
> but now that they are indeed
> apart, winnowed from failures,
> they withdraw to an orbit

> and turn with disinterested
> hard energy, like the stars.

In his later books Gunn sometimes reverts to regular metres, and at other times gives himself over to a meanderingly disordered lay-out which reflects an equally meanderingly disordered content (one such poem is dedicated to the meanderingly disordered American poet Robert Duncan). One realises, in long retrospect, that metres are for Gunn something like a formal equivalent of the protective gear of his motorcyclists; that his difficulty in evolving his own rhythms, or in getting them to hold up for very long, parallels the problem – which increasingly becomes his theme – of his impotence to find any way of accepting or believing in himself as a finite individual or determinate character within a world of other finite individuals or determinate characters – to find any mode of existence between pure existential will, unable to open itself up to or to receive anything from the world around it, and a kind of sentimental emotionalism which longs to recover the unity of pre-individualised primal state; also that while Gunn's Californianism panders to this sentimentality it also makes inevitable the Charles Manson-ish violence which tends to erupt within its illusory paradise. This dissociation of sensibility dominates *My Sad Captains*; while one poem tells how 'purposeless matter hovers in the dark', another ('From the Highest Camp') focuses explicitly, but not without a degree of exhilaration, on the diseased condition of the disembodied and loveless consciousness. (Another poem on the same theme is actually called 'The Monster'.) In *Touch* the concerns are similar, though there are also moments where one seems to glimpse the possibility of the evil spell being broken; in *Moly* there are drug experiences which reach towards mysticality (and therefore escape) but where the lateral drifting and tenuousness of the imagery are really either still under the sign of conscious manipulation or else seem merely wandering and inconclusive (there are poetically effective moments in both books). . . .

   In *Jack Straw's Castle* there are some early-autobiographical poems which have predictable lost-idyllic qualities about them but which might be the beginning of a move in this direction. In other poems Gunn's old toughness is equally in evidence (in one of them called 'The Geysers', he tells us 'I do recognise / – For what such recognition may be worth – / Fire at my centre, burning since my birth / Under the pleasant flesh. Force calls to force'). The main progress of the

book is probably in the directness with which it faces up to what
Gunn now clearly sees as his central problem: its title-sequence
shows a protagonist trapped within the empty castle of the self and
trying to decide whether the outside world – which breaks in on
him only through a teasing interlocutor, one Charlie Manson – (for
it is he) – is real or only a dream. One of the most fascinatingly
readable poems, on the other hand, is a dramatic monologue in the
person of a black Newfoundland dog whose not-yet-emerged-from-
nature simplicity, together with his faithful acceptance of his master's
authority ('I am confused, I feel loose and unfitted.//At last deep
in the stairwell I hear a tread,/it is him, my leader, my love'),
makes it possible for him to live a richly fulfilled life:

> I investigate tar and rotten sandwiches, everything, and go on.
> And here a dried old turd, so interesting
> so old, so dry, yet so subtle and mellow.
> I can place it finely, I really appreciate it . . .
>   . . .
> My leader looks on and expresses his approval.

If it would be silly to say that this was a poem about fascism, it
might be just as silly to say that it wasn't (it perhaps does for dogs
the same kind of thing that a Georgian favourite. Harold Monro's
'Milk for the Cat', did for cats). One of the most encouraging things
about *Jack Straw's Castle*, apart from its particular poetic successes,
is the sense it conveys – and therefore the faith it sustains – that on
some appropriately primitive level Gunn continues to know what
he is doing and is getting on with doing it.

Whether Gunn can move from his Dostoevskyan vision which
locates the point of disbelief – or wonder – on the near side of the
individual's unity with the world to a Tolstoyan vision which accepts
this unity as an underlying faith and as an assured basis for quite
different kinds of disbelief or wonder is not yet clear. One might
almost say that there is no reason why – *qua* artist – he should, were
it not for the fact that Gunn himself seems so persistently and deeply
to want to. Intellectual convolutedness ('I am the man on the
rack./I am the man who puts the man on the rack./I am the man
who watches the man who puts the man on the rack.' makes up one
entire section of 'Jack Straw's Castle') may not in itself be a way of
reaching a new simplicity but it may help in coming to terms with
the obstacles that lie in the way. The real growing-points for Gunn's
poetry itself, on the other hand, must almost certainly be the points

where the human faith and sympathy he longs for are already faintly
present (act as though you believed, as Pascal might have said . . .).
In *Touch*.

> There is a girl in the train
> who emulates the bee-hive
> of the magazine stars of
> four years ago.
> 　　　　　　I blush at
> the jibes that grow inside me,
> lest someone should utter them.
> Why was something evolved so
> tender, so open to pain?

– and one feels a pity at the heart of the poet's toughness and
something almost approaching a tenderness at the heart of the pity.
In 'An Amorous Debate' in *Jack Straw's Castle*. 'Leather Kid' and
'Fleshly' end their debating ('You have/a hard cock', she tells him,
'but there is/something like the/obduracy of leather/still in your
countenance/and your skin, it is like/a hide under hide') by melting
'one/into the other forthwith/like the way the Saône/joins the
Rhône at Lyon' – though the melting, so far as the poem lets us go
with it, seems to be only sexual. The last poem of *Jack Straw's Castle*
is a poem of bereavement, and it wrings real feeling from the poet
in a way that comes courageously close to, but by sheer honesty
manages to avoid, an old-fashioned kind of sentimentality; it also
achieves its final effect by resolving itself into the Renaissance idiom
('Shee/is gonn, Shee is lost,/Shee is found, shee/is ever faire')
which first fired Gunn's imagination. . . .

Source: extracts from 'Uncertain Violence' in *New Review* (Nov. 1976),
pp. 37–9, 39–40, 40–1.

NOTES

1. Thom Gunn, in *Poetry Book Society Bulletin*, 90 (Autumn 1976).
2. John Bayley, *Times Literary Supplement* (24 Sept. 1976).
3. Martin Dodsworth, in *New Review*, 18 (April 1968).

Terry Eagleton   'Shifting Myths'
(1972)

. . . In a fairly loose sense of the term, Gunn has been equipped
with a myth from the outset – that of Sartrian existentialism. Its
advantage, as in Sartre's early philosophical work, has been its
ability to bring the contingencies of personal and social history into
some kind of relation with an underlying ontology. That relation
has rarely been an easy one in Gunn's actual poetry: the specific
action of a poem too often merely stiffly bodied out (a recurrent
Gunn verb) an *a priori* metaphysic. But the Sartrian myth did allow
a limited kind of transaction to take place between the variable
texture of experience and a framing vision. At the same time,
however, that transaction was often of a negative sort: the poetry
centred on a nameless *néant* which intervened between a watchful
consciousness aware of its large general meanings, and the swarming
bits of specific reality within which it moved. In the earlier volumes,
the tactic of a particular poem was then either to dramatise that
sickening sense of disparity, or, as in a poem like 'Waking in a
Newly-Built House', to rest satisfied with the alien self-possession
of things, strictly curbing the turbulent, subversive questions which
consciousness addressed to them.

In one or two of the final poems of *My Sad Captains*, however,
another sort of myth began to emerge – one almost antithetical in
tendency to the existentialist dilemma. It is there, for instance, in
the closing lines of *Loot*:

> I am herald to tawny
>
> warriors, woken from sleep, who
> ride precipitantly down
> with the blood towards my hands, through
> me to retain possession.

It is the fusion, not the disparity, between man, nature, and history
which is central here: a sub-Lawrentian myth of the individual as
passive transmitter of primordial forces which fill and possess him
with their own richness. If Gunn is, notably, the poet of emptiness

and lack, it is also true that he is the poet of fullness: cramming, blooding, bodying are recurrent images. Consciousness either stands impotently apart from its object, fending off the invasion of chaos, or allows its vigilance to be sensually dissolved into a moment of mindless surrender to an impersonal natural force. This can only be risked, of course, if the force is somehow friendly, as the dog in 'The Vigil of Corpus Christi', whose tongue licks a stiff sentry into 'unsoldierly joy', is friendly. If the Sartrian myth stresses alienation, this primitivistic vision emphasises man's rootedness in the cosmos: it offers – in my view, in a mystifying and merely assertive way – a natural solution to social breakdown.

This second mythology seems to have grown stronger in Gunn's recent poetry – grown, indeed, to the point where, in a discussion of *Moly*, he can talk gravely and explicitly of certain 'powers' friendly to man, in whom trust can be placed. In *Touch* [1967] the impulse towards an edgy, defensive hardening of the self underwent some sardonic questioning, as images of melting dissolution and momentary merging began to creep in; and that tendency becomes even more affirmative in *Moly* [1971]. One reason for this is that Gunn's sense of what sustaining 'poise' involves seems to have been modified. The surf-riders in San Francisco bay keep their balance, but they do so by moving with, not against, natural forces:

> Their pale feet curl, they poise their weight
> With a learn'd skill.
> It is the wave they imitate
> Keeps them so still.

The sharp disjunctions between controlling mind and chaotic matter of the earlier books seem superseded here: it's by rooting himself responsively in the flow of natural forces, not by fending them off, that man can master them. And so, whereas Gunn's previous use of werewolf imagery sometimes suggested a potentially tragic discontinuity between man and nature, the imagery of man-beast metamorphosis in *Moly* seems to express a sense of some organic, ecological *rapport* between man and the forces he moves among. The Circe myth to which the book's title refers still underlines the need for an alert self-awareness which allows man to master the bestial; but a number of 'centaur' poems in the volume view the frontier between man and beast as blurred and indefinite, a merging rather than sharp dividing. In a similar way, the mind must acknowledge

the dependency of its sharpened perceptions on an amorphous
undertow of mindless natural merging:

> On the stream at full
> A flurry, where the mind rides separate!
> But this brief cresting, sharpened and exact,
> Is fluid too, is open to the pull
> And on the underside twined deep with it.

It seems fanciful to relate *Moly* to Davie's *Six Epistles to Eva Hesse*
[1970]; yet a relation of an indirect kind can be asserted. Davie,
comfortably ensconced in his Californian cat's-cradle, and Gunn
confidently poised on a Pacific wave, have a more than geographical
contiguity: they share a tentative trust, reached through different
uses of myth, that man can be at home in the universe. Man can be
at home because entwined with the present in which he lives are
threads or forces from elsewhere, buoying him up, binding him to
Nature or geography, history or space. And because this is so, the
individual can, once again, become *representative*. This is the condition
of Gunn's lonely survivor in 'Misanthropos':

> If he preserves himself in nature,
> it is as a lived caricature
> of the race he happens to survive.
> He is clothed in dirt. He lacks motive.
> He is wholly representative.

Source: extract from 'Myth and History in Recent Poetry', in Grevel
Lindop and Michael Schmidt (eds), *British Poetry since 1960* (Manchester,
1972), pp. 236–7.

Clive Wilmer   Definition and Flow
(1978)

. . . In the introduction to his selection of Ben Jonson's verse, Gunn
praises that master for his formal and stylistic versatility: throughout
his career, Jonson tried 'every "style" he could, not feeling bound
to stick with one and develop within it'. Then, as if striking back at

his own critics, he challenges the orthodox identification of 'style' with 'personality'. Just as there are 'many Ben Jonsons' in Gunn's selection, so there are many Thom Gunns in *Jack Straw's Castle*. They are most readily identifiable in terms of the forms they deploy: there are rhymed stanzas, heroic couplets, songs and free verse both in the cadenced Whitmanesque long line and in the short, tense, run-over line associated with William Carlos Williams. It is, in short, a strikingly experimental book; and experiment is not only a quality of the writing but, in a sense, a theme of the poems too. Gunn has always liked the word 'risk'.

Jack Straw's Castle is not a showy book. . . . It is clear that Gunn, though never a lazy writer, no longer sets great store by perfection – may even feel that it is a form of dishonesty, that reality cannot be so neatly encapsulated as seemed possible in the most Parnassian of his previous poems. When Gunn, as he often does, slips into some gaucherie of rhythm or expression, we should remember that we are reading work by the author of 'Innocence', 'Pierce Street' and 'From the Wave'. We should remember too that one of the poets Gunn most values is Thomas Hardy. In a lecture on Hardy he praises him for the 'precision and vividness' with which he records particulars. Noting that two examples which he cites are neither 'positively euphonious' nor 'elegant-sounding', he asks why we should care, since 'They present things with immediate authority' so that we focus more on the things than on the means. The means are therefore adequate to the things and, as Gunn goes on to suggest, the clumsiness authenticates much of the poetry: 'you never feel, even in Hardy's most boring and ridiculous poetry, that he is pretending – he is never rhetorical.' The same might be said of Gunn himself.

Frequently he has commended to his readers' attention the American edition of D. H. Lawrence's *New Poems* (1920). In the Preface to that edition, Lawrence writes of free verse as pre-eminently the medium of present-tense meditation, of perception in the process of taking form. The essay is characteristically portentous but, on the whole, wiser than its rhetoric. Most poetry, says Lawrence, deals with ends and beginnings, with past and future.

It is in the realm of all that is perfect. It is of the nature of all that is complete and consummate. This completeness, this consummateness, the finality and the perfection are conveyed in exquisite form: *the perfect symmetry, the rhythm which returns upon itself like a dance* where the hands link and loosen and link for the supreme moment of the end . . . But there is another kind of poetry: the poetry of that which is at hand: the immediate present. In the immediate present there is no perfection, no consummation, nothing finished. The strands are all flying, quivering, intermingling into the web, the waters are shaking the moon. There is no round, consummate moon on the face of running water, nor on the face of the unfinished tide.

It is not only the substance of this that needs considering, but the imagery too. For, though Gunn's poetry is hardly dance-like, it certainly used to be remarkable for rhythms returning upon themselves, for the finality of its meditations; and yet it celebrated risk, flux, the unpredictable future, the unfinished artefact. Lawrence's 'unfinished tide' is equivalent to the 'Cool seething incompletion that I love' in one of Gunn's recent poems (he is talking of a river). Part of the excitement of his poetry has always lain in the tension between form and content. And yet it is hardly surprising that Gunn has come increasingly to admire a poetry which possesses the very qualities which move him in life: the poetry of Whitman, Pound, Williams, Crane, Creeley and Snyder. All that such a poetry must have lacked to so skilled and deliberate an artificer as Gunn was a sense of the necessary and inevitable artificiality of poetry, the supreme fiction.

His first attempt to confront this problem involved a compromise. About half the poems in *My Sad Captains* (1961) are written in syllabic verse, a form in which arbitrary structure imposes discipline – felt more by the writer than the reader – upon rhythms as unpredictable as those of free verse. Indeed, Gunn has since admitted that he finds 'the virtues of syllabics indistinguishable from those of free verse'. He has now given them up, since they were 'only a way of teaching myself to write free verse', which he succeeded in doing in *Positives* (1966). Now, in *Jack Straw's Castle*, there are signs that the two kinds of verse have begun to influence one another. In the metrical poems the rhythms are looser, the language more conversational, the structures based more on sequences of perception than on patterns of logical thought. But a sense of the limits of both flux and artifice is built into the poetry. It is that sense of how a poem is made and how its making must relate to what already exists that gives the free verse its authenticity. There is none of the Black Mountaineer in Gunn, though some poets of that school have affected his newer work. He knows that a poem cannot *be* life, that it is a formulation and therefore a fiction; that if a poem includes non-grammatical pauses, for example, those pauses *imitate* the natural pauses of speech – they are not 'breaths' of the spirit. . . .

As Lawrence suggests, 'metrical' verse retains its own function; it will continue to be called upon to embody the products of concentrated thought, to give the semblance of immutable form to immutable verities. For this, it depends on an element of predictability in its movement. But in free verse, however formal in the deep sense it may be, one can never predict the rhythmic outcome. Gunn, like Williams and Creeley, plays on this, tantalising the reader with weak line-endings and long sinuous sentences broken into short lines. This procedure emphasises the overall rhythm (as against the line-as-unit) and suggests the hesitancy of the human voice shaping its utterances. Gunn's free verse seems to discover its meanings as it proceeds, as if the poem is a sequence of thought enacted before us, affected by the moment: a sense of thought (and poem) as *process*.

'Touch', the title-poem of Gunn's 1967 volume, evokes a situation which is almost a metaphor for this process of discovery. The poet, cold and naked, gets into a bed already occupied by his lover. In sleep, the lover turns round to embrace him. Gradually, through human tenderness, the isolated self comes to rediscover its place in the objective world, the 'dark/wide realm where we/walk with everyone'. He begins in simple language with a perception of his lover's otherness: 'You are already/asleep'. But from the outset the versification is working against the syntax to generate diverse potentialities of meaning. (The prosodic norm of the poem is a line of two major stresses, with occasional departures from that norm.) The implicit pause at the line-end mimes the poet's discovery of the sleeper. This dramatic use of the line-end is sustained throughout the poem, but in long, intricate sentences. Here it has a secondary effect: it isolates (temporarily) part of the sentence: 'you are already' – as if the poet were saying, 'you exist already'. The same clause recurs – as a single line again – towards the end of the poem as part of a highly elaborate period which moves towards the idea of 'touch', human contact, as generating a process of 'continuous creation'. The implications of the verb 'to be' in that first line are now remarkably expanded, for, though the phrase 'continuous creation' refers specifically to the growth of shared personal awareness, it is also a quasi-technical term. It is one of the theories of how the universe comes to *be*. The world was not *made* in the beginning, but has always been and is always becoming. The idea of poem as process is more than usually apt.

> You turn and
> hold me tightly, do
> you know who
> I am or am I
> your mother or . . .

Each line acquires a different significance if isolated from its syntactical context, yet each of them has the kind of line-ending which compels us to read on within that context. This method of versification enables Gunn not only to describe the world, the incompletion that he loves, but at the same time to dramatise the ways in which we come to know it, in terms which point ultimately to his own beliefs about its nature. This is not quite Lawrence's 'incarnation . . . of the ever-swirling flood'. We are concerned here with the most sophisticated form of artifice. The lines may seem spontaneous but it is the semblance of spontaneity that we are offered, just as in a stanzaic poem we are offered – among other things – the semblance of uniformity.

Or is this going too far? Surely between sonnet and sonnet, say, there is *some* uniformity – why should poets bother to write sonnets otherwise? There is some truth, too, in the semblance of spontaneous process in a free-verse poem. It is easier to 'think aloud' in free verse, to write without a clear end in view. The metrical poem, though also a 'form of discovery' (in Winters's phrase), has to be the product of prior consideration. In both cases, though, there is discovery and we should bear in mind that all experiments have results – even if the results are negative – and that, if only by virtue of being printed, the free-verse poem becomes a stable artefact.

But the discoveries Gunn has been making are not new; on the contrary, they are based on ideas associated with the adolescence of the modern movement. Their importance to us is that he has re-discovered them for himself, and – this is really the point – that he is a poet many readers associate with quite different attitudes to the function of poetry. When his poetry was first noticed in the 1950s, it was seen as typical of the anti-Romantic 'Movement', and much the most important influence on it was Yvor Winter's. . . .

Gunn is now closer to Whitman than to Winters. And yet he still appears to concur with the art/life dualism implicit as much in Winters's politics as in his poetics. Poems are supposed, not to partake of life (though inevitably to some extent they do), but to comment upon it. Gunn has, over the years, developed away from his former teacher, but he has in no way reneged on former loyalties. Winter's influence can severely constrict lesser poets, but the force of his argument often adds sinew to poetry that is strong enough to use him and take issue with him. Insofar as Gunn's recent poetry still owes a debt to Winters, it seems to me to attempt a synthesis rather than a compromise. For, great as Winters was, the principles he developed, and the restricted tradition he derived from them, were determined largely by his need to defend his own practice and beliefs. And his application of those principles – as Thom Gunn appears to agree – was narrower than it need have been.

In his youth, Winters was associated with the second generation of 'modernism'. But from the outset, as his early essays and reviews show, poetry was only of value to him if its end was the *understanding* of experience. At the end of his life he wrote, with characteristic pessimism, 'Unless we understand the history which produced us, we are determined by that history; we may be determined at any event, but the understanding gives us a chance.' Gunn has often endorsed this point of view. It marks the most radical of his recent poems. Contributing to a symposium on violence in contemporary art some years ago, he declared,

What we write must always constitute an attempt to understand. Experience in itself is meaningless. If our nostalgia for violence is also an obsession . . . we must attempt to master it without abandoning it . . . with the imagination and intelligence working at their keenest and hardest.

Winters himself might almost be speaking. The vigilant poet must understand with his intelligence, but his imagination too. . . .

. . . Gunn wrote that Gary Snyder 'like most serious poets . . . is mainly concerned at finding himself on a barely known planet in an almost unknown universe, where he must attempt to create and discover meanings. Discovery of a meaning is also the creation of it, and creation is an act of discovery.' Then, of one specific poem, 'it is . . . a series of pictorial perceptions made by a man embedded in time, who advances into the sensory world opened up by his waking'. This conception of poetry, and the terms Gunn uses, are largely dependent on Winters's example. What Gunn adds is a greater respect for the force of sensuous and instinctual awareness. Gunn's poetry has always attempted to balance the value he sets on rational intelligence with his respect for our more elementary, animal consciousness. The resulting tension is at the heart of many of his best-known poems, such as 'On the Move', 'The Allegory of the

Wolf-Boy' and 'Misanthropos'. He has described 'Wrestling' in *Jack Straw's Castle* as, 'An attempt to deal with the way we acquire knowledge intuitively (as, for example, an animal does).' In the earlier poems the tension was a source of pain; in the new book, though the conflict is not resolved, it has become ground for celebration.

Gunn would, I suspect, sympathise with Donald Davie's attempt to enlarge our understanding of the word 'idea' in relation to the work of Ezra Pound. In Davie's recent Fontana study of Pound, he takes issue with Winters, but finds his objections to the *Cantos* illuminating. Winters, he writes,

conceiving of an idea as that which could be stated in the form of a proposition, recorded his experience of reading the *Cantos* by saying, 'we have no way of knowing whether we have had any ideas or not' . . . if we take account of what he understood 'idea' to be, Winters's remark is one of the few valuably exact formulations that we have, of what reading the *Cantos* amounts to, and feels like.

It is illuminating because, as Davie has just argued, an idea need not be an exact proposition at all. He relates Pound's use of 'The *forma*, the immortal *concetto*' to a passage from Allen Upward which includes these words: 'The idea is not the appearance of a thing already there, but rather the imagination of a thing not yet there. It is not the look of a thing, it is a looking forward to a thing.'

Gunn rejects Wintersian 'propositions' in favour of something rather like Pound's *forma* in 'The Outdoor Concert' in *Jack Straw's Castle*. The title includes a pun: the 'concert' is both a musical performance and an experience of unity. The poem describes a 'secret' at the core of a shared experience, a kind of synthesis. The act of discovery is not a lonely individual's quest but one man's participation in a group.

> The secret
> is still the secret
>
> is not a proposition:
> it's in finding
> what connects the man
> with the music, with
> the listeners, with the fog
> in the top of the eucalyptus,
> with dust discovered on the lip.

A proposition will not embrace the multiplicity of experience – nor indeed will any formulation – but to perceive *connections* is also a form of understanding. The poem constructs a *web* – one of Lawrence's images – or, in more mechanical terms, a diagram. The web is an organic image and the poem is in free verse; a diagram is an artefact, so it is not surprising that the poem Gunn calls 'Diagrams' is in that artificial form, the heroic couplet. Its fourteen lines recall the still more elaborate artifice of the sonnet. We can now perceive how Gunn's old preoccupation with reason and volitional form has developed: he is now concerned with 'models' of thought. This interest is as Poundian as it is Wintersian, for what are Pound's ideograms but 'models', the matrices on which ideas are formed?

In Pound's theory, the ideogram, though related to rhythm, is primarily a matter of content, of images and ideas. It was of no interest to Yvor Winters. And I doubt that Winters's scrupulous distinctions between rhythm and metre would have appealed to Pound – though he would certainly have understood them:

Metre is the arithmetical norm, the purely theoretic structure of the line; rhythm is controlled departure from that norm. The iambic pentameter norm, for example, proceeds as follows:
   One *two*, one *two*, one *two*, one *two*, one *two*.
Yet no other line in the language corresponds exactly to that just given . . .

However incompatible Pound and Winters may have seemed, both conceptions are relevant to Gunn (as to many more of us). If Gunn's web is a kind of Poundian ideogram, his conception of metre is every bit as mathematical as Winters's. Responding to the question, 'How dead is the pentameter?' in an *Agenda* questionnaire, Gunn wrote, 'It is nonsense to say that metre is dead. It was never alive, it is an unbodied abstraction: it's the poem that has to be alive, and if a metrical poem *is* alive then the metre is the muscle of the living thing as much in 1972 as in 1600.' For both Gunn and Winters metre is abstract and artificial, yet both stress that the life of the poem depends on it. It is a kind of skeleton. And for both, all structures, whether of language or of society, are frameworks which sustain life, though – of their very nature – quite separate from it.

Gunn first appeared before the public – and seems thus fixed in many readers' minds – as the champion of the tough, solitary individual, living by the will and concerned only with the release of his own energy. Gunn's early heroes are in opposition to or in conflict with nature, and within themselves experience a similar conflict between consciousness and instinct. His attitudes had already changed radically by the time he published his third book in 1961 at the age of thirty-two. Yet the wound of that divided solitary is still in many ways the source of his later work. The stance I have described was consciously epitomised in 'On the Move', which opens *The Sense of Movement* (1957), and by implication revised and challenged in 'From the Wave', the centrepiece of *Moly* (1971). In the earlier poem, a gang of motorcyclists submerge their individuality in the uniformed group to assert the power of human will over nature. Man creates his own identity through choice (the philosophy is plainly existentialist) and here the symbol for that process is a manufactured object, the motorcycle.

> They scare a flight of birds across the field;
> Much that is natural to the will must yield.
> Men manufacture both machine and soul
> And use what they imperfectly control
> To dare a future from the taken routes.

We should not miss the suggestion here that, in scaring the birds, the motorcyclists act in accordance with nature as well as against it. But the main impression is of man at war with nature. In 'From the Wave', however, the protagonists are surfers who establish their identity by choosing the 'right waves' to ride. They too become what they are through 'movement', but a movement now at one with nature. Moreover, to do so they need 'skill' and 'balance', which require a harmony between knowledge and instinct, consciousness and action. And though they act as a group – in concert, one might say – their individual identities are not suppressed beneath a uniform.

Of *Moly* Gunn said, 'It could be seen as a debate between the passion for definition and the passion for flow'. That book appeared to mark a retreat from the 'open' forms he had developed in *Touch* (1967), and nowhere has he used his 'passion for definition' with greater elegance and skill. The first section of *Jack Straw's Castle* continues that debate, but the significance of formal artifice is more deliberately explored. The poem is a fiction in which language and experience are given the illusion of permanence. It is a permanent object attempting to contain an impermanent, fluctuating reality. Free verse may be equally 'permanent' but it attempts mimetically to adapt itself to a world in which things change, to imitate ways in which we come to know the world. 'The Plunge' tries in its language to enact the process of acquiring knowledge by total immersion. A diver plunges into a pool and stays under till he can take no more, reaches the limits of the self. This discovery of limits is a discovery of necessary definition, essential form. 'How much more can the body / take?' he asks, driving himself to the point where process must stop and formulation begin. In 'Thomas Bewick', immersion in the detail of the natural world leads to a kind of spiritual rebirth, a return to the womb in which the individual is not yet free, not yet cut loose from the rest of the material universe. Again, immersion in process reaches its limit in a new kind of permanence, the book for which Bewick's name is remembered, capitalized and visually set apart from the rest of the poem. The rhythm enacts the flow of experience into record:

> Drinking from
> clear stream and resting
> on the rock he loses himself
> in detail,
> he reverts
> to an earlier self, not yet
> separate from what it sees,
>
> a selfless self as difficult
> to recover and hold as to
> capture the exact way
> a burly bluetit grips
> its branch (leaning forward)
> over this rock
> and in
> The History of British Birds.

'Saturnalia' describes an orgy, another kind of immersion. There the senses

> roam at play through
> each organ as if
> each were
>
> equally
> a zone of Eros

So the poem ends with the last phrase, as in 'Thomas Bewick', visually set apart from the rest.

If these poems are composed in 'open' form, what are we to make

of those that conform to the rules of traditional prosody and how
are the two kinds kept distinct? What Gunn has discovered through
free verse has affected his standard metre, sometimes to its detriment
in the rhythms and the organization of content. A surprising
gaucheness is apparent in the rhythms. I find that Gunn's use of
metre is most effective when he sticks to the rules. In this book he
attempts looser metres and, when he fails, the result is disappointing.
For example, the line 'It doesn't matter tomorrow. Sleep well.
Heaven knows' is only theoretically a pentameter. It is impossible
to hear five feet, iambic or otherwise. His attempts at the conversational can be banal: 'More meteors than I've ever set eyes on' or 'I
saw them radiate from the barracks/Into the town that it was in'.
But, just at the edge of clumsiness, there are some felicitous
variations, as in a mimetic view of a water-snake: 'I see a little snake
alert in its skin/Striped head and neck from water, unmoving,
reared'. The precariousness of such successes and failures are part
of the whole debate between flux and definition, the intrusion of
'natural' rhythms into the fixities of traditional prosody.

The debate is directly opened by the first three poems in the book,
'The Bed', 'Diagrams' and 'Iron Landscapes'. 'Diagrams' explores
the illusion of permanence and the containment of flux. It presents
a skyscraper being built. In its unfinished state it looks like a 'mesa',
as if it were not an artefact but a permanent feature of the landscape.
To the European reader, both mesa and skyscraper suggest the
American landscape. Gunn, though an Englishman by birth, is
now deeply concerned with the United States as a political and
geographical entity. It is significant that the men at work on this
building are aboriginal Americans: 'On girders round them, Indians
pad like cats,/With wrenches in their pockets and hard hats.'
Their agility expresses their closeness to the environment, mesa or
skyscraper. The human embodiment of American 'nature', they are
engaged in creating the human contribution to that landscape. They
are, I believe, the presiding deities of *Jack Straw's Castle*, moving like
animals among provisional human artefacts, yet equally at home in
the 'given' world. They are poised between permanence and flux:
'They wear their yellow boots like moccasins,/Balanced where air
ends and where steel begins,/Sky men'. The diagrams of the title
are cranes, 'Angled top-heavy artefacts'; they are also the exposed
girders; and they may be taken as an allusion to the poem's metric
too. The 'sky men' – there is a Renaissance suggestion of man poised

between earth and air – wear yellow boots, a product of industrial
society, to work among that society's structures; yet they wear them
like the moccasins they would use on a real mesa. The building they
are erecting, intended as a fixed and stable thing, appears nonetheless
to absorb and transform the energies that surround it as it grows.
It becomes a 'giant' that 'grunts and sways', rising into the air.
'And giving to the air is sign of strength.' The final line is gnomic,
mystical. As in 'From the Wave', to bend to the power of the
elements is to derive strength from them. But the ordinary meaning
of 'to give' is also present: the building appears to seep energy into
the air. Energy has always been Gunn's central concern. The first
phase of his work, which he consciously concluded with the title
poem of *My Sad Captains*, was concerned with solitary heroes: They
were men/who, I thought, lived only to/renew the wasteful force
they/spent with each hot convulsion.' The consumption of their
energy was magnificent but, ultimately, waste; but for Gunn today,
the transformation of energy is 'sign of strength', the adaptation of
self to environment.

In these metrical poems Gunn is concerned with moments in
which fluidity takes permanent form. Such permanence is illusory but
necessary. American permanence, in a political sense, is embodied in
a constitution which has its origin in revolutionary change. Gunn is
not a political poet in the 'committed' sense – he is primarily
concerned with identities and relations we think of as pre-political:
'he is mainly concerned at finding himself on a barely known planet
in an almost unknown universe'. But as Camus (one of his heroes)
discovered, 'freedom' and 'choice' do not exist in abstract purity;
once a man is oppressed, he discovers his political nature, whether
he will or no. If the existentialist Sartre is, with Winters, the main
influence on *The Sense of Movement*, the more humanistic Camus
presides over *My Sad Captains*. There for the first time Gunn shows
how individual choices may operate in society. Like Camus, he was
thinking of an extreme kind of society, though unlike Camus he had
not lived in one. His political positions are limited in application,
but clear: specifically anti-fascist, broadly anti-totalitarian. They
elude positive definition, though the rational individualism of 'Claus
von Stauffenberg, 1944' might be called 'liberal'. Curiously, Gunn
has himself been accused of fascism. It must be stressed that the
violence of the early poems is examined outside a social context and
not proposed as a good; that the dissolution of self in the group and

the adoption of various 'uniforms' are choices made voluntarily by individuals, and that the heroic stance is precisely that: a stance, a posture by which a man attempts to define himself. It is frozen action, the fluid given the appearance of permanence. If Gunn was obsessed with Nazism – its history, its postures, its regalia – this has something to do with his growing up in time of war and reaching manhood when the struggle was over. *Not* having fought in that war is the context a recent poem like 'The Corporal' requires. So, in *My Sad Captains* and *Touch*, Gunn criticizes his earlier stances in such a way as to acquit himself of this accusation. Since *Touch*, Gunn's politics – such as they are – have become decidedly American. It is possible to read the Arcadian world of *Moly* as a new version of the American dream – the New World as the second Eden. But that Arcadia becomes merely escapist in the years of the Vietnam war and the Nixon years if actual political issues are not faced. *Jack Straw's Castle* is Gunn's first book to show the need to deal with contemporary history. 'Nixon's era', with its corruption and rigidities, is portrayed as a betrayal of the system of institutionalised change on which the United States was founded. 'Iron Landscapes', the one poem which deals with these issues directly, is brilliant but flawed and problematic.

It is a metrical meditation on an old iron pier and a girdered ferry-building beside the Hudson River. Gunn's newly-acquired modernism is apparent not least in the rhythmic flexibility:

> A girdered ferry-building opposite,
> Displaying the name LACKAWANNA, seems to ride
>
> The turbulent brown-grey waters that intervene:
> Cool seething incompletion that I love.

In these lines, the iambic pentameter is the norm from which the rhythm departs. The first and fourth lines are regular. The other two depart from the pattern, as the non-verbal facts they attempt to evoke elude formulation. In the first case, the capitalised name fits so awkwardly into the line that the hard physical intractability of the other artefact comes alive for us (Gunn's praise of Hardy comes to mind). Variation in the third line achieves a different effect: we feel the elusive fluidity of the perception by contrast with the formulaic precision of the regular line that follows. Regularity, of course, is appropriate to commentary – formulations necessarily of the mind.

It is not just a matter of rhythm. Free verse enacts a different kind of thought and thinking from metrical verse. If we look at 'Innocence', a mature early Gunn poem, or 'The Annihilation of Nothing', we are struck by the exactness of the metre (in contrast with the awkwardness of 'Iron Landscapes') but, more, by the perfection of the argument. Too perfect, too coherent to allow for the fluidities, the innate contradictions of the subject. Life is imprisoned, not enlarged. But in this poem we are able to follow the poet's train of thought as the different elements that compose the argument are brought together. But it is not, as in the free verse poems, a poetry of process. The different elements are prefabricated. Our attention is drawn less to thought-as-process than to the way experience is shaped into form and formula, becomes idea, concept, belief, opinion.

The poem begins with the 'bare black Z' of the pier and the poet beneath it, looking across the river to the ferry-building. The zigzags of the iron structures 'come and go' in the water, become fluid in the reflection. Separate perceptions are brought together not by volition but contingency. Contingency provokes the poem's main paradox: the conflict between Gunn's passion for definition and for flow. Then a third perception comes into play. Downstream, the poet glimpses the Statue of Liberty. It provokes reflections on the present state of the nation. He has declared his 'passion for definition', having earlier declared his love for its opposite, 'Cool seething incompletion'.

> But I'm at peace with the iron landscape too,
> Hard because buildings must be hard to last
> – Block, cylinder, cube, built with their angles true,
> A dream of righteous permanence, from the past.
>
> In Nixon's era, decades after the ferry,
> The copper embodiment of the pieties
> Seems hard, but hard like a revolutionary
> With indignation, constant as she is.
>
> From here you can glimpse her downstream, her far charm,
> Liberty, tiny woman in the mist
> – You cannot see the torch – raising her arm
> Lorn, bold, as if saluting with her fist.

Thus from stability and flux, iron and water, the poem moves to an historic plane: the rigidity of reactionary government is set against the principle of change on which the Constitution is founded. In the first stanza here, identification between buildings and institutions is made: the dream from the past is, among other things, the dream of the original revolutionaries whose Utopia is embodied in another metal artefact, the statue. The difficulty is that they created their liberal revolution in the image of the old order: they tried to institutionalise change. Today's revolutionaries aspire to base new societies on change, but they fail to recognise the human need for fixities. The final image here is of the old revolution (the statue) transformed into the new (the clenched-fist salute), and 'Liberty' is neither permanent nor fluctuating but *constant*, a principle existing in time when changing manifestations, itself unchanging.

This sort of writing raises questions. These are matters about which we argue, yet the poem – though it appears to take sides – is unresolved. This is a case where we *need* Wintersian propositions but are left with a web of gestures, even prejudices. For example, the poem depends on the belief – which I share – that the Nixon era was a bad time; but this needs substantiation. A similar doubt infects the poem's technique. Is Gunn being relaxed and flexible, or clumsy? Does the rhyme 'ferry'/'revolutionary' work? Yet the rhythmical counterpoint in the last stanza is as beautiful and assured as anything in Gunn's work. His gaucheries sometimes seem Hardyesque authentications of his honesty; here he is most fluent where difficulties need to be raised, where the thought should meet with most resistance from the verse. It is a convincing conclusion to a line of thought but, finally, no more than a gesture – and it is many years now since he first decided to question the validity of 'the large gesture of solitary man'. In his earlier work, stance, pose and gesture were important as moments of stasis in which people established an identity, breaking free from 'movement' temporarily. The earlier stances, though they involved commitment to action, did not involve action in terms of the stance. The fetishistic dandy with the swastika-draped bed in 'The Beaters' is in no sense a Nazi. But in this later poem, the emotion compels us to identify with a pose which is intended to issue in specific actions with public implications and, even if one agrees with the poet's premises, one must ask what essential difference there is between the clenched fist and the Nazi salute. True, one is a gesture of resistance, the other of oppression. But both are salutes; both call for public violence; both deny the validity of rational discussion. It is not Gunn's purpose in the poem to declare a commitment or invoke the detail of political argument. It is one of his best poems because it provokes these questions and because it shows historical patterns growing from the matrices of feeling the landscape represents. It shows American society as based on the dialectic of permanence and change, the dialectic which determines the creative tensions of Gunn's poetry.

We have reached a stalemate – one that is at the root of modern poetry. 'Iron Landscapes' attempts to reconcile the fluidity of the modern (free verse and the rest of it) with the monumental qualities of the classical (the metred stanza). Whatever one makes of the metric, the internal structure is modernist, Poundian. It is concerned not with ideas but with the raw material of thought. It is significant that the internal structure resolves itself in a gesture. And that is precisely the weakness of some of Pound's poetry. But what Gunn brings to his newly discovered 'modernism' is respect for the classical as a living concern. Whatever we make of the clenched fist, there is no mistaking the fundamentally liberal position of 'Iron Landscapes', a position reinforced by, for example, his version of colonisation in 'The Geysers' sequence. The Indian workers of 'Diagrams' belong to a race displaced and humbled by colonialism, yet – as 'The Geysers' shows – *all* human habitations are colonies. The perpetual challenge to the liberal is how to make such colonies humane and establish a harmony between man the artificer and man the creature. Gunn is a highly civilised artist – hence his continuing loyalty to the old forms. Despite his enthusiasm for the new, he does not welcome – as some writers whose names have been misleadingly linked with his appear to do – the collapse of our civilisation. Rather, he sees change and the capacity for change as the essential quality of a living civilisation, and he celebrates its continuity.

Source: excerpted from 'Definition and Flow: A Personal Reading of Thom Gunn', in *PN Review*, 5, no. 3 (1978), pp. 51–2, 52–3, 53, 54–7.

Merle E. Brown　　A Critical Performance of 'Misanthropos' (1973)

. . . It is not possible to work out the critical performance of a poem by means of director encounter, by what children call a 'stare-down', and thus it is that I have moved with indirection toward Thom Gunn's 'Misanthropos,' in spite of the lines with which Gunn concludes the poem:

> You must
> If you can, pause; and, paused,
>
> Turn out toward others, meeting their look at full,
> 　Until you have completely stared
> On all there is to see. Immeasurable,
> 　The dust yet to be shared.

Each of the seventeen poems of which 'Misanthropos' [in *Touch*, 1967] is composed echoes the others, and all of them interinanimate each other. But if one would sense the surge of feeling that gives life and unity to the whole, he must attend to the interlinking action of Gunn's mind. Just as the final man of the poem, who has become its first man, can affirm that you must 'Turn out toward others, meeting their look at full,/Until you have completely stared/On all there is to see' . . . .

The skeletal pattern of 'Misanthropos' is not hard to discern, nor is discerning it important when compared with the question, 'do these bones live?' But noting it has mnemonic value and is a first step in coming as close to the poem as possible. The pattern is derived ultimately from Vico's eternal course and recourse of nations. The decadence of any nation or civilisation is a state of disintegration. In the final stage of Rome, the citizens retreat to the hills, each one a final man upon his final hill. The accepted hierarchy of value collapses, each man carries off his own fragmentary version of it to his own hill, no one sees anyone else, and it is only the wind that utters ambiguous orders from the plain. Chaucer's pilgrims may stand as representative of another such recourse of decadence. But

such decadence is virtually indistinguishable from the innocence
with which a new recourse of nations begins. Thus, as Toynbee
has shown, the Holy Roman Empire springs out of the isolated
monasteries and mountain citadels and Germanic tribes which
represent the final stage of the fall of the Roman Empire. And
Chaucer's pilgrims are full of innocent exuberance and self-confidence. Now Gunn, in 'Misanthropos', is working with just this
moment of transition in the eternal course and recourse of nations, the
moment of decadence as it turns into the moment of innocence. . . .

With all his misanthropy and with all the sympathy he shows for
this American form of misanthropy. Gunn is able to resist this
deepest revulsion for men with a disgust more intense than the
sympathy he feels for it. Gunn articulates this complex mixture of
sympathy and disgust in the twelfth poem, 'Elegy on the Dust',
which is the high point of 'Misanthropos', the point at which the
last man turns into the first man. The poem is a stunning articulation
of the vision of men in society as a bowl of dust, 'vexed with constant
loss and gain', 'a vaguely heaving sea', a graveyard which is a sea
of dust. At the beginning of 'Misanthropos', the final man was being
a temporary Englishman in his refusal to build a watch tower. But
here he has moved to America and looks outward from his retreat,
taking into his view the hill, the wooded slope, and the vast expanse
of dust beyond it. He has made the transfer which Lawrence's Lou
Witt makes at the end of *St Mawr*[1].

'Elegy on the Dust' ends with this visionary judgment on man in
a modern mass nation state:

> Each colourless hard grain is now distinct,
>   In no way to its neighbour linked,
> Yet from wind's unpremeditated labours
>   It drifts in concord with its neighbours,
> Perfect community in its behaviour.
>   It yields to what it sought, a savour:
> Scattered and gathered, irregularly blown,
>   Now sheltered by a ridge or stone,
> Now lifted on strong upper winds, and hurled
>   In endless hurry round the world.

The poem might seem to be merely a vision of man's ultimate form
of decadence, that last stage in a Platonic cycle of degeneration at
which a mobocracy turns into tyranny. Men are seen in the poem
at their very lowest, averaged out in indistinguishable 'grains of
dust/Too light to act, too small to harm, too fine/To simper or

betray or whine'. In such a mobocracy, where even those who
sought distinction hard are levelled with the rabble, in absolute
uniformity, men are ready for a savior, a tyrant, who will windily
hurl them 'In endless hurry round the world'. But instead of sharing
this vision of Marcuse of the complete bankruptcy of our civilisation,
Gunn attends to its articulation with his keen, critical ear and turns
the poem into a condemnation of that vision for which he has so
much sympathy. The ultimate form of decadence turns out to be
not what is seen, but the vision itself. As Raymond Williams has
argued so persuasively, men exist as a mass only in the eye of the
beholder. It is the beholding of men as a bowl of dust, as a mobocracy
turning into a tyranny, not the men beheld in such a way, which is
decadent. . . .

My reading of 'The Elegy' as an expression of disgust for the
vision of men as a bowl of dust instead of as a direct expression of
that vision is reinforced by echoes in the 'Elegy' from the poem just
before it, the Epitaph for Anton Schmidt, and by the echoes of the
'Elegy' itself in the poem which follows it, 'The First Man'. There
is no irony in Gunn's admiration for Anton Schmidt, whose greatness
depends on his not having mistaken 'the men he saw,/As others
did, for gods or vermin'. The vision of the 'Elegy' clearly mistakes
the men viewed for vermin and the viewer for a god. Furthermore,
the first man of the thirteenth poem is presented as Gunn's vision
of the man who has had the vision of the 'Elegy', 'An unreflecting
organ of perception'. *That* man can perceive men as a disgusting
smudge because he does not reflect on what such a vision implies
about himself. What it implies for Gunn is that, just as the men
viewed in the 'Elegy' disappear into the dust of a society blown 'In
endless hurry round the world' by a windy tyrant, so the visionary
of the 'Elegy', that imperial self, that 'transcendental eyeball', is
finally to be seen 'darkening in the heavy shade/Of trunks that
thicken in the ivy's grip'. And this image of the first man, of this
American innocent, this barbarian who may be what must follow
after the decadence of Europe, this appals Gunn as much as it did
the poet here being echoed, Wallace Stevens. The eleventh poem of
Stevens's 'The Man With The Blue Guitar' is the rejection of its
vision of men dissolving into a thicket of time, where they are caught
as flies, 'Wingless and withered, but living alive'. At this point Gunn
must make his final choice: to accept the disappearance of man as
an individual into the dust of society or the heavy shade of nature

or to reaffirm the value of that man as distinctive. His choice, as is obvious from the fourteenth poem, is the second: he must stare upon men as a smudge until they come so close to him that the outlines of the smudge break away from it and the men turn into individuals.

Only as a result of doing this does he realise in direct experience that as he gazes upon a man, he is himself gazed upon, as he touches another, he is himself touched, and that his own self and his whole world are enlarged and enlivened by this interaction. Gunn does not simply assert this but works it out experientially by means of echoes. The first man's affirming in the seventeenth poem that you must pause, if you can, echoes and is even learned from the scratched man's pausing in the sixteenth poem. The first man's revulsion from the stale stench, the hang-dog eyes and the pursed mouth of the scratched man in the sixteenth poem echoes the scratched man's response to the first man when he first sees him in the fifteenth poem:

> The creature sees him, jumps back, staggers, calls,
> Then, losing balance on the pebbles, falls.

The effect of Gunn's restraint in this passage – we aren't quite sure what the lines imply and may even feel them to be empty – is that our sense of the repulsiveness of the first man and Gunn's sense of his own repulsiveness coincide with the first man's momentary revulsion from the scratched man even as he grips his arm. Although Gunn's movement out of isolation at the end of 'Misanthropos' includes such moments of felt insight, it is harsh and painful. There is no moment of explosive joy as there is at the end of Stevens's 'Esthétique du Mal', when Stevens realises that human life is made up of

> So many selves, so many sensuous worlds,
> As if the air, the mid-day air, was swarming
> With the metaphysical changes that occur,
> Merely in living as and where we live.

Gunn's use of the word 'stared' to express the way in which we must connect with others suggests harshness. And his last words, 'Immeasurable/The Dust yet to be shared' come out with a grudging sigh. But Gunn has made his recognition and affirmation. And the poems which follow 'Misanthropos' in *Touch*, especially the last one, 'Back to Life', and many poems in . . . *Moly* [1971] show that he meant it.

The innermost sense of experience which forces Gunn to pull himself out of his isolation still remains to be explained. What forces him to affirm the value of human community is, I believe, his sense that his own nature as an individual is communal, even when he is most isolated. Observing the first man, in the thirteenth poem, 'darkening in the heavy shade/Of trunks that thicken in the ivy's grip', he sees that his very existence as an individual, composed of himself as self-aware observer and himself as a rudimentary man, is about to be annihilated. It is his commitment to himself as a community, as both spy and spied on, which forces him finally to turn out toward others. The final choice is between dissolving into nature and rejoining men. Gunn chooses the second because of his growing awareness that the very essence of himself as an individual is communal and that he will not survive in any form at all if he becomes one with nature.

As early as the second poem of 'Misanthropos', Gunn reveals the doubleness of his individuality as poet and the last man quite emphatically. In contrast to the first poem of the sequence, in which Gunn as poet talks out his sense of himself as the last man, presented in the third person, in the second poem Gunn speaks as the last man in the first person to his echo, which of course is Gunn as poet. This conversation concludes thus:

> Is there no feeling, then, that I can trust,
> In spite of what we have discussed?
>
> > Disgust.

The form of the whole of 'Misanthropos' is implicit in these lines. The experience of the last man is based upon disgust, upon misanthropy. But the nature of this disgust is articulated in marvellously varied discussions carried on between the last man and his echo or, to reverse the coin, between Gunn as poet and himself as last man. Gunn's shifting from poem to poem between the last man as objectively third person and as subjectively first person can be explained in no other way. It is in passing through 'what we have discussed' that Gunn is enabled to move from disgust to trust and thus begin the last poem with:

> Others approach. Well, this one may show trust
> Around whose arm his fingers fit.

The trust of this last poem never breaks free from a need that it be discussed or even, for that matter, from an element of disgust. Thus, the poet, in expressing the last-man-become-first-man's willingness to trust the scratched man, also implies his grave doubts as to whether the man is worthy of such trust. Even the internal community of the second poem, moreover, is itself full of disgust. To get the tone of the poem right one needs to add to each echoing word the phrase 'you poor fool'. Thus, even though the basic movement of 'Misanthropos' is from isolated disgust through discussion to communal trust, there is an internal community involved in the initial disgust just as there is an element of disgust in the trust of the final external community.

Once the reader recognises the explicitly communal nature of the isolated individual as presented in the second poem, he can then see this community as implicitly present even in the first poem, which begins:

> He avoids the momentous rhythm
> of the sea, one hill suffices him
> who has the entire world to choose from.

> He melts through the brown and green silence
> inspecting his traps, is lost in dense
> thicket, or appears among great stones.

Although one probably begins the poem merely spying on the last man, who 'lives like/the birds, self-contained they hop and peck', further readings are sure to convince him that the poem contains, along with the man we spy on, its own spy, the echoing, controlling presence of the poet. Unlike the last man, the last man's echo, the poet Thom Gunn, proves himself capable of the momentous rhythm of the sea. The first clause of the poem, with its anapestic rhythm and with the first line running on into the second is a sea-like rhythm. But having set this rhythm in motion, the poet then drops it abruptly, with the second clause, 'one hill suffices him', working iambically and in a syntax at odds with that of the first clause, so that there is no build-up by way of clauses rhythmically and syntactically parallel. Similarly, in the second stanza the first line is a return to the momentous rhythm of sea-like anapests, but here the expected run-on effect of the first stanza is frustrated; one must pause after 'silence' and begin again with 'inspecting his traps'. The poet as spy does, in other words, have a watch tower. He is not self-contained as the spied-upon man is; he looks beyond that self-containment to glimpse the rhythm the last man avoids, introducing it only to break it down, so that we sense not just the isolation of the man, but also that from which he is isolated.

The communal nature of 'Misanthropos' is shared, it seems to me, by all genuine poems, and is why John Crowe Ransom was wrong when he said: one cannot write a love poem while he is in love and that is why Elizabeth Barrett Browning's sonnets are loving but unpoetic. The truth is rather that one must be both in love and out of love to write a love poem. To write a poem on himself as a man who widens his solitude till it is absolute, Gunn had to be both in that solitude and in community. In other words, the very writing of the poem forces him into internal communal relations which work against his desire for absolute solitude. 'Misanthropos' is distinctive because it is a genuine poem based upon the realisation of the communal doubleness inherent in all poetic sincerity. The very form of the poem, the way its parts echo each other, grows out of Gunn's sense that the poet's individuality, in the act of composing the poem, is communal. And it is this sense of the communal nature of the poet as individual, even when pushed to an extreme isolation by disgust, which leads Gunn to reject the American desire for dissolving into nature and to turn out towards other human beings. . . .

SOURCE: extracts from 'A Critical Performance of Thom Gunn's "Misanthropos"', in *Iowa Review*, 4 (1973), pp. 75–6, 80–1, 83–6.

NOTE

1. See Richard Poirier's superb analysis of *St Mawr* in *A World Elsewhere: The Place of Style in American Literature* (Oxford, 1966), pp. 40–9.

Patrick Swinden   Thom Gunn's
Castle   (1977)

. . . Gunn's poems might be described as elegant queries about their right to exist, meditations on the inadequacy of language to express the related inadequacy of most descriptions of personal identity. In

... 'For a Birthday', Gunn pictured words as tiny yelping dogs snarling around his trouser bottoms, 'a weight upon my haste'; they were 'tons which I am detaching ounce by ounce' so that eventually he would be able to rest in 'springs of speech, the dark before of truth'. ...

[His] first two volumes [*Fighting Terms*, 1954, and *The Sense of Movement*, 1957] and the first half of the third (*My Sad Captains and Other Poems*, 1961), for the most part skirmish at the edges of the problem. This may strike some of Gunn's readers as an odd way of putting it, because his reputation was established on a basis of what was usually conceived to be a sort of poetic thuggery. He was the poet who set aside the finer feelings of his fellow Movement poets in favour of less discriminating and more simplifying postures. He 'praised the overdogs from Alexander / To those who would not play with Stephen Spender', in a celebrated couplet from one of the least self-questioning poems. He also evinced a tough admiration for aggressive folk heroes of the 1950s – the Marlon Brando of *The Wild One*, Elvis Presley, even the Abominable Snowman. But even at that time, with the Brando prototype of 'On the Move' in mind, it was possible to see that what Gunn admired about the Boys was not merely their aggression. Their violence was described as 'uncertain', the words forming themselves out of the 'dull thunder' of their machines were 'approximate'. And their robustness was no more than skin deep since their gleaming jackets 'strapped in doubt' as they committed themselves to an irresistible movement that divides and breaks those who fail to join in. In *Jack Straw's Castle* the skinhead hero reappears as Leather Kid in a poem called 'An Amorous Debate'. Here his leather outfit is described as 'a firm defence of hide against / the ripple of skin'. This excites Fleshly, the female side of the relationship, until she zips him open and finds that his skin underneath is like leather too: ' "Strange", she said, "you / are still encased in your / defence" ', and she has a hard time of it moving him on from the debate to the serious business that is to follow. Significantly, in the light of what is happening in these later volumes, he achieves orgasm only after he makes accidental sexual contact between parts of his own person (his lips suck at his arm).

During the 1950s Gunn was preoccupied with the contrivances erected by the poet's will and intelligence to cope with what would otherwise have been the intolerable pressures of self-consciousness.

Perhaps 'contrivances' is not the best word, since these gestures, which I have described as functions of the will, are often difficult to distinguish from a sort of psychological reflex action, tricks played by consciousness to keep the reality that underlies it at bay. They also keep the world outside consciousness, especially other people, other minds and demands, at bay. Gunn is very astute in poems like 'Carnal Knowledge' or 'Captain in Time of Peace' about the diplomacy of emotional, and usually sexual, relationships. His 'poses', 'games' and 'performances', his 'moves' and 'tactics', are plotted with a scrupulous accuracy that recalls Donne, or Shakespeare in his sonnets: 'When my love swears that she is made of truth/I do believe her, though I know she lies' – except that in Gunn it is the poet who lies and the other person who may, or may not, believe.

The issue is complicated in Gunn's work where the poet himself is the other, a secret sharer in his own psychological and emotional strategies.

In poem after poem this importunate *doppelgänger* appears. His the 'strange head' in 'The Secret Sharer'; and the strange eyes in the pier-glass in 'The Corridor' watching the man who in turn watches 'The couple in the keyhole' who themselves seem hardly separate from that apparently infinite recession of observers. He is 'The Monster' of *My Sad Captains*, 'the man who never can get in' to the room the poet has just left and to the supple love-making the poet has achieved in a small bed where, now, he fears, his other self will be found awake. In *Touch* he is glimpsed in a painting, his back turned towards us, but still identified as 'my monstrous lover, whom/I gaze at/every time I shave'. Little wonder that, in [*Jack Straw's Castle*], the animals of 'The Geysers' are admired for their combination of verbal taciturnity and lack of self-reflection: a fly disappears in the flicker of a snake's tongue – 'What elegance! it does not watch itself.'

Gunn attaches great importance, in these early volumes, to elegance – elegance in the postures taken towards life which are the subjects of the poems, and elegance in the verbal expression of those subjects. But his elegance catches him out, because it catches him watching himself. In 'The Court Revolt' the just king is senselessly overthrown, and his subjects are deprived of an order which, whilst transcending themselves, is still personal and magnanimous. But:

> The subject's real subjection, though, was near:
> Coming from justice without face or shape
> Was self-subjection which has no escape.

Gunn developed his notion of self-subjection in a poem from *The Sense of Movement* called 'A Plan of Self-subjection'. Here the political allegory of 'The Court Revolt' has given place to a dramatic psychological analysis on the Donneian model. The analysis has to do with problems that are bound to arise when a poet uses language to define his personal identity. The main problem in this case arises out of what Gunn calls 'contentment'. This is the habit of resting in false certainties, in rigid categories of self-explanation. It is Gunn's view that the drift towards 'contentment' is likely to be increased rather than dispelled by the formalising, structuring activities of verse:

> I put this pen to paper and my verse
> Imposes form upon my fault described
> So that my fault is worse.

The opening of the third line is deeply ambiguous, and is meant to be. Is Gunn intending us to take 'So that' to mean 'with the result that', as it does so often in common speech, and therefore his fault is made worse as an unlooked-for consequence of an attempt to improve it? Or is he intending us to take it for what, strictly grammatically, it is supposed to mean, implying that there is some deep impulse in his psyche that drives him to make his fault worse by imposing that compromising 'order' to 'form' which, in the next line of the poem, is identified as a 'bribe' (He puts his pen to paper 'Not for condonement but from being bribed/with order')? The grammatical pun – do the words open an adverbial clause of purpose or result? – encapsulates the dilemma out of which the poem has been formed. . . .

In the early sixties Gunn stood at an intellectual watershed. He had created a poetic landscape in which what was distinctively human was thrust painfully into a world of natural forms that were imbued with some instinctive, 'hidden purpose', rank with growth and promiscuity; and into a world, also, of human artefacts, sharp cornered and angularly planned, a world of rectangular buildings rising high over their foundations; 'cosmetic light' illuminating 'The longest streets, desire that never ends'; recessive corridors, rooms within rooms, locked doors. And behind the contemporary, man-

made world, often penetrating its brittle geometrical forms, lay a
more elegant but deteriorated past: 'failing stonework'; 'a carved
head that you fish from slime'; 'a carved cherub' crumbling in the
streets of a decaying town; 'two moulded garden urns' at an edge of
the gentle lawn of a country house.

Usually Gunn's people were most admired when they simplified
their condition by committing themselves most wilfully to the
machinery of a man-made world set against nature. 'You control
what you can, and/use what you cannot' is one of the confessions
of the life artist in *Touch*. He looks back to the wilfully ignorant
aggression of the Boys in 'On the Move', 'using what they imperfectly
control' as they 'scare a flight of birds across the field'.

But as early as *The Sense of Movement* [1957] there were meditations
on other kinds of movement, more internally disturbing, less
evidently willed and simplified. Those 'moulded garden urns', for
example, occupy part of the landscape of 'The Allegory of the Wolf
Boy', whose 'loose desires' are 'hoarded against his will'. Clear
outlines of a human personality, grasped and defined, are 'gone
beyond'. The poem broods on the moment of transformation from
boy to beast, a moment at which the 'seeds of division' hidden in
the 'firm tissues' of his body, 'play us in a sad duplicity'. In *Moly*
[1971] this duplicity has itself divided, and, from the point of view
of the man who experiences it, is less cause for despondency or
alarm. 'The Sand Man', having been beaten into a simple-minded
innocence thirty-five years ago, now rolls round in the sand near
the Golden Gate bridge in San Francisco:

> He rocks, a blur on ridges, pleased to be
>   Dispersing with the sands
> He feels a dry cool multiplicity
>   Gilding his feet and hands.

It is, I suppose, the same blur that confronted the speaker in 'Vox
Humana'. But now it does not call the mind to definition and choice.
Instead it disperses consciousness into an apparently beneficent
multiplicity, making the sand man almost saint-like in his withdrawal
from single identity. The same point is made, more beautifully I
think, by the landscape of 'Flooded Meadows' in the same volume.
Here, after weeks of rain, sunlight pours down on meadows where
definition has been 'suspended'. A 'level listlessness' cancels the
detail of the valley floor, creating 'the unity of unabsorbed excess'.
Duplicity or duality, multiplicity, the unity of unabsorbed excess.

The breaking down of clear definitions means that they lack fixed identity, the sort of identity, that is to say, that issues from those willed and formal interferences that were deprecated in 'For a Birthday'.

In the second part of *My Sad Captains*, Gunn turned more frequently to natural forms for hints about how this relaxation of will and purpose might combine in a single poem the formal integrity and capacity for growth, change, even dispersal, that were sinister in the wolf boy, seductive in the San Francisco sand man. He addresses himself to the problem explicitly in 'The Value of Gold'. Lying on the grass of what I suppose is a public park, Gunn looks up at the flowers in the border, towering high above him, and asks:

> Can this quiet growth
> Comprise at once the still-to-grow
> And a full form without a lack?
> And, if so, can I too be both?

The question is Gunn's way of posing the familiar Romantic problem of identity, the same that Yeats also tried to answer by contemplating an image of growing things – in the form of a chestnut tree at the close of 'Among School Children'. How can the poet, whilst using words that of necessity confer form and order on the world, find a way of expressing the unformed *processes* of experience? And how can he do this at the same time as he shows how these processes are a part of the completed structure of an experience to which it might not be correct to say they aspire, but which, from a certain vantage point outside the process, it must be said that they belong? Now the growth is not silent but 'quiet'; and that quiet process, and the hesitant, undeclarative syntax and verse movement which are to be its linguistic expression, must gather so imperceptibly into themselves the multiple strands of thought, feeling, intuition, that no 'lack' will be felt. There is to be no faltering gap between the moment-by-moment evolution of the poet's language, and the sum total of those moments as they are finally viewed from the end of the poem.

The appropriate form for a poetry of this kind turned out to be an extension into syllabic measures of the seven-syllabled line, usually in stanza units of six rhyming lines, Gunn has begun to use as early as 'Tamer and Hawk' (in its six-syllabled variant), and brought to its most satisfying expression so far in 'Vox Humana'. In a conversation with Ian Hamilton in 1964[1] he said that 'in syllabics I can much more easily record the casual perceptions, whereas with metrical verse I very often become committed to a particular kind of rather taut emotion, a rather clenched kind of emotion'. I want to look into this matter of 'casual perception' as the proper subject matter of poetry later. The syllabic verse that Gunn had decided to use as its vehicle of expression was not altogether new to him in the early sixties. He had already experimented with it in a short poem called 'Market at Turk', another treatment of the 'tough guy' theme, which interestingly anticipates Leather Kid and Fleshly:

> It is military, almost,
> how he buckles himself in,
> with boot straps and Marine belt,
> reminders of the will, lest
> even with that hard discipline
> the hardness should not be felt.

Like the speaker in 'The Nature of an Action', a few pages above, this boy at the street corner has found that in 'Testing my faculties I found a stealth/Of passive illness lurking in my health' – that is to say, a 'lack' or, to substitute another word Gunn is fond of using in [*Jack Straw's Castle*], a 'need' (which is a more positive way of putting it). But more to the present purpose, this lack, this irresolution encased in the flaunted poses and insignia of resolution, is mirrored in the hesitant, almost furtive movement of the line endings over half rhymes and muted sound patterns.

This same hesitancy and strangely unpurposive-seeming fluency is reproduced and refined in many of the poems in the second part of *My Sad Captains*. Those that answer strictly to the definition I have offered so far – of seven syllabled syllabics in stanzas of six lines (rhyming, as a matter of fact, abcabc – like 'Market at Turk') – are 'Considering the Snail', 'Hotblood on Friday', 'Lights Among Redwood', 'A Trucker', and 'My Sad Captains'. They are among the best poems in the volume, and as it happens there is a very precise way in which their accomplishment can be measured. The title poem has much in common with a poem in *Fighting Terms* called 'Lerici', which is a reflection on heroic death occasioned by a visit to the scene of Shelley's drowning in 1822. Turning from this death, which is described as 'submissive' (Shelley was 'but a minor conquest of the sea'), Gunn contrasts Byron's more dignified end at

Missolonghi (though the context remains that of 'the sea's pursuit')
in the terms of this final stanza:

> Byron was worth the sea's pursuit. His touch
> Was masterful to water, audience
> To which he could react until an end.
> Strong swimmers, fishermen, explorers: such
> Dignify death with thriftless violence –
> Squandering with so little left to spend.

Contrast this with the second stanza of 'My Sad Captains', on a
similar theme:

> . . . before they fade they stand
> perfectly embodied, all
>
> the past lapping them like a
> cloak of chaos. They were men
> who, I thought, lived only to
> renew the wasteful force they
> spent with each hot convulsion.
> They remind me, distant now.

The force that was wasteful in the second poem has much in common
with the violence that was squandered and thriftless in the first, but
the incorporation of the rhetorical phrases into the prepared context
of the verse is very different. In the earlier poem heavy stresses bear
down on both beginning and end of the two last lines with their
pyrrhic or trochaic feet shifting the energy forward down each line,
the last carefully alliterated to draw attention to the link between
squandering and spending. In the latter the rhetorical gesture is
allowed to fall back into the surrounding meditation ('I thought')
because the rhymes fall on lightly stressed and syntactically light-
weight words, like 'a', 'to', 'now'; the second sentence, most relevant
to this particular comparison, comes to rest with the low-key rhyme
of the third syllable of 'convulsion' with 'men' three lines back. The
effect is that instead of standing out as separate statements occupying
set positions in an argument or a train of thought, the phrases in
the later poem feel inseparable from the movement of the poem as
a whole, details that cannot be detached from the completed poem
in which they are discovered to be realising their present potential.

Gunn's most successful poem in this vein is, I believe. 'Lights
Among Redwood'. This is not so much a description as a shared
involvement in the response to light settling in the streams, ferns,

and Redwood trees of Muir Woods, California. The poem needs to be quoted in full for its rare, musing and discreet power to be appreciated:

> And the streams here, ledge to ledge,
> take care of light. Only to
> the pale green ribs of young ferns
> tangling above the creek's edge
> it may sometimes escape, though
> in quick diffusing patterns.
>
> Elsewhere it has become tone,
> pure and rarified; at most
> a muted dimness coloured
> with moss-green, charred grey, leaf-brown.
> Calm shadow! Then we at last
> remember to look upward:
>
> constant, to laws of size and
> age the thick forms hold, though gashed
> through with Indian fires. At once
> tone is forgotten: we stand
> and stare – mindless, diminished –
> at their rosy immanence.

It opens as if already half complete, with where we are ('here') understood and made present in whatever preceded 'And' before that first line. The light that has descended into the streams, and accurately touched the veins of the young ferns nearest the water, is now absorbed in other things, present but transformed. Involvement in the diffusion of the light into changing patterns, tones and dimness is achieved by the appeal to visual sensations alone (there is no Keatsian tactile richness or synaesthesic narcosis). Then this diffusing detail, muted and soft edged, gives way to the forms of the trees that rise from it, freeing those who stare at them, by what is with a Marvellian delicacy called a 'rosy immanence', from the constraints of personal and linguistic identity. 'Immanence' is simply an indwelling quality – the trees are in the world, firmly there, and 'rosy' in a way that suggests comfort, beauty, and, perhaps, a resistant toughness (in view of the Indian fires only four lines away). But the word also has religious connotations – not clamorous but lingering somewhere at the edges of our consciousness of the trees. The poem successfully releases us into an experience hardly our own, moving through sensory involvement to something at the other side of it, where the self that perceives suddenly becomes as if perceived, and gratefully diminished in the process. Those quiet passages over the muted rhymes and the unemphatic carriage of the syllabic metre have a great deal to do with this lapse out of self and will into the immanence of the scene.

These syllabic poems are among the best Gunn has written, but it is a condition of their being that they must fail to incorporate several important aspects of his poetic character. They withdraw from personal contacts and relationships at the same time as they withdraw from the circle of self-consciousness Gunn has spent so much time drawing and evading in the past. Their quiet visual concentration manages to assimilate what is seen to what is thought with no intrusion of more immediate and, perhaps, cruder sense impressions – of taste, smell and, above all, touch. . . .

[The title poem in] *Jack Straw's Castle* is Gunn's latest metaphor of self-consciousness. It contrasts starkly with that other castle back in 'Human Condition', which suggested a containment in individuality that was more guardedly aggressive than confining. In any case, in the earlier poem Gunn soon left behind the image of the castle to 'stay or *start from*, here', and at the end of it he was able to 'Walk through hypothesis / An individual'. In the new poem, individuality is much more of a problem. Why can't I leave my castle? Jack Straw asks:

> isn't there anyone
> anyone here beside me
>
> sometimes I find myself wondering
> if the castle is castle at all
> a place apart, or merely
> the castle that every snail
> must carry around till his death

Inside the castle Jack explores room after room, down to the cellars and foundations. The verse cannot dispel his uncertainty as to whether these are real rooms or areas of psychological disturbance (populated by 'dream sponsors' like Medusa or Charles Manson) or simply consciousness of body as the palpable and inescapable evidence of physical confinement. When he is consumed in the glow of a naked light bulb, which has become the dazzle of Medusa's gold hair in one of his fantasies, Jack sinks into the darkness of his foundations, into cellars which again fail to locate themselves as inner or outer, a part of or separate from Jack's self-consciousness:

> And when later
> I finger the stickiness along the ridges
> Of a large central block that feels like granite
> I don't know if it's my own, or I shed it,
> Or both, as if priest and victim were only
> Two limbs of the same body

This involvement in the foundations of personality, the basis out of which identity is formed, and which it includes, is defined as 'the seat of needs', the area far below consciousness where the lacks, incompletenesses and metaphysical hungers of these and earlier poems arose. The place is so deep, so old

> That even where eye never perceives body
> And where the sharpest ear discerns only
> The light slap and rustle of flesh on stone
> They, the needs, seek ritual and ceremony
> To appease themselves.

'To appease themselves.' Confidence in a world beyond the castle, however disordered and obscured by the fog that was so disturbing in 'Human Condition', has given way to a repeated withdrawal from even the hypothesis of an otherness, somewhere outside the speaker's own skin. After his visit to the cellar Jack speculates that there is 'nothing outside the bone/nothing accessible',

> I sit
> trapped in bone
> I am back again
> where I never left, I sit
> in my first instant, where
> I never left
>
> petrified at my centre

Then Manson reappears, breaking into Jack's 'long solitude', a dream that insists it came from nowhere but his own head. But though the sadistic fantasies that summoned Manson originate in the castle, Jack for a time believes that their embodiment in the figure of Manson must imply that there is a real Manson outside the castle, and that there really is an outside of the castle after all. This possibility of otherness, or a movement towards it, offers itself in the image of a staircase. No sooner, however, has Jack started to

climb the staircase than the cold awakes him, and what he calls his
spectre continues the climb until the staircase ends at a sheer drop.
Beneath it 'bone-chips which must/at one time have been castle'
lie under broken slabs. Even in the wakened man this creates a
panic, which is only partially calmed by this assertion that the castle
is still here. He needs the castle – so long as it will remain familiar,
habitually lived in – as a protection against dreams of what is either
inside or outside its confinements. Yet the urge to make contact
with what lies beyond it, beyond the body and the dreams, remains,
and impinges on Jack's half-waking state in the form of an intruder
in his bed. Like Gunn and his fellow sleeper in 'Touch', perhaps,
Jack Straw and the man to whom he claims he gave his key lie 'bare
and close/Facing apart, but leaning ass to ass'. With slightly less
extreme ambitions than the sleeping partners of that earlier poem,
the two men make contact which is 'sufficient touch,/A hinge, it
separates but not too much'. At the end of the sequence, Jack is
unsure as to whether the man is real or a part of a dream. Either
way the sense of hinged separation, of 'Thick sweating flesh' which
combines an experience of merging and of setting off one thing or
person against another, is the nearest Jack comes to satisfaction in
the poem. Even if he were a dream, he says, 'With dreams like this,
Jack's ready for the world'.

The volume as a whole dwells on these facts of merging and
separation. Many of the poems celebrate occasions of mystical or
narcotic unity and community. The fourth poem in the sequence
called 'The Geysers' describes another experience of self-diffusion,
where the 'hinge' of 'Jack Straw's Castle' is no longer there to
separate one self from another. Instead there is a dissolving of self
into the shared consciousness of others. In the bath-house of a
Californian commune, Gunn no longer knows for certain who is
who among the naked bodies 'locked soft in trance of heat'. The
eyes are empty and other senses break down to touch alone, 'touch
of skin of hot water on the skin/I grasp my mind squeeze
open touch within'. At the end, through a process of entry into
others, which is at the same time a yielding, Gunn loses all sense of
self by becoming 'part of all', returning to a state of being he must
have experienced in the womb, before 'caesarian lightning lopped
me off separate'.

As he puts it in another, wittier poem, 'one thing follows from
another/Things were different inside Mother.'

Origins, the fact of unitary being before the inevitable separation into identity, are sought in a variety of ways. Often, as in 'Jack Straw's Castle', they are discovered in cellars or foundations, or what lies beneath the foundations of 'Bringing to Light', 'bringing a raft of tiny/cellars to light of day'. Even here, however, the facts of division are present. The 'Common Root' in the last cavern with its foundations merely the Earth, is

> nothing
>   but a faint
> smell, mushrooming, thin
> as if something
>   even here
> were separating from its dam
>
> a separating
>   of cells

The earliest self, 'not yet/separate from what it sees,/a selfless self' ('Thomas Bewick') is lost to consciousness, and poems cannot help expressing consciousness. So Gunn has still to find a way out of the difficulties he suggested in 'Touch', how to write poems expressive of a movement towards and into undifferentiated being, 'the dark before of truth', when the last thing consciousness would be capable of doing in such a state of self-abnegation, would be to reflect on itself as an identity, something set apart as an object of attention. The moment the poem is found doing this, it fails to ratify the unitary experience out of which it tries to convince us it has been born. On the other hand, the moment 'we/have thrown off/the variegated stuffs that/distinguish us one from/one' ('Saturnalia'), poems disappear, because there is no poet left to exert any personal control over the arrangement of words. No poet can articulate that roar of the pouring from 'At the Centre' which, we recall, is 'unheard from being always heard'. It might be possible, as Gunn says it is in 'The Outdoor Concert', to live for a while

> at that luminous intersection
> spread at the centre
> like a white garden spider
> so still
> that you think it
> has become its web

but it is not possible to write about it at the same time as living it, and to write about it with hindsight to make it over into an object of consciousness, what is what it essentially is not.

Nevertheless there are some fine poems taking as their subject experiences which are at least approximations to this unreflecting, and unreflective, life at the centre. Gunn is evolving a language which enables him to speak from experiences which are immediately physical, which bypass reflection in favour of an involvement, from the inside as it were, in activities where consciousness is no more than rudimentary and sensational: a dive into and out of water in 'the plunge'; 'The Cherry Tree''s flowering and fruiting, 'Yoko''s walk with his master to the piers on the New York waterfront, investigating the varied detritus of the pavements and the streets – these are the most successful poems of the volume. . . .

SOURCE: extracts from review-article, 'Thom Gunn's Castle', in *Critical Quarterly*, 19, no. 3 (Autumn 1977), pp. 43–5, 48–53, 56–60.

NOTE

1. Thom Gunn in interview with Ian Hamilton, *London Magazine*, IV, 8 (1964).

A. E. Dyson   'Watching You Watching Me . . .': A Note on 'The Passages of Joy'   (1989)

At the end of 'My Life Up To Now', included in *Thom Gunn: A Bibliography 1940–78* (1979), Gunn writes:

I do not either like or dislike myself inordinately. I have just had *Jack Straw's Castle and Other Poems* published. I cannot guess what my next book will be like.

The element of risk, chance, exploration is strong in Gunn, counter-balancing his love of clarity, order, hardness, in art and life. In numerous interviews and as a theme of various essays, he has stressed discontinuities, not continuities, in his work. No one poetic

voice or oracle is trusted blindly; though the 'sad captains', now in
orbit, 'One by one . . . appear'; 'and turn with disinterested / hard
energy, like the stars'.

Exploring, moving on, trusting luck and will – here is Gunn's
breathing space; here, the source of those gleams, chasms, mirages
which light up his art. His forms are tough, rooted in early classicism,
made for precision, but the content is imagist, or more exactly
symbolist: the peculiar spell is easier exemplified than described:

> On the other drinkers bent together
> Concocting selves for their impervious kit,
>   He saw it as no more than leather
> Which, taut across the shoulders grown to it,
>
>   Sent through the dimness of a bar
> As sudden and anonymous hints of light
>   As those that shipping give, that are
> Now flickers in the Bay, now lost in night . . .
>   (from 'Black Jackets', *My Sad Captains*, 1961)

Gunn admits also, in 'My Life Up To Now': 'I know that we all
continue to carry the same baggage: in my world, Christian does
not shed his burden, only his attitude to it alters'. His view of the
earlier volumes as stepping stones to the later is typical. They chart
a personal voyage, valid at every stage, however tinged with self-
irony; flexible enough for certain favourite poems – and a favourite
volume – to remain. (The latter is *Moly*, from that charmed moment
in the 60s when intangibles could almost be grasped, Dionysus
almost seemed simple. Dionysus, of course, is true god and must be
worshipped; but his apotheosis in history has always been rare and
fleeting.)

From Cambridge days, Gunn has been an intellectual poet, nearer
to the late Elizabethan and Jacobean 'metaphysicals' than Eliot ever
was (as near, say, as Auden); and with something of the deliberate
cleverness (in *Fighting Terms*, mainly) that could mar even Donne.
But, more important by far than 'intellectual', he is intuitive and
unified. Experience matters, art matters, and the two become one.
The much-discussed 'Philosophy' (existentialism, commitment-in-
alienation and the rest) is a servant, fused with Image irrevocably:
apart from which, it would be mere idle chatter, of no interest at
all.

The world Gunn lives in – or the aspects of it which turn to creation, and so become public – involves vivid tensions. For instance, intense joy in friendship, in New York and London, in erotic sex, in 'loud, boisterous men', in a friend's dog, in great spaces and deserts, are in balance (though also somehow continuous) with great longing for the withdrawal of self, before things-in-themselves. No doubt compassionate irony, beating back pessimism, is a note we could point to; along with astringent observation, and sheer delight in diversity, colour, sensation, in life itself. This is specially pertinent, since artists of joy are not thick on the ground these days. They must face the whole modern tug to despair, to negation, if they are at all to ring true. (In their distinctive ways, R. S. Thomas and Ted Hughes have a place with Gunn, in this rare achievement; so my yoking them is not as much a yoking of disparates as might first be thought.)

It must be added that Gunn's 'voice' is always his own, however many and varied his 'influences' (this aspect has led far too many critics an unholy dance). Of course the influences are there, who could miss them? Brando's 'The Wild One' (directly behind 'On the Move'?: but look at Gunn's ironies!); the Beat Poets; the Black Mountain Poets – these Americans were important long before Gunn settled in the States, interacting with an exceptionally rich (and scholarly) English brew: late sixteenth-century and early seventeenth-century poets; Hardy, Yeats, Auden, and indeed, a great many more. There are debts less often remarked upon, for instance, to Tennyson. The *In Memoriam* stanza is adapted for 'Modes of Pleasure: 2' (*My Sad Captains*) and 'The Garden of the Gods' (*Moly*) – both fine, pioneering poems, at first glance far removed from Tennyson, yet pointing to homoerotic and hypnotic instincts which both poets share. The point I emphasise is that Gunn never uses a source for frivolous reasons, and he never diminishes it. Even 'The Victim' in *The Passages of Joy* – an odd instance indeed – somehow enhances Betjeman: though it is slight in itself, and may seem handmade to mock.

Is Gunn a moralist? Eager for life, ruthlessly observant, loving, reckless, amused by human folly and endlessly subtle, how could he not be? His distinction is to be devoid of all malice and cant. Consider 'Adultery', 'The Girls Next Door', 'Donahue's Sister': these may not be vintage, but the hallmark is Gunn's. His poems of detached social attention can disconcert readers, especially those in whom antipathy too simply leads on to satiric disdain. True, fools

are not suffered gladly or in any way whitewashed; but a poet who
does not 'like or dislike' himself 'inordinately' is an unusual man.
Even 'Slow Waker' receives some residual support from his poem's
title; and the poet watching is the poet, too, of 'Talbot Road'. At
this moral level, we who read are most at risk, really; we may not
grasp Gunn's game, or its rules, or its place for ourselves, until some
trap is sprung. We may not grasp that an 'us'-and-'them' stance is
a treacherous business – particularly with a poet whose least
flattering images may be in mirrors we at first fail to see. (It is worth
revisiting two of the finest early poems from *The Sense of Movement*:
'The Nature of an Action', and 'The Corridor'.)

   The Passages of Joy has one theme, cropping up everywhere: literally
child's play, to which adults adapt, in many odd, off-beat ways.
This image closely links with labyrinths, and may dawn on us
gradually. Best start with the poem that declares the game in its
title, particularly since it embodies much that is positive and healing
in Gunn's own moral stance: 'Hide and Seek'. The poem records a
day of play, now passing to evening; it is the closing images I wish
to quote:

> In their fathers' gardens
> children are hiding
> up in orchard trees, seeking
> to be lost and found.
>
> Mother comes down
> for the youngest
> and as the dark thickens
> for the oldest too.
>
> Indoors, under a naked bulb,
> eight puppies sleep
> close against the huge hairy body
> of their mother. The bees
> have returned to their Queen.
> The crescent moon rises
> nine-tenths of it still hidden
> but imperceptibly moving
> below the moving stars
> and hugging the earth.

   In 'Sweet Things', Gunn befriends a mentally retarded youngster
with a child's I.Q., without at all liking him. He uses irony against
the child, which may seem cruel if we miss the honesty; then, the

same irony rebounds on himself, with disarming effect. He is taking both seriously, child and himself, in one equal measure. Both like sweet things, both are hypocrites – and what does Gunn care? Seek sweet things single-mindedly, and maybe you get them; don't seek, or hold back at all, and you certainly won't. Such a poem offers the stuff of judgement, the sharp feel of it; but judgement may bear lighter on acts, than on lives left unlived.

Lost threads, on-the-move endings, the drift of mortality: all these come anyway. But to turn them to virtue, to discover 'sweet things' early, then chase them and get them: this is success in life. 'Live all you can': Pater advised this; so did James's fictional Strether (*The Ambassadors*); Eliot denounced it, as a *fin-de-siècle* snare. For Gunn it seems gloriously obvious and there for the taking: just so long as we know it is art to be worked for, and to savour just as long as we can. Like daylong child's play, things darken towards evening; all passages of joy are envied, by powers destined to win:

> Time hovers o'er, impatient to destroy,
> And shuts up all the Passages of Joy'.
> (Johnson: *Vanity of Human Wishes*)

Johnson made heavy going of life, for all his energy. Gunn's 'Transients and Residents', to whose poem this eponymous quotation is prefixed, do better; and are more like Gunn.

In 'Interruption', a metrical poem in Gunn's earlier style, the poet speaks of his poems as 'snapshots', His overriding urge is to get them 'accurate': which is, as nearly as possible 'images', in the Imagist sense. But then, accurate snapshots are art, and within art's kingdom: 'the truest poetry is the most feigning . . .' (and consider the Family Album, for a simple test). There are necessary dislocations in the medium, in focus and viewpoint; in degree of light chosen: above all, in the artist's feelings for the subject itself.

'Song of a Camera' is a poem clearly related, with Isherwood's seed (the title) rerooted in Gunn's fertile soil. Again crisply metrical, the poet claims that his snapshots are necessarily detached from self – one moment of 'truth', now single, and transposed to the different timescale of art. Impersonality caught, by an artist in self-effacement: emotion recollected in tranquillity, one might almost say?

Then, before we can argue, the poem goes into swift reversal, disarming us: 'very well – make your own space too, don't stint yourself; be generous. You need to attend – to the snapshot; or at the very least, to what you see, what you feel there. You need to look for the pattern in the carpet. The art needs it, too'. Without recreation and its dance, the snapshot lies dead, for all its potency. Only let it live, and fluidity runs wild after all:

> Find what you seek
> find what you fear
> and be assured
> nothing is there
>
> I am the eye
> that cuts the life
> you stand you lie
> I am the knife

The 'knife' is more surgeon's than butcher's? (Yet the image is violent.) The camera is 'I', not 'it', so irony modifies; as it most often does, when 'beauty untouched by personality' (cf. 'Interruption') is the theme. Or, as Gunn wrote of William Carlos Williams in an essay dated 1965:

His stylistic qualities are governed, moreover, by a tenderness and generosity of feeling which makes them fully humane. For it is a human action to attempt the rendering of thing, person, or experience in the exact terms of its existence.

'Find what you seek': more than a free-for-all game, but not less than one: ('. . . We know our charm. / We know delay makes pleasure great. / In our eyes, on our tongues, / we savour the approaching delight / of things we know yet are fresh always. / Sweet things. Sweet things.') On the cover of *The Passages of Joy* is a crudely drawn maze, as if in contrast with Gunn's meticulous artistry. This maze, which reproduces a graffito found in Pompeii beside which is scrawled 'HIC MINOTAURUS HABITAVIT', does have a centre which can be reached. In this aspect, it symbolises the point of rest, where the dance is complete (the point of danger also, one might judge . . .) The centre might even hint at a common (i.e. a human) route, for accurate reading – or at a key theme or themes amid variations (such as the hide-and-seek *motif* already suggested here). But in the larger perspective, there is no centre: the 'passages of joy' all narrow and close towards the same, looming dark. The maze of Gunn's art is a structure from Borges, our modern master of labyrinths: where

one wanders in dizzying spirals of space/time, world without end.
Gunn, like Ted Hughes and R. S. Thomas, is indeed a Modern: he
writes in a world where God must be joking or hiding or dead. All
passages of joy are joyful through the joy *we* give them: maybe easy
in childhood; in youth, marvellous, given courage and energy
(otherwise, fading). In age, if we reach it, Yeatsean frenzy, sustained
to the end, might just do the trick.

'Find what you seek' – Gunn's blessing? (his warning also). All
the more urgent, since the balancing 'Find what you fear . . .' is
our birthright, do what we will. The circumstance surrounding life
is, simply, Nothing: Nothing before birth, Nothing after death; life
vibrant between. Some people find this thought mockery, some,
beckoning promise. For Gunn it is *datum*, context, for creation and
life:

> The power that I envisaged, that presided
> Ultimate in its abstact devastations,
> Is merely change, the atoms it divided
>
> Complete, in ignorance, new combinations.
> Only an infinite finitude I see
> In those peculiar lovely variations.
>
> It is despair that nothing cannot be
> Flares in the mind and leaves a smoky mark
> of dread.
>   Look upward. Neither firm nor free,
> Purposeless matter hovers in the dark.
>   (closing lines from 'The Annihilation of Nothing',
>   *My Sad Captains*)

In 'Flying above California', the same polarities cohabit: first,

> names of places I have not been to:
> Crescent City, San Bernardino
>
> – Mediterranean and Northern names.
> Such richness can make you drunk . . .

and in balance:

>   Sometimes
> on fogless days by the Pacific,
> there is cold hard light without break
> that reveals merely what is . . .

Both spread below the poet, flying over; it is the second which leads back to and enhances the first:

> ... That limiting candour
> that accuracy of the beaches,
> is part of the ultimate richness.

Gunn feels kin with rich lives, whether or not in his heroes; flaws in character, in circumstances dwindle, if the lifestyle is sure. In *The Passages of Joy*, 'BALLY Power Play' is an exuberant rollercoaster ride on erotic imagery, carrying Gunn's affinity with a creative loner who creates no more than his life. 'Taut control', 'brief fortunes': 'Bally's drama absorbs him'. 'Bally' is a specific type of pinball machine, absorbing the player, while he waits for his real game to circle round, with the night. Between games,

> he recognizes me, we chat,
> he tells me about broken promises
> with a comic-rueful smile
> at his need for reassurance
> which is as great as anybody's ...

Gunn's poem is celebration of a casual acquaintance, a man like himself, good to relax with: no mysteries between them, a shared understanding of 'sweet things' as with Chuck ('Sweet Things') ... or was it John?

Now for a finer poem, more personal, probing deeper (and here, let me make clear that the word 'persona' has no place in Gunn, on my reading – or in R. S. Thomas, or in most poets; it was almost always a refuge for timid critics, in its 70s phase). 'The Menace' starts in 'stifling passages', a psychic underground where 'an opposition lurks . . ./haunts the brain hunts the sleeper . . .'. It is the setting of two of the best poems from Gunn's previous volume – 'The Geysers' and the eponymous 'Jack Straw's Castle' – where syllabics mutate to the free-flowing, archetypal logic, revisited here. So, through 'stifling passages' to this dangerous territory for all modern pilgrims:

guard	father
executioner	angel of death
delivering doctor	judge
cop	castrator

the-one-who-wants-to-get-me

> Come out, come out, wherever you are,
> come on out of your hiding place,
> put on a body, show me a face . . .

'So, to objectify', the poem continues, 'He congeals / from what had seemed sheets / of fallen rainwater. . . . / He leaps from the night / fully armed'.   Then fleeting impressions: 'The flash of his leap' . . . 'helmet and sunshades' . . .

> . . . Both hands hang heavy
> gloved for obscure purpose.
> There is menace, perhaps cruelty . . .
>
> But I stand against him,
> and he settles reluctantly
> into a perturbed gleam . . .

The technique is cinema ('film noir', in current critical jargon), the setting, shadows: 'Suddenly, by passing headlights, I can see . . .' and this 'menace' is revealed as a shop-window mannequin. First alarm, false.

But no turning back here . . . if we start at all on this path, ahead are real terrors:

> I am, am I,
> the-one-who-wants-to-get me

This question, as punctuation, is now adult hide-and-seek: 'The quick air of a new street / hits my face', and the quest continues, as grammar leads back to its fracturing, in the chaos of search

> Romantics in leather bars
> watch the play of light and dark
> on the shine of worn wood,
> bottles and badboy uniforms,
>
> frame fantasies like the beginnings
> of sentences, form opening clauses,
> seeking a plausible conjunction
> that a sentence can turn on
> to compound the daydream . . .

And now, the real thing, menace and quarry . . . macho man, flesh and blood, in the wood where fear hardens to lust, lust dissolves towards eros . . . All to fight for, as the shadowside takes over, prepares for the challenge, for the known, uncharted risks of hunting by night.

Gunn's imagery retains perspective – a certain irony, as in
dreaming – the setting, 'theatre', the 'exemplary figure' real, but
playing to rules:

> He is not a real soldier
> but a soldier
> inducted by himself
> into an army of fantasy
> and he greets another.
>
> This time the glitter
> pulls me after it.
> In a little room
> we play at large
> with the dull idea of the male
> strenuous in its limitations.
> We play without deceit,
> compressing symbol into fetish,
> which is as it were
> an object vivified
> from inside, a lamp
> that abruptly wakens desire
> in the night,
>   we play
> with light and dark . . .

So, the 'dull idea' – a last fading of daylight – gives way to intensity:

> From imagination's forcing-house
> my man produces
> surprise after surprise.

The imagery of light and dark, reversed by eros, is familiar from
Tristran and Isolde, that key masterpiece at the start of modern music,
in William Mann's estimate; the start of The Modern *per se*, I have
argued elsewhere.[1] Gunn does not derive from Jung, but their
insights are close. Gunn goes further than Jung, as befits a poet.
Metaphors are ends through a means, not the usual reverse of this,
in 'The Menace': which is to say, the poem releases adrenalin,
leaving all structural aspects secondary in our reading response.

> And we sleep at the end
> as a couple. I cup
> the fine warm back,
> broad fleshed shoulder blades.
> We give the menace
> our bodies: his arms

were our arms . . .
His terror became
our play.
. .   . .   . .

Silt settles: windows clear.
The great piers are being searched
by the wind, but their secrets hide
deep in the meshed gleam of the river.

The process of love – described earlier, then interspersed with a
grammatical prose inset quoted from *Steps to an Ecology of Mind*
(1973) by George Bateson and further distancing images – resumes,
with great power, the healing of 'menace' in 'play' (love's hide-
and-seek). Then, the row of dots – space for sleep – leads to a
beautiful image – cold, clean; baptismal secrets of cleansing, revealed
and still hidden. And there follows the parting, the metamorphosis
from night's mysteries to 'the ordinary', renewed and made whole:

The 'exemplary figure'
strides away, i.e.
a cheerful man in workclothes
stumbles off grinning
'Bye babe gotta get to the job'.

I see as he goes
how admirably the loose
or withholding stuff of his clothing
has adapted to his body, revealing
what he has become.

the-one-who-wants-to-get-me

guard   angel
guardian   delivering

No, this is not Tristran, not meant to be; not the fever of love
(ecstasy wilder, destruction love's logic): but the healing of eros
itself – partners driven, then free. The rule of the hunt, through
menace to wholeness: then goodwill, casual untroubled parting is
the end of *this* game. It is a pivotal poem, the theme of hide-and-
seek at its most positive: seeking, finding, keeping; a happy ending.
At a very deep level, it is a poem of healing; one way (not for
everyone). But these protagonists need no analysis, no psychiatrist's
couch. This (I imagine) is why analysis has its place in the structure,

but seems largely peripheral. 'The Menace' initiates through resonance – hunt, risk, plunge, this time lucky. If we resist it, the healing asserted will remain mere abstract words.

So 'guard' turned to 'guardian', 'angel of death' to 'angel', 'delivering doctor' to 'delivering'. 'Judge', 'cop', 'father' (him especially) cancelled, for the psyche's healing: 'executioner', 'castrator' cancelled too (here, the luck matters?): and the-one-who-wants-to-get-me is a hound from heaven not hell; an agent of union.

I want to turn, for a close, to the two greatest poems in this volume, which take their place with Gunn's best work, up to now. As it happens, these have within them a feel of prophecy; the 80s to come throwing dark shadows before. They are marked by the rare moral fineness concealed in Gunn's amoral hedonism which he seemingly finds, without seeking, when passages finally close for men he is drawn to or loves. First, 'A Waking Dream':

> They are massing at the bank
> On the slippery mud, the only light
> leaking from the world behind them.
> In the middle of the crowd
> not in the front pushing but not laggard
> on his way to the grey river
> one figure catches my eye.
> I see in a strong glint of light
> a thick neck half curtained
> by black hair, and the back of a head
> that I dare recognise,
> though knowing it could be another's.
> Fearfully, 'Tony!' I call.
> And the head turns: it is indeed his,
> but he looks through me and beyond me,
> he cannot see who spoke,
> he is working out a different fate.

Tony White was a friend of Gunn's who died in a sporting accident, in his mid-forties (and for his living part in Gunn's life, see 'Talbot Road'). Whether this poem records an actual 'waking dream' (near vision?) or is pure distillation is not an important question (as it might be, in Yeats). The scene is the Styx. The crowd flows inexorably towards Charon. The underlying myth is as eerie as in Hardy's use of it in 'The Shadow on the Stone', though naturally different (Hardy's marvellous poem is for Emma, of course).

The tug of images half-create (reinforce certainly) the poet's polarities – half, impressions of life still; half, of parting and loss.

There is the vibrant reality of a vivid life, cut off without warning: 'massing', 'light', 'In the middle', 'on his way', 'catches my eye', 'strong glint of light', 'black hair', 'the head turns', 'looks . . . beyond', 'working out'. And in balance, enforced retreat, encroaching darkness: 'slippery mud', 'leaking', 'grey', 'back', 'could be another's', 'cannot see', 'different fate'. The dead man moves, unbowed, to the ultimate crossing (that ancient image of crossing as if new-minted in this context, where there is neither hope nor hope-beyond-hope to soften the truth). Like other 'sad captains', Tony leaves simply; as Borges puts it, 'Everything happens precisely, precisely now'. Consciousness and work are left solely for the poet, grief turning to icon where private compulsion and public duty meet.

Not defeated, not 'laggard', but 'not . . . pushing' either: 'in the middle', 'on his way' – as if the game is not really over, if the new icon holds. And looking 'beyond', making the exit with calmness, uniquely himself still, as the poet's 'I dare to recognise' records and affirms.

This is a poem of bereavement, not of fearfulness: the contrast with Larkin's 'Aubade' (another fine poem from the same period) is instructive to make. Larkin's line 'Death's no different whined at than withstood' is objective in context, but resonates otherwise: fear for one's own end is surely craven; but who – at four in the morning, mortal illness burrowing there – will rush in to judge? Gunn's own 'end' doesn't concern him – it is part of his living; but the bitter aura of 'Nothing' does haunt him when others burn out. Tony's 'passages of joy' are closed; no appeal against Charon; and the poet will not diminish his friend by any pollution of homage from himself. The one presses on, unbroken in spirit, not whining; the other turns to his craft, to translate and transform:

> True, they are not at rest yet
> but now that they are indeed
> apart, winnowed from failures,
> they withdrew to an orbit
> and turn with disinterested
> hard energy, like the stars . . .
>   (Final stanza of 'My Sad Captains')

If there is eerieness (as there is) it is all in the image: exact, and universal, as a ground of response. Note the sureness of touch:

'Fearfully . . . I call' is personal ('purely' personal, could it be?), 'I dare to recognise' public: an act of courage (poet/reader as nearly one as the reader will reach). The Imagist ideal of one, complex emotion pared down to words fully adequate is seldom achieved, but we find it here. The head 'turns', as though somehow conscious (surely, he must be?), but 'looks through me'; 'cannot see' is the truth. The poet does not expect to charm the dead back, like Orpheus. It is the dead whose head turns, not his; no charm is unwound. And does the head turn, really? It does in the poem. If as readers, we move inside this, sharing, as we can, fully; then to this degree, the poem exists.

Life and love in one balance, death in the other. Fear of death and pain must often be fear of life and love also: this insight is the 'moral fineness' in Gunn's amoral hedonism to which I referred. 'A Waking Dream' is a true verbal icon, testing the health of its culture, its readers; as great art will.

My second poem, the first in the volume, is not dissimilar; it is placed as a touchstone, I would imagine, for celebration to come. 'Elegy' has the death of an acquaintance for subject. 'I can almost see it . . .' so the poem opens, as the poet imagines a man deciding on, then enacting, his own ending – this death by suicide tinged for Gunn with a dreamlike haze. At first hearing it is almost descriptive, as if drained of emotion except that the details noted, 'half-handsome', 'hungry sweetness' merge, with precise details, to evocation: 'thin pointed boots', 'crackling eucalyptus leaves' (the word 'eucalyptus' is a sure sign of sensuous heightening in Gunn). We may then note the word 'thin', three times repeated, in dispersed usage; achieving a subtle colour, as if by stealth:

> I can almost see it
> Thin, tall, half-handsome
> the thin hungry sweetness
> of his smile gone
> as he makes up his mind
> and walks behind the barn
> in his thin pointed boots
> over the cracking eucalyptus leaves . . .

This image has haunted me since I read it first, as the whole poem does. As an image of the 80s (my image), it reached all ways.

This man is not a friend of the poet, nor a close acquaintance. The phrase 'Though I hardly knew him . . .' is held back to the

third section; first, the poet supplies a more general reflection, as if
the death were his own:

> Even the terror
> of leaving life like that
> better than the terror
> of being unable to handle it.

Well, not 'his own', since Gunn can handle life as this unnamed
man couldn't; still, there is a time when luck could run out for us
all.

Some of Gunn's heroes were taken (cf. 'A Waking Dream') without
warning; the others mostly defied death in their passion for life.
That fear of life and fear of death are near allies is a constant Gunn
subtext; but so too is the personal subtext, which 'Elegy' is. We are
in the area of Tennyson's 'Frater Ave Atque Vale', of Arnold's
'Thyrsis', of *In Memoriam* even; poems often feared today (how else
explain the neglect of outstanding art?). The sting of bereavement –
and the sting of estrangement, its sad *simulacrum*. Well, some signposts
are needed, when our own words drop into clichés and dismally fail.
Fears for our own death are one realm, best explored with some
caution; fear of bereavement is its own sovereign kingdom – different
customs and laws. That 'Elegy' is a touchstone of human civility,
for any culture worth having, seems to me certain; and it in no way
surprises me that an atheist is more likely to fulfil this need than a
'believer' in our present time. But it cannot be easy, for reasons too
numerous and menacing, familiar and threatening to list, let alone
to discuss. Perhaps the poems of bereavement that 'work' are not
really neglected, but regarded as sacred? Best just to return, to
Gunn's pared-down words:

> They keep leaving me
> and they don't
> tell me they don't
> warn me that this is
> the last time I'll be seeing them
>
> as they drop away
> like Danny or
> slowly estrange themselves . . .

And here, a transition occurs, in its logic magic and dreamlike, to
an image akin to a major incident, the canal party, in 'Talbot Road'.
In *that* poem (the fourth section) we experience a perfect moment of

happiness, a moment 'unqualified by subsequent attrition' (to borrow from Eliot) though the next section, fifteen years later, is in bleaker mood. Even so, this last section of 'Talbot Road' moves to another great image, wholly life-affirming, confronting life in a stream far surpassing any one, transient 'self'.

In 'Elegy', the image from 'Talbot Road' appears in inversion, speaking here of the never-can-be:

> There will be no turn of the river
> where we are all reunited
> in a wonderful party
> the picnic spread
> all the lost found
> as in hide and seek
>
> An odd comfort
> that the way we are always
> most in agreement
> is in playing the same game
> where everyone always gets lost

'Get lost . . .' Have we ever (or often) said this? Perhaps sometimes we mean it; no other way, as our own human story maps out. More often, 'get lost' is simple inattention to people, to life, death, joy, sorrow, to simple self-interest. It violates whatever we have, between the Nothings. It is, of course, in absolute antithesis to art.

'Elegy' might lead us, through this ending, to useful moralising; but maybe as a way of evading the poem itself.

I have suggested that 'The Passages of Joy' has one important thematic image, 'hide-and-seek'. Like its maze on the cover, and its title from Johnson, this child's-play is fruitful in variants, wherever we look. For the most part, the volume is much about finding, if and while our luck holds; provided we don't hold back too long: dare play this game at all.

'Watching me watching you watching me . . .' or its converse – from *Fighting Terms* onwards, this too is Gunn's game. I suppose that my fascination with Gunn and high critical claim for him is apparent. Let me end with another image, to which I have alluded already; where he offers a perfect entrée to his own major work:

> But I do clearly remember my last week,
> when every detail brightened with meaning.
> A boy was staying with (I would think)

his grandmother in the house opposite.
He was in his teens, from the country perhaps.
Every evening of that week
he sat in his white shirt at the window
– a Gothic arch of reduced proportion –
leaning on his arms, gazing down
as if intently making out characters
from a live language he was still learning,
not a smile cracking his pink cheeks.
Gazing down
at the human traffic, of all nations,
the just and the unjust, who
were they, where were they going,
that fine public flow at the edge of which
he waited, poised, detached in wonder
and in no hurry
before he got ready one day
to climb down into its live current.

> (From 'Talbot Road' – final lines)

SOURCE: A. E. Dyson, June 1989. Written for this Casebook.

NOTE

1. A. E. Dyson: Introduction to *Poetry Criticism and Practice: Developments Since the Symbolists* (Macmillan Casebook).

PART TWO

Ted Hughes

1. HUGHES ON HIMSELF AND POETRY

i On Violence

... Every society has its dream that has to be dreamed, and if we go by what appears on TV the perpetual tortures and executions there, and the spectacle of the whole population, not just a few neurotic intellectuals but the whole mass of the people, slumped every night in front of their sets . . . in attitudes of total disengagement, a sort of anaesthetised unconcern . . . watching their dream reeled off in front of them, if that's the dream of our society, then we haven't created a society but a hell. The stuff of pulp fiction supports the idea. We are dreaming a perpetual massacre. And when that leaks up with its characteristic whiff of emptiness and meaning-lessness, that smell of psychosis which is very easy to detect, when it leaks up into what ought to be morally responsible art . . . then the critics pounce, and convert it to evidence in a sociological study. And of course it does belong to a sociological study.

On the other hand it's very hard to see where that type of violence becomes something else . . . a greater kind of violence, the violence of the great works. If one were to answer that exam question: Who are the poets of violence? you wouldn't get far if you began with Thom Gunn . . . and not merely because his subject is far more surely gentleness. No, you'd have to begin with Homer, Aeschylus, Sophocles, Euripides, etc., author of Job, the various epics, the Tains, the Beowulfs, Dante, Shakespeare, Blake. When is violence 'violence' and when is it great poetry? Can the critic distinguish? I would say that most critics cannot distinguish. The critic whose outlook is based on a rational scepticism . . . simply . . . cannot distinguish between fears for his own mental security and the actions of the Universe redressing a disturbed balance. Or trying to. In other words, he is incapable of judging poetry . . . because poetry is nothing if not that, the record of just how the forces of the Universe try to redress some balance disturbed by human error. What he can do is judge works and deeds of rational scepticism within a closed society that agrees on the terms used. He can tell you why a poem is bad as a work of rational scepticism, but he cannot tell why it is good as a poem. A poem might be good as both, but it need not be. Violence that begins in an unhappy home can go one way to produce a meaningless little nightmare of murder etc. for TV or it can go the other way and produce those moments in Beethoven. . . .

. . . The poem of mine usually cited for violence is the one about the Hawk Roosting, this drowsy hawk sitting in a wood and talking to itself. That bird is accused of being a fascist . . . the symbol of some horrible totalitarian genocidal dictator. Actually what I had in mind was that in this hawk Nature is thinking. Simply Nature. It's not so simple maybe because Nature is no longer so simple. I intended some Creator like the Jehovah in Job but more feminine. When Christianity kicked the devil out of Job what they actually kicked out was Nature . . . and Nature became the devil. He doesn't sound like Isis, mother of the gods, which he is. He sounds like Hitler's familiar spirit. There is a line in the poem almost verbatim from Job. . . .

II   ON SYMBOLS

. . . It is my belief that [elemental] symbols work. And the more concrete and electrically charged and fully operational the symbol, the more powerfully it works on any mind that meets it. The way it works depends on that mind . . . on the nature of that mind. I'm not at all sure how much direction, how much of a desirable aim and moral trajectory you can fix onto a symbol by associated paraphernalia. A jaguar after all can be received in several different aspects . . . he is a beautiful, powerful nature spirit, he is a homicidal maniac, he is a supercharged piece of cosmic machinery, he is a symbol of man's baser nature shoved down into the id and growing cannibal murderous with deprivation, he is an ancient symbol of Dionysus since he is a leopard raised to the ninth power, he is a precise historical symbol to the bloody-minded Aztecs and so on. Or he is simply a demon . . . a lump of ectoplasm. A lump of astral energy.

The symbol opens all these things . . . it is the reader's own nature that selects. The tradition is, that energy of this sort once invoked will destroy an impure nature and serve a pure one. In a perfectly cultured society one imagines that jaguar-like elementals would be invoked only by self-disciplinarians of a very advanced grade. I am not one and I'm sure few readers are, so maybe in our corrupt condition we have to regard poems about jaguars as ethically dangerous. Poems about jaguars, that is, which do have real summoning force. . . .

. . . Blake's great poem 'Tyger! Tyger!' is an example, I think, of a symbol of this potentially dangerous type which arrives with its own control – it is yoked with the Lamb, and both draw the Creator. Yeats's poem about the Second Coming is very close – and the control there is in the direction given to the symbol in the last line – 'towards Bethlehem'. Not so much a control as a warning, an ironic pointer – but fixing the symbol in context.

Behind Blake's poem is the upsurge that produced the French Revolution, the explosion against the oppressive crust of the monarchies. Behind Yeats's poem is the upsurge that is still producing our modern chaos – the explosion against civilisation itself, the oppressive deadness of civilisation, the spiritless materialism of it, the stupidity of it. Both poets reach the same way for control – but the symbol itself is unqualified, it is an irruption, from the deeper resources, of enraged energy – energy that for some reason or other has become enraged. . . .

III   ON ENERGY

. . . Any form of violence – any form of vehement activity – invokes the bigger energy, the elemental power circuit of the Universe. Once the contact has been made – it becomes difficult to control. Something from beyond ordinary human activity enters. When the wise men know how to create rituals and dogma, the energy can be contained. When the old rituals and dogma have lost credit and disintegrated, and no new ones have been formed, the energy cannot be contained, and so its effect is destructive – and that is the position with us. And that is why force of any kind frightens our rationalist, humanist style of outlook. In the old world God and divine power were invoked at any cost – life seemed worthless without them. In the present world we dare not invoke them – we wouldn't know how to use them or stop them destroying us. We have settled for the minimum practical energy and illumination – anything bigger introduces problems, the demons get hold of it. That is the psychological stupidity, the ineptitude, of the rigidly rationalist outlook – it's a form of hubris, and we're paying the traditional price. If you refuse the energy, you are living a kind of death. If you accept the energy, it destroys you. What is the alternative? To accept the energy, and find methods of turning it to good, of keeping it under control – rituals, the machinery of religion. The old method is the only one. . . .

IV   ON POETIC INFLUENCE

. . . Well, in the way of influences I imagine everything goes into the stew. But to be specific about those names. Donne . . . I once learned as many of his poems as I could and I greatly admired his satires and epistles. More than his lyrics even. As for Thomas, *Deaths and Entrances* was a holy book with me for quite a time when it first came out. Lawrence I read entire in my teens . . . except for all but a few of the poems. His writings coloured a whole period of my life. Blake I connect inwardly to Beethoven, and if I could dig to the bottom of my strata maybe their names and works would be the deepest traces. Yeats spellbound me for about six years. I got to him not so much through his verse as through his other interests, folklore, and magic in particular. Then that strange atmosphere laid hold of me. I fancy if there is a jury of critics sitting over what I write, and I imagine every writer has something of the sort, then Yeats is the judge. There are all sorts of things I could well do but because of him and principles I absorbed from him I cannot. They are principles that I've found confirmed in other sources . . . but he stamped them into me. But these are just the names you mentioned. There are others. One poet I have read more than any of these is Chaucer. And the poet I read more than all other literature put together is Shakespeare. More than all other fiction or drama or poetry that is. . . .

I read Lawrence and Thomas at an impressionable age. I also read Hopkins very closely. But there are superficial influences that show and deep influences that maybe are not so visible. It's a mystery how a writer's imagination is influenced and altered. Up to the age of twenty-five I read no contemporary poetry whatever except Eliot, Thomas and some Auden. Then I read a Penguin of American poets that came out in about 1955 and that started me writing. After writing nothing for about six years. The poems that set me off were odds pieces by Shapiro, Lowell, Merwin, Wilbur and Crowe Ransom. Crowe Ransom was the one who gave me a model I felt I could use. He helped me get my words into focus. That put me into production. But this whole business of influences is mysterious. Sometimes it's just a few words that open up a whole prospect. They may occur anywhere. Then again the influences that really count are most likely not literary at all. Maybe it would be best of all to have no influences. Impossible of course. But what good are they as a rule? You spend a lifetime learning how to write verse when it's been clear from your earliest days that the greatest poetry in English is in the prose of the Bible. And after all the campaigns to make it new you're stuck with the fact that some of the Scots ballads still cut a deeper groove than anything written in the last forty years. Influences just seem to make it more and more unlikely that a poet will write what he alone could write. . . .

v   ON PHILOSOPHY

. . . I can't say I ever quested deliberately for a philosophy. Whatever scrappy knowledge of Indian and Chinese philosophy and religious writings I have picked up on the way . . . tied up with the mythology and the folklore which was what I was mainly interested in. And it's the sort of thing you absorb out of pure curiosity. The *Bardo Thödol*, that's the *Tibetan Book of the Dead*, was a special case. In 1960 I had met the Chinese composer Chou Wen-chung in the States, and he invited me to do a libretto of this thing. He had the most wonderful plans for the musical results. Gigantic orchestra, massed choirs, projected illuminated mandalas, soul-dancers and the rest. . . . I got to know the *Bardo Thödol* pretty well. Unfortunately the hoped-for cash evaporated, we lost contact for about nine years, and now of course we've lost the whole idea to the psychedelics. We had no idea we were riding the zeitgeist so closely. . . .

The only philosophy I have ever really read was Schopenhauer. He impressed me all right. You see very well where Nietzsche got his Dionysus. It was a genuine vision of something on its way back

to the surface. The rough beast in Yeats's poems. Each nation sees
it through different spectacles. . . .

VI ON SHAMANISM

. . . Basically, it's the whole procedure and practice of becoming
and performing as a witch-doctor, a medicine man, among primitive
peoples. The individual is summoned by certain dreams. The same
dreams all over the world. A spirit summons him . . . usually an
animal or a woman. If he refuses, he dies . . . or somebody near
him dies. If he accepts, he then prepares himself for the job . . . it
may take years. Usually he apprentices himself to some other
shaman, but the spirit may well teach him direct. Once fully-fledged
he can enter trance at will and go to the spirit world . . . he goes to
get something badly needed, a cure, an answer, some sort of divine
intervention in the community's affairs. Now this flight to the spirit
world he experiences as a dream . . . and that dream is the basis of
the hero story. It is the same basic outline pretty well all over the
world, same events, same figures, same situations. It is the skeleton
of thousands of folktales and myths. And of many narrative poems.
The Odyssey, the Divine Comedy, Faust etc. Most narrative poems
recount only those other dreams . . . the dream of the call. Poets
usually refuse the call. How are they to accept it? How can a poet
become a medicine man and fly to the source and come back and
heal or pronounce oracles? Everything among us is against it. The
American healer and prophet Edgar Cayce is an example of one
man who dreamed the dreams and accepted the task, who was not
a poet. He described the dreams and the flight. And of course he
returned with the goods. . . .

VII ON 'CROW'

. . . The first idea of *Crow* was really an idea of a style. In folktales
the prince going on the adventure comes to the stable full of beautiful
horses and he needs a horse for the next stage and the king's
daughter advises him to take none of the beautiful horses that he'll
be offered but to choose the dirty, scabby little foal. You see, I throw
out the eagles and choose the Crow. The idea was originally just to

write his songs, the songs that a Crow would sing. In other words, songs with no music whatsoever, in a super-simple and a super-ugly languge which would in a way shed everything except just what he wanted to say without any other consideration and that's the basis of the style of the whole thing. I get near it in a few poems. There I really begin to get what I was after. . . .

SOURCE: excerpts I–VII are drawn from Ekbert Faas's interview with Hughes in 1970; reproduced in Appendix 2 of Faas's *Ted Hughes: The Unaccommodated Universe* (Santa Barbara, California, 1980); pp. 198–9, 199–200, 200–1, 202, 203–4, 205, 206, 208.

VIII   ON JOHN CROWE RANSOM

. . . His is not a world you can explore for ever and ever. But his best poems are very final objects. . . . I think his best poems have an extreme density where every movement and every word in the line is physically connected to the way it's being spoken. There is a solid total range of sensation within the pitch of every word. There are moments in Ransom's work which have a Shakespearean density to that sort – and that's quite unique in American poetry and, I think, modern poetry generally. . . .

. . . It's all a matter of the ear. I guess the poems have very limited content. 'Tawny are the leaves turned but they still hold.' I mean, how does that strike you? It had my hair stand on end when I first read it. It was the first line I ever read of Crowe Ransom's where I felt that there was something extraordinary there. It seems to be completely commonplace and yet it's very weirdly planned. 'Tawny are the leaves turned but they still hold.' It's still a mystery to me how that line should have stirred me so much after I'd read acres and acres of Wallace Stevens and William Carlos Williams who never had any of the like effect on me. . . .

IX   ON THE WRITING OF 'OEDIPUS'

. . . I did that in the middle of writing those Crow pieces. And that turned out to be useful. Because it was a simple story, so that at every moment the actual writing of it was under a specific type and weight of feeling. It gave me a very sharp sense of how the language had to be hardened or deepened so it could take the weight of the feeling running in the story. After a first draft I realised that all the language I had used was too light. So there was another draft and then another one. And as I worked on it, it turned into a process of more and more simplifying, or in a way limiting the language. I ended up with something like three hundred words, the smallest vocabulary Gielgud had ever worked with. And that ran straight into *Crow*. However, it was a way of concentrating my actual writing rather than of bringing me to any language that was then useful in *Crow*. It simply concentrated me. That was probably its main use. It gave me a very clear job to work on continually, at top pressure. You knew when you had got it and when you hadn't, and it was lots of hours you could put into it. And all that momentum and fitness I got from it, I could then use on those shorter sprints. . . .

x   On the Underworld Plot of 'Gaudete'

. . . It tied itself all together in 1971 or so when I began to look at the *Gaudete* material again. Then I realised that that was the more interesting part of the story. And my first hope was that I'd somehow or other manage to do it all together. But then I became more interested in doing a headlong narrative. Something like a Kleist story that would go from beginning to end in some forceful way pushing the reader through some kind of tunnel while being written in the kind of verse that would stop you dead at every moment. A great driving force meeting solid resistance. And in order to manage that I had to enclose myself within a very narrow tone, almost a monotone, so that the actual narrative trimmed itself down more and more. The original story was much more complicated in detail and had many more characters and irrelevant novelistic digressions. . . .

SOURCE: excerpts VIII–X are drawn from the 1977 interview of Ekbert Faas with Hughes; reproduced in Appendix 2 of Faas's study of the poet, op. cit., pp. 211, 212, 214.

xi   A Reply to Critics   (1979)

I haven't seen Aidan Coen's article about my verse, but reading Mr

Brinton's letter, where he volunteers some opinions of his own, it occurred to me – not for the first time – that I should perhaps have taken more trouble to bridge the culture gap that seems to render my poem *Crow* nearly inaccessible to some readers.

Maybe I assumed too confidently that readers would share my weakness for the particular literary tradition in which the poem is set – or in which I tried to set it. I realise now that a reader who is unfamiliar with the Trickster Tales of early and primitive literatures, or who can't concede that those folk productions have any place in the canon of serious literary forms, is going to try to relate my poem to something more familiar; what usually comes up is Black Comedy of the modish, modern Continental sort. I think this is misleading, and I will try to say why.

Black Comedy (as I understand it) and Trickster Literature have superficial apparent resemblances, to be sure. But they are fundamentally so opposite that those seeming resemblances are in fact absolute opposites, as negative and positive are opposites.

Black Comedy is the end of a cultural process. Trickster Literature is the beginning. Black Comedy draws its effects from the animal despair and suicidal nihilism that afflict a society or an individual when the supportive metaphysical benefits disintegrate. Trickster Literature draws its effects from the unkillable, biological optimism that supports a society or individual whose world is not yet fully created, and whose metaphysical beliefs are only just struggling out of the dream stage.

In Black Comedy, the despair and nihilism are fundamental, and the attempts to live are provisional, clownish, pathetic, meaningless, 'absurd'. In Trickster Literature the optimism and creative joy are fundamental, and the attempts to live, and to enlarge and intensify life, fill up at every point with triumphant meaning.

In Black Comedy, great metaphysical beliefs lie in ruins, and the bare forked animal has nothing but a repertoire of futilities. In Trickster Literature metaphysical beliefs are only just being nursed into life, out of the womb and the soil, and the bare forked animal has a repertoire of all untried possibilities.

It is easy to confuse the two with each other, because historically they sometimes co-exist, and psychologically they often do so – or at least they do so up to the point where the negative mood finally crushes out all possibility of hope, as very often demonstrated in our day, so that the biological processes of reproduction and renewal

cease. Black Comedy expresses the distintegration and misery of
that, which is a reality, and has its place in our attempts to diagnose
what is happening to us. But Trickster Literature expresses the vital
factor compressed beneath this affliction at such times – the renewing
sacred spirit, searching its depths for new resources and directives
exploring towards new emergence and growth. And this is how the
worst moment comes closest to the best opportunity. 'When the
load of bricks is doubled, Moses comes' etc.

But an alert sensitivity can distingush between the two easily
enough. In Black Comedy, the lost hopeful world of Trickster is
mirrored coldly, with a negative accent. In Trickster Literature, the
suffering world of Black Comedy, shut off behind thin glass, is
mirrored hotly, with a positive accent. It is the difference between
two laughters: one, bitter and destructive; the other zestful and
creative, attending what seems to be the same calamity.

In the individual life, Black Comedy corresponds to the materialist
disillusionment of inescapable age and illness, as if it were founded
on the breakdown of the cells. Trickster Literature corresponds to
the infantile, irresponsible naivety of sexual love, as if it were founded
on the immortal enterprise of the sperm.

At bottom, this is what Trickster is: the optimism of the sperm,
still struggling joyfully along after 150 million years.

Cultures blossom round his head and fall to bits under his feet.
Indifferent to all the discouragements of time, learning a little, but
not much, from every rebuff, in the evolutionary way, turning
everything to his advantage, or trying to, being nothing really but a
total commitment to salvaging life against all the odds, perpetuating
life, renewing the opportunities for all the energies of life, at any
cost. Plenty of other qualities, some of them dubious enough, spin
around that nucleus, but the trajectory is constant. The sperm is
looking for the egg – to combine with every human thing that is not
itself, and to create a new self, with multiplied genetic potential, in
a renewed world.

In the literature, the playful-savage burlesque of Trickster's
inadequacies and setbacks, which is a distinguishing feature of the
style, is an integral part of the deep humane realism. And it is this
folk-note of playfulness, really of affection and fellow-feeling, which
does not date, no matter how peculiar and extreme the adventures.

All the annihilations and transformations that befall Trickster are
reminiscent of what used to happen to some gods. This agon is like

the perpetual replay archive of all that ever happened to living organisms, as if all life could pool its experience in such beings, and it defines the plane Trickster lives on, the dimension of psychic life through which he fares forward, destruction-prone but indestructible, and more than happy, like the spirit of the natural world, a green endlessly resurrected god in a wolf-mask, only intermittently conscious perhaps, blundering through every possible mistake and every possible sticky end, experimenting with every impulse, like a gambling machine of mutations, but inaccessible to despair. And rescuing through everything the great possibility.

The morality of the sperm is undeniably selfish, from all points of view but its own and the future's ('A standing cock knows no conscience' – Scots proverb) and innate in it is a certain hardness of ego, over-purposeful, nickel-nosed, defensively plated, all attention rigidly outward and forward: the ego of the sign for Mars. But the paradox is, this spirit has at the same time no definable ego at all – only an obscure bundle of inheritance, a sackful of impulses jostling to explore their scope. And from beginning to end, the dynamo of this little mob of selves is a single need to search – for marriage with its creator, a marriage that will be a self-immolation in new, greater and other life.

This spirit of the sperm, as Trickster, may be generalised, simultaneously base and divine, but it is not at all abstract. His recurrent adventure is like a master plan, one of the deepest imprints in our nature, if not the deepest, and one of our most useful ideas. We use it all the time, quite spontaneously, like a tool, at every stage of our psychological recovery or growth. It supplies a path to the God-seeker, whose spiritual ecstasy hasn't altogether lost the sexual *samadhi* of the sperm. A little lower, like the hand of his Fate, it guides the Hero through his Hero-Tale, embroils him, mortal as he is, in tragedy, but sustains him with tragic joy. Beneath the Hero Tale, like the satyr behind the tragedy, is the Trickster Saga, a series of tragicomedies. It is a series, and never properly tragic, because Trickster, daemon of phallic energy, bearing the spirit of the sperm, is repetitive and indestructible. No matter what fatal mistakes he makes, and what tragic flaws he indulges, he refuses to let death detain him, but always circumvents it, and never despairs. Too full of ideas for sexual *samadhi*, too unevolved for spiritual ecstasy, too deathless for tragic joy, he rattles along on biological glee.

Each of these figures casts the shadows of the others. The

Trickster, the Hero, and the Saint on the Path, meet in the Holy Fool. None of them operates within a closed society, but on the epic stage, in the draughty wholeness of Creation. And each of them, true to that little sperm, serpent at the centre of the whole Russian Doll complex, works to redeem us, to heal us, and even, in a sense to resurrect us, in our bad times.

This particular view of the Trickster Tale was my guiding metaphor when I set out to make what I could of *Crow*. The form proposed itself, by way of the unique possibilities of the style and tone, as a means of domesticating many things that interested me, and that were interested in me, and that I could find no other way of coming to terms with at the time. And I was conscious, too, that the overall theme offered a good outcome for me personally.

I don't know if this account will modify readings of such pieces as 'Truth Kills Everybody'. That poem seems to attract particularly sharp dislike.

'Truth Kills Everybody' records one of Crow's face-to-face encounters with the object of his search: the spirit link with his creator. It is an inner link, naturally, and the meeting is internal.

The hostility and energy of the confrontation are the measure of a gap – the difference in electrical potential between the limited, benighted-with-expectations-and-preconceptions ego of Crow at this point, and the thing he seeks to unite himself with. Much is projected. The mood is the appropriate one of the Old Adam *in extremis* – where shocking things are done and undergone in a sort of dreadful, reckless glee, with wild laughter.

Since Crow's understanding is so inadequate, and his procedure so mistaken, the thing defends itself with successive cuttlefish ink-clouds of illusion – composite symbols, each one recombining the various changing factors of the fight, in a progression.

Crow can either give up, and escape back into his limited self-conceit, or he can press on till he breaks through to what he wants. But since what he wants – to lose himself in that spirit-link with his creator – means the end of his ego-shell, then that breakthrough will destroy him as the Crow he was. But he does break through, and he is duly exploded. That is the chief positive step that Crow ever takes, but even this he takes wrongly.

Taking it too suddenly, unprepared and ignorantly, by force, he can't control the self-transformation. The spirit-light emerges as shattering flame. So his momentary gain destroys him, and is itself lost. He reappears elsewhere as the same old Crow, or rather as not quite the same. A Crow of more fragments, more precariously glued together, more vulnerable.

In this context, the annihilation has nothing to do with the annihilations in Nazi Germany, or even in a fox-hunt. The images were all taken from memorable dreams, which in this poem I tried to set in an interpretative context. It's possible, I suppose, that I interpreted wrongly, but remembering the physical effect the assembling of this poem had on me, I believe not. That's neither here nor there, I know, in what a reader finds on the page, but it persuades me that any sense of ease in the contemplation of annihilation, in this poem, is not mine.

Crow is like most of us – he directs involuntary blinkered aggression against what he most wants to unite with in himself, and what most wants to unite with him. But at least he doesn't displace his distorted attack sideways, and deflect it from himself, against some outer substitute. In this case he has the wit to recognise the cause of his fear and fascination, and to hang on to it. So he gets somewhere, for a while.

The Annihilation in this poem is part of 'the fury of a spiritual existence', in Blake's sense. It is like all the other misfortunes Crow undergoes, the deaths he dies, throughout his adventures. They are the sort that pass, maybe, without the flicker of an eyelid, but which nevertheless decide, I think, our minute by minute ability to live.

Naturally, what isn't there in the verse will have to stay invisible, (just as what isn't there in the reader will never be found in any verse) no matter how the intended drift is explained. But a more graphic idea of the context – of the traditional convention I set out to exploit, as far as I could, and of the essential line and level of the narrative, which might make some misreadings less likely – ought to have been part of those published fragments.

'Close reading' is evidently not enough to save us from misreading, or to break through the projection of fixed ideas, conditioned reflexes, preconceptions, etc. which often seem to be the only lenses we have – witness Mr Brinton's misquotation of 'Truth Kills Everybody'. In one main sense, that poem is about just the sort of misreading it seems to provoke: the cuttlefish ink-clouds, behind which the real nature of the thing escapes, are Rorschach blots, of a kind.

SOURCE: reply from Ted Hughes to an enquirer (letter dated 7 Nov.

1979); reproduced in *Books and Issues*, no. 3, as 'A Reply to My Critics'. Approved by the poet as the correct version of his letter.

XII   ON IMAGES IN 'CROW'   (c. 1980)

. . . Your remarks about 'Truth Kills Everybody' make me think I haven't made some important things very clear in that book. What Crow is grappling with is not 'something dangerous', but what becomes – at the end of his mistakes and errantry – his bride and his almost-humanity. To every action an equal but opposite reaction. In their alarming aspect, the images are mirror images of his method of interrogation – the hidden thing defends itself with these.

The 'violence' of the poem, therefore, is in Crow's attitude. And in the difference in electrical potential between his mentality and the nature of what he's trying to grasp – which is the difference between his ego-system and the spirit dimension of his inner link with his creator. The first cannot in any way cope with or know the second. For Crow to 'know' the second, he will have to go through the annihilation of the first.

The images are all from a series of dreams I once had – memorable to me for the shock they came with, and the interpretation of them which presented itself. They are all equivalents of each other: the situation is fixed, impasse. But in the poem I grade them. There is a progression. At the end of the poem Crow makes his single greatest step. Though it's not the only time he makes it. And he keeps regressing.

The components of each image are: one aspect of the nature of the hidden thing, a mirror-image of Crow's own mood, motive and expectation, a representation of the incompatibility between Crow's mentality and the hidden thing, and a representation of the escape or momentariness of his glimpse of the hidden thing: the hidden thing is a simple existence, but the images it throws up are compound metaphors, dream-symbols. As Crow persists, the proportions of the components in each image change: there is less of one thing and more of another; Crow's determination is itself an advancing thing.

The deadlock can only end in two ways: Crow either gives up, or he breaks through to what he wants and is exploded – his ego machinery is exploded. That he explodes is positive. If he had withdrawn, he would have remained fixed in his error. That he pushes it to the point where he is annihilated means that now nothing remains for him but what has exploded him – his inner link with his creative self: a thing of spirit fire.

In this context, I would argue that the images are not hackneyed, they are simply in place. Christ's heart, sure enough, is hackneyed everywhere except the one place where it belongs – i.e., where it has personal meaning. Parables of this sort, I know, are bald fantasies without a certain sort of subjective experience in the reader.

And I know, too, that in all writings of this sort it is very difficult to tell what is authentic and what is only imagined, unless you're on the inside of it. Or unless you have the whole of the author's life to judge it by. Very difficult. The only rule for a commentator – or at least for one who wants to transmit to his readers a creative response – is goodwill, readiness to give the benefit of the doubt, where there is doubt. And if the doubt is too intrusive – silence and watchfulness. . . .

SOURCE: letter (date uncertain but probably written at about the same time as the previous letter) from Ted Hughes in response to a correspondent's queries about the Crow poems; reproduced with the poet's permission.

2. CRITICAL STUDIES

A. E. Dyson 'Power Thought of Absolutely' (1959)

... Born in 1930, at Cambridge in the early 'fifties, and now based in New York, Ted Hughes has become widely known through poems in various journals, and especially through *The Hawk in the Rain*. This volume, published by Faber in 1957 ... is, to my mind, the most distinguished volume of verse by a poet of Mr Hughes's generation to have appeared .... . The most obvious immediate influences are Hopkins and Dylan Thomas, possibly because like these poets Ted Hughes is concerned to recreate and participate in experience, not to reflect upon it from a distance. But the tone and mood are too distinctive to be derivative. The deeper influences are Donne, Webster and the early seventeenth-century writers generally. Ted Hughes's values are much nearer to those of this period than they are to either Hopkins or Dylan Thomas; reading him, one is aware of closer affinities with the seventeenth century than even the poets of the twenties and thirties, with their rediscovered admiration of the Jacobeans, offered.

The major theme in the poems is power; and power thought of not morally, or in time, but absolutely – in a present which is often violent and self-destructive, but isolated from motive or consequence, and so unmodified by the irony which time confers. For Ted Hughes power and violence go together: his own dark gods are makers of the tiger, not the lamb. He is fascinated by violence of all kinds, in love and in hatred, in the jungle and the arena, in battle, murder and sudden death. Violence, for him, is the occasion not for reflection, but for *being*; it is a guarantee of energy, of life, and most so, paradoxically, when it knows itself in moments of captivity, pain or death. He looks at the caged jaguar, as it hurries 'enraged Through prison darkness after the drills of its eyes', and finds victory in its untamed will

> there's no cage to him
> More than to the visionary his cell.
> His stride is wildernesses of freedom

Beast and visionary are linked in the triumph of will over circumstance; in 'The Martyrdom of Bishop Farrar' he goes further, and finds triumph in a moment of martyrdom. The flame 'shrivels sinew and chars bone', but the spirit rises superior to suffering. The bishop's victory is one of pure stoicism, creating in the flames a timeless moment of glory, which is the currency of heroism, and so good coin long after his own flesh is consumed

> His body's cold-kept miserdom of shrieks
> He gave uncounted, while out of his eyes
>   Out of his mouth, fire like a glory broke,
> And smoke burned his sermons into the skies.

One is reminded here, and often in the other poems, of Yeats's 'Easter 1916'. Essentially ordinary men are taken, by one act of heroism consummated in death, out of the humdrum world 'where motley is worn' into the lasting world of symbols. The cause they died for may be unnecessary, it may fail, but this matters little, since the heroic exists neither in its motives nor its consequences, but in itself

> . . . changed, changed utterly,
> A terrible beauty is born.

So in Ted Hughes's poems, there is a constant striving towards moments of significance; moments of greatness which will last, as symbols if not as facts; ideal events more enduring than their agents, whose death, indeed, is their own occasion to be. Love, like death is valued for its power of providing such moments. First, there is the violence of encounter, restless, compulsive, pitiless

> There is no better way to know us
> Than as two wolves, come separately to a wood.
> Now neither's able to sleep . . .

but after, the lovers break through to a moment of glory; they duck and peep,

> And there rides by
> The great lord from hunting . . .

Ted Hughes values such moments for their intensity; but he has to isolate them from past and future, cause and effect, reflection and evaluation before he can savour them to the full. Hence the absence of compassion, anger, humility, nostalgia, disgust and the other attitudes belonging to the perspectives of time. His intelligence is often wholly absorbed in the battle to embody moments of power in words: it is the purity of intoxication, not the complexities of hang-over, that engage him. The poem 'September' is about the timeless sense of union which desire can bring.

> When kisses are repeated and the arms hold
> There is no telling where time is . . .

'Incompatibilities' is about the no less timeless disunion which can come from the same impulse

> Desire's a vicious separator in spite
> Of its twisting women round men . . .

The Song, 'O lady, when the tipped cup of the moon blessed you', explores the tenderness and romance of love, 'The Decay of Vanity' explores its transience and hollowness.

Instead of the opposites coming together, and generating the complexities which modify them in sober reflection, they are resolutely segregated, and so kept pure and strong. In this way, the poems recreate the intensity, the absolute quality of each state – union and disunion, romanticism and cynicism – treating experience not as parable or text but as sacrament. Articulation itself becomes a mode of participation, at least for the moment when feeling is being grasped.

All of this, of course, is exactly similar to Donne. And as in Donne, one finds explosiveness of utterance; imagery which is developed intellectually, but assimilated at every point to the central emotional experience; vividness and even grotesqueness of phrase and metaphor; metre which twists and turns in its wrestling with meaning

> Love you I do not say I do or might either.
> I come to you enforcedly . . .

and a general sense of being at the white-hot moment of experience: directly involved, so that the experience of the words is inseparable from the insight with which they grapple, and is, indeed, the high point of awareness itself.

When this is said, one can see the poems dividing into two groups; those in which the poet seems wholly identified with some moment

of power and violence, and vicariously elated; and those in which
he realises such a moment fully, but remains a human and time-
bound intelligence outside the experience, aware of the unbridgeable
gulf between symbol and fact, eternity and time. In the former
group, one can mention the very fine poem 'Hawk Roosting' . . . .
The hawk's victorious moment of triumph – might without mercy,
conquest without effort, privilege without responsibility, energy
without consciousness of end – is explored in vividly memorable
phrases (the words and statements suggesting animal consciousness
deeper than either words or statements); and remains, without any
specific comment from the poet, but unanswerably, the embodiment
of one possible mode of being

> I kill where I please because it is all mine.
> There is no sophistry in my body:
> My manners are tearing off heads—
>
> The allotment of death.

This is at one pole: other poems, as one would expect, hold such
a moment of triumph, ruthless and timeless, in balance against a
more human sense of time, with the knowledge both of complexity,
and of limitation, which this brings. In the other fine hawk poem,
the title poem of 'The Hawk in the Rain', the poet also enters
imaginatively into the hawk's victory, this time as it rides 'Effortlessly
at height' above the storm. But here, he remains conscious, also, of
the 'habit of the dogged grave' which keeps him earthbound, and
which in the end will smash the bird, too – though in the hawk's
'own time', a choice that enables the bird to submit to its fate, and
so snatch a martyr's triumph even in destruction

> . . . maybe in his own time meets the weather
> Coming the wrong way, suffers the air, hurled upside down,
> Fall from his eye, the ponderous shires crash on him,
> The horizon trap him; the round angelic eye
> Smashed, mix his heart's blood with the mire of the land.

In this poem, the striving towards the 'master-Fulcrum of violence
where the hawk hangs still' is balanced by awareness of time: the
hawk's holding of 'all creation in a weightless quiet' is 'steady as a
hallucination', and the word 'hallucination' pinpoints the ambivalence which a human intelligence cannot help feeling about the
reality of such moments. The poem 'Six Young Men' confronts this

ambivalence directly. The poem is about a photograph of six young men who went to the war and were all killed. Because of their death, the photograph becomes in one sense eternal. The dead men, as heroes, remain living symbols, 'mightier-than-a-man dead bulk and weight'. Yet the photograph itself is already 'faded and ochretinged', the clothes that the dead men wear in it are now unfashionable. The intense guarantee of life that is felt in their death has to be balanced against 'Forty years rotting into soil' and the other erosions of time. So the poem's final statement is a paradox – similar in content to that of Keats's 'Ode to a Grecian Urn', even though tone and mood could scarcely be further removed

> That man's not more alive whom you confront
> And shake by the hand, see hale, hear speak loud,
> Than any of these six celluloid smiles are,
> Not prehistoric or fabulous beast more dead;
> No thought so vivid as their smoking blood:
> To regard this photograph might well dement,
> Such contradictory permanent horrors here
> Smile from the single exposure and shoulder out
> One's own body from its instant and heat.

'Grief for Dead Soldiers', a poem equally fine, avoids the ambivalence by separating three 'griefs' about death in action, and exploring each in isolation. The 'secretest' grief, which is that of the widow, is one thing:

> Closer than thinking
> The dead man hangs around her neck, but never
> Close enough to be touched, or thanked even,
> For being all that remains in a world smashed . . .

the 'truest' grief, which is that of the calm craftsmen digging graves for the unburied dead as they wait 'like brides to surrender their limbs', is another. But apart from these, unmodified by them, and 'mightiest', is the public grief at the cenotaph. Here, the deaths are ideally celebrated. The dead become symbols, as enduring as the marble of the cenotaph itself; pure heroism, protected from the irony which the other two more human griefs would undoubtedly generate if allowed to mix, is celebrated as enduring magnificence

> their souls
> Scrolled and supporting the sky, and the national sorrow,
> Over the crowds that know of no other wound,
> Permanent stupendous victory.

In almost any other post world-war-II poet one can think of, these lines could scarcely be anything other than ironic; and the 'griefs' of the widow, and of the agents of oblivion, would be among the stuff of irony. Ted Hughes alone manages to isolate the heroic – not denying the other facts, but denying their power to negate the quality of heroism itself. Perhaps it is no surprise that he should write of the first rather than the second world war, and be obsessed by such types of warfare (bayonet charges, trench fighting) as belong to the pre-hydrogen age . . . . The quality of violence he writes of, however, is sufficiently up-to-date; one cannot write off his achievement as mere nostalgia for the good old days of meaningful slaughter.

'The Casualty' well illustrates the themes discussed here. At its start, the doomed airman is caught into the loneliness of violent death. His burning aircraft removes him from the company of the indifferent living, who watch from below, into the company of the more meaningful dead. In falling 'out of the air alive' he becomes of unique interest. The price is immediate death, the breaking of his body beyond repair ('Now that he has No spine, against heaped leaves they prop him up'). Yet it is the living, confronted by his death, who stand 'helpless as ghosts', and the dead man, by virtue of his sudden death, who 'Bulks closer greater flesh and blood than their own'. The word 'alive', with its serious, non-ironic application to the dead man falling, is pivotal, enabling death to take on its full ambivalence as an event both terrible and glorious:

> A snake in the gloom of the brambles or a rare flower.

This 'either/or' in the fact of death is the dichotomy which Ted Hughes takes care never to resolve. It is by segregating the two possibilities, and stopping them from meeting, that he is enabled to enter into both as he does: exploring the 'rare flower', in particular, undiverted by that ironic no-man's-land between the 'either/or' where most of his contemporaries are to be found.

It is of interest that the onlookers, in this poem, should be seeking to enter into the airman's experience

> Greedy to share all that is undergone,
> Grimace, gasp, gesture of death

but that their 'sympathies' should be described in terms of greed, and the parasitic. In 'Famous Poet', Ted Hughes describes the poet as one who, like these onlookers, tries to 'concoct The old heroic bang' from the deeds of others – but who is himself 'wrecked' in the attempt, and ends, not united with his object, but exhausted and diminished, 'like a badly hurt man, half life-size'. Perhaps, we may feel, the irony which Ted Hughes resolutely keeps out of heroic events he cannot wholly exclude from heroic people. Events partake of eternity, as poems do; but people, and poets, can never be free of the turning world.

Hence he celebrates, in his own poems, the frozen moments of greatness – the photograph, the cenotaph, the martyr burning, the hawk riding the storm, the jaguar free in his cage, the lover at the moment of consummation. To remember these things can give meaning to birth and life, and incite to vigour and endurance. To some degree it can put magic back in life, and also meaning; but no human can stay on such heights for long.

What, then, can be a provisional judgment on these poems? . . . Ted Hughes's control of words and metre in his best poems is profoundly mature already; the style is clearly the expression of a serious and adult intelligence . . . . Poetry need not always *evaluate* experience. Sometimes its main function is to extend awareness, creating new areas which the reader can assimilate into his own total morality later . . . . Ted Hughes, more than any recent poet I can think of, has the skill to do this. The quality of violence, which many of our finest novelists (Angus Wilson, William Golding and others) explore as moralists, is presented *in* Ted Hughes's poems in a manner which makes us more alive to what certain forces in modern politics and life really are.

His own obvious values are not unimportant – the quest for resilience and endurance, the response to birth as miracle, the sense that being able to ask 'Why?' may still be more important than hearing answers. But beyond these, he offers us the *feel* of power, as something inescapably to do with life, however we may feel its deadly qualities too. The God of the tiger must be known today, whether we choose to worship or not. Refusal to worship might . . . itself be a kind of death.

Ted Hughes's present achievement is within fairly narrow limits, but . . . his voice is the most distinctive we have heard in poetry since Dylan Thomas, and this marks him out – especially since he is swimming against the prevailing currents of detachment, irony, urbanity and neo-Augustan influences generally. Our present literary

scene is full of very *good* poets . . . but Ted Hughes offers more. . . .
I judge that, hydrogen bombs and his own ethos of violence
permitting, he will be one of the select few to be read a hundred
years from now.

SOURCE: extracts from review-article discussing *The Hawk in the Rain* among
other new poetry books, in *Critical Quarterly*, 1, no. 3 (Autumn 1959),
pp. 220–6.

M. L. Rosenthal   'Early Hughes' (1967)

The most striking single figure to emerge among the British poets
since the last war is undoubtedly Ted Hughes. . . . In [*The Hawk in
the Rain*], published when he was twenty-seven [1957], . . . there
are moments – a single stanza or phrase, perhaps – when the
smoldering fire blazes forth savagely. But only in one of the poems,
'The Thought-Fox,' does it dominate the whole poem and give it a
consistent, passionately vivid life throughout. Uncharacteristically,
the poem embodies an abstraction, suggested by the title: a thought
coming to life on the printed page, like a wild beast invading the
speaker's mind. The process is described in exquisite gradations,
from the first moment when

> I imagine this midnight moment's forest:
> Something else is alive
> Beside the clock's loneliness
> And this blank page where my fingers move.

After an interval, the living metaphor moves into the poem:

> Cold, delicately as the dark snow,
> A fox's nose touches twig, leaf;
> Two eyes serve a movement. . . .

The movement is completed in the last stanza:

> Till, with a sudden sharp hot stink of fox
> It enters the dark hole of the head.

> The wind is starless still, the clock ticks,
> The page is printed.

Something like the effect in this poem of the physical realization of a meaning, quick with its own rank presence, occurs in all the best work of Hughes. One other poem, 'Wind,' comes close to it in *The Hawk in the Rain*. But this poem is more representative of Hughes in the sense that it presents literal reality (though through the distortion of metaphor) rather than an abstraction made tangible. Nevertheless, it takes on symbolic meaning through the very accuracy and intensity of its literal presentation. The opening stanza will illustrate:

> This house has been far out at sea all night,
> The woods crashing through darkness, the booming hills,
> Winds stampeding the fields under the window
> Floundering black astride and blinding wet. . . .

In both these poems, we have examples of the authority that stamps this poet's work. The stage of the imagination is set with such sureness that one does not quarrel with its rightness. The 'thought-fox' is alive in its own way; the reader has no more choice than the protagonist as to whether or not he will make room for it. The conception of the house as a ship on a wildly treacherous sea is equally uncontestable, given the initial figure that launches the poem.

   . . . The title poem of the volume, 'The Hawk in the Rain', carrying echoes of Hopkins and Dylan Thomas, places the speaker – a man slogging through the sucking, clinging mud in a heavy rain – in a curiously independent polar relationship with a hawk in the distant sky that 'effortlessly at height hangs his still eye'. The speaker 'strains towards the master–/Fulcrum of violence where the hawk hangs still'; yet the hawk may one day view the earth from a victim's standpoint and feel 'the ponderous shires crash on him.' The poem attempts too much, but reflects better than any other in the book the obsession of the poet with one aspect of nature – the power and the gift of animals to make the kill, and behind that the intransigent force of being itself that is so indifferent to suffering and weakness. The symbolic application to man is fairly clear. Hughes picks up cues from Lawrence and Thomas, including the latter writer's artistic creed: 'Man be my metaphor'. More than either Lawrence or Thomas, he carries them to unsentimental limits in his best poems.

The second volume, *Lupercal* [1960] includes a half-dozen or more
poems that fulfill the first book's promise superbly. No poet of the
past has quite managed to 'internalize' the murderousness of nature
through such brilliantly objective means, and with such economy,
as Hughes in poems like 'Esther's Tomcat', 'Hawk Roosting', 'To
Paint a Waterlily', 'View of a Pig', 'An Otter', 'Thrushes', and
'Pike'. Like Lowell, he has the gift of presenting image and thought
in a context of hurtling action; there is a strong narrative and
dramatic element in all his projections, and the pacing is of the
varied, shifting kind employed by a skilled narrator impatient of
any description or comment that is in any way inert.

> A tomcat sprang at a mounted knight,
> Locked round his neck like a trap of hooks
> While the knight rode fighting its clawing and bite.
> After hundreds of years the stain's there
>
> On the stone where he fell, dead of the tom. . . .

Or the hawk, characterizing itself:

> I kill where I please because it is all mine.
> There is no sophistry in my body:
> My manners are tearing off heads. . . .

Or the poet contemplating a dead pig:

> Once I ran at a fair in the noise
> To catch a greased piglet
> That was faster and nimbler than a cat,
> Its squeal was the rending of metal.
>
> Pigs must have hot blood, they feel like ovens.
> Their bite is worse than a horse's –
> They chop a half-moon clean out.
> They eat cinders, dead cats.
>
> Distinctions and admirations such
> As this one was long finished with.
> I stared at it a long time. They were going to scald it,
> Scald it and scour it like a doorstep.

A passage like the one just quoted would have been less likely to
appear before the last war. Its bloodymindedness is a reflex of recent
history, the experience of the Blitz, the Bomb, and Auschwitz – an
expression of them, a recoiling from them, an approach to experience
by way of their implications. Hughes resembles Sylvia Plath closely

in such a passage. His Nature is Nazi, not Wordsworthian. Even
the 'attent sleek thrushes on the lawn' are terrifying, he says.

> More coiled steel than living – a poised
> Dark deadly eye, those delicate legs
> Triggered to stirrings beyond sense – with a start, a bounce, a stab
> Overtake the instant and drag out some writhing thing. . . .

> Is it their single-mind-sized skulls, or a trained
> Body, or genius, or a nestful of brats
> Gives their days this bullet and automatic
> Purpose? Mozart's brain had it, and the shark's mouth
> That hungers down the blood-smell even to a leak of its own
> Side and devouring of itself. . . .

It would be false to say that this fierce turn of mind is all there is
to Hughes. This very poem. 'Thrushes', is as a matter of fact
unusually contemplative for him. Despite the allusion comparing
Mozart's brain to the murderously triggered thrush, which would
suggest that the great artist's sureness of method and insight is a
more sophisticated functioning of the same process as is involved in
the kill, the poem ends by saying that 'with man it is otherwise'.
Time and waste, depths of distraction, and the essential distinction
between man himself and his acts are, he tells us, characteristic of
human effort. So we must distinguish between the implications of
Hughes's most telling poetic method (the comparison of Mozart
with the thrush and the shark gives away the feeling about existence
with which he must deal as an artist) and his thought outside the
context of that method.

Despite this necessary consideration, which only reminds us that
Hughes is, after all, humanly free to dissociate himself from the
vision of terror whose literal acceptance would constitute a form of
madness, the bias of the poetry lies in another direction. In such
magnificent poems as 'An Otter' and 'Pike' – poems that with
'November' and possibly the mysterious poem 'Lupercalia' approach
the full articulation of great art – it is sheer bitter endurance and
the devouring ferocity lurking in every depth and crevice of life that
obsess him. His empathy with the animals he contemplates is so
thorough and so concretely specific that the effect is of magical
incantation, a conjuring up of another possible kind of self. Both
otter and pike, though they *can* be caught and killed by man,
are given supernatural attributions by the language that Hughes

sometimes employs in describing them, and by his awestruck feeling
of the mystery of their existential reality, so different from our own
though constantly suggestive of the human. 'Neither fish nor beast
is the otter', who carries 'the legend of himself' wherever he goes
and seeks 'some world lost when first he dived'. He is 'like a king in
hiding' – a note Lawrence would have recognized, as he would have
seen in Hughes a kindred seeker for the deepest identity of the
submerged physical self. The pike, 'killers from the egg, the
malevolent aged grin', have

> A life subdued to its instrument;
> The gills kneading quietly, and the pectorals.
>
> Three we kept behind glass,
> Jungled in weed: three inches, four,
> And four and a half: fed fry to them –
> Suddenly there were two. Finally one
>
> With a sag belly and the grin it was born with. . . .

'Pike' is Hughes's supreme construct, a series of descriptions,
anecdotes, impressions building up the single theme. . . .
    'November' and 'Lupercalia' give us other, though related, views
of this young poet that should be noticed. In 'November' our
attention is directed, not to the animal world but to the human in a
degraded form. Its subject is a tramp observed sleeping in the rain –
'I took him for dead' – in a farmland ditch. The close-up view the
poem gives us is as accurate and detailed as those of the beast-
poems; indeed, the tramp is but one of a myriad beings watersoaked
in the woodland countryside: 'weasels, a gang of cats, crows', a hare
that 'crouched with clenched teeth', and such lesser objects as 'the
buried stones, taking the weight of winter', 'the bare thorns', 'the
rotting grass'. The poet admires the sleeping tramp's 'strong trust',
lying there with his face covered by his beard, 'in the drilling rain'
and the 'welding cold'.
    'November' recalls at least one poem, 'The Hawk in the Rain', in
the earlier book; and two others, 'Things Present' and 'Everyman's
Odyssey', in *Lupercal*. All these poems have in common the figure of
the beggar or of a rain-beaten, bedraggled speaker hammered into
nonentity by the elements. 'I drown in the drumming ploughland',
says the speaker in 'The Hawk in the Rain', who describes himself
also as a 'bloodily grabbed dazed last-moment-counting / Morsel in

the earth's mouth'. 'Things Present', the opening poem of *Lupercal*, projects an image of the speaking self as 'a bare-backed tramp' in a 'ditch without fire / Cat or bread'. The next poem, 'Everyman's Odyssey', sees the Homeric tale of the despised beggar who turned out to be the evil-destroying Odysseus as an embodiment of the common dream. Underlying the recurrent beggar figure in these poems is a humiliated sense of human loss, of a falling off from a previous exalted state, that justifies the hostile, death-wielding tone of the books. In the rather difficult poem 'Lupercalia' itself, we have a series of powerful images of the 'declined blood' of man and beast, then a glimpse of something beyond brute grossness in the images of dancing fauns, and a prayer for transformation out of the 'frozen' spiritual state of the speaker. . . .

SOURCE: extracts from section on Ted Hughes in *The New Poets* (Oxford, 1967), pp. 224–5, 226–30, 231–2.

Keith Sagar   'Poet at the Limit: The place of *Lupercal*'   (1975)

. . . In a British Council interview in 1963, Peter Orr asked Hughes: 'Is there a consistent "you" that emerges in all your poems – you as a poet, as Ted Hughes, with a certain attitude to life?' Hughes replied:

Not really, no. I tend to suspect that my poems are written by about three separate spirits or three separate characteristic states of mind, which are fairly different. They are obviously all written by the same person, but if they went under different names it's possible they'd deceive most people as being written by different people.

The poems are explorations, 'reconnaissances', bulletins from an internal internecine battleground.

All great writers are mapping unknown lands, that is, bringing more and more of the unknown into consciousness. These maps are then available for later writers. But the great writer will eventually reach a point where the old maps will take him no further. He is on

his own. The old maps may even become an encumbrance or begin
to divert him from his true path – the path which leads to the centre.
They must be jettisoned, with everything else.

His most difficult task is to remove the obstacles, the clichés of
thought, feeling and expression to bring himself into a state of full
awareness, openness, excitement, concentration. The rest is a gift,
but a gift not so uncommon as the emphasis of our education and
culture on language as rational discourse has led us to believe.

The gift is partly metaphor:

Metaphor, for the authentic poet, is not a figure of rhetoric but a
representative image standing concretely before him in lieu of a concept
. . . All one needs in order to be a poet is the ability to have a lively action
going on before one continually, to live surrounded by a host of spirits
(Nietzsche, *The Birth of Tragedy*).

I believe Hughes to be a great poet because he possesses the kind
of imagination which issues in the purest poetry, charged poetry,
visionary, revelatory poetry that sees into the life of things, that
takes over where all other modes of apprehending reality falter.
Words, though controlled up to a point, are allowed to retain a life
of their own and express more than the poet consciously knows.
His imagination, which draws on his unconscious, on the racial
unconscious, on his sixth sense and perhaps innumerable further
senses, speaks through him. He is, in a word, 'inspired', though the
word is not now fashionable. He performs a function essential to
the race, a function analogous to that performed in more 'primitive'
cultures by the shaman, whose function is to make the dangerous
journey, on behalf of his society, into the spirit world, which is to
say, into his own unconscious:

In preparing his trance, the shaman drums, summons his spirit helpers,
speaks a 'secret language' or the 'animal language', imitating the cries of
beasts and especially the songs of birds. He ends by obtaining a 'second
state' that provides the impetus for linguistic creation and the rhythms of
lyric poetry. Poetic creation still remains an act of perfect spiritual freedom.
Poetry remakes and prolongs language; every poetic language begins by
being a secret language, that is, the creation of a personal universe, of a
completely closed world. The purest poetic act seems to re-create language
from an inner experience that, like the ecstasy or the religious inspiration
of 'primitives', reveals the essence of things. It is from such linguistic
creations, made possible by pre-ecstatic 'inspiration', that the 'secret
languages' of the mystics and the traditional allegorical languages crystallize.
(M. Eliade, *Shamanism*, pp. 510–11)

The 'secret language' is partly metaphor; it is also 'the animal language' in the sense that words can communicate as sheer sound beneath their meanings. They can, as Lawrence put it, 'sound upon the plasm direct'. It is the language of another being within us buried much deeper than the repressed self psycho-analysis seeks to let speak:

And in fact this other rarely speaks or stirs at all, in the sort of lives we now lead. We have so totally lost touch, that we hardly realise he is absent. All we know is that somehow or other the great, precious thing is missing. And the real distress of our world begins there. The luminous spirit (maybe he is a crowd of spirits), that takes account of everything and gives everything its meaning, is missing. Not missing, just incommunicado. But here and there, it may be, we hear it.

It is human, of course, but it is also everything else that lives. When we hear it, we understand what a strange thing is living in this Universe, and somewhere at the core of us − strange, beautiful, pathetic, terrible. Some animals and birds express this being pure and without effort, and then you hear the whole desolate, final actuality of existence in a voice, a tone. There we really do recognise a spirit, a truth under all the truths. Far beyond human words. And the startling quality of this 'truth' is that it is terrible. It is for some reason harrowing, as well as being this utterly beautiful thing. Once when his spirits were dictating poetic material to Yeats, an owl cried outside the house, and the spirits paused. After a while one said: 'We like that sort of sound.' And that is it: 'that sort of sound' makes the spirits listen. It opens our deepest and innermost ghost to sudden attention. It is a spirit, and it speaks to spirit. ('Orghast: Talking Without Words', *Vogue*, Dec. 1971)

From the beginning Hughes is searching for a way of reconciling human vision with the energies, powers, presences, of the non-human cosmos. At first his main concern is to identify these energies and describe them, not only in human terms but in their own, that is in Nature's terms. And the discrepancy between these two descriptions gives the most powerful of his early poems, for example the hawk and jaguar poems, their characteristic tension. Hughes is also concerned to discover whether negotiations are possible between man and Nature, that is between man and his Creator, and, if so, why they have so completely collapsed in our time and what the consequences of this collapse have been and may yet be. The destructiveness of Nature is so clearly seen and deeply felt that it seems in many of the poems in *Wodwo* and *Crow* that negotiation is impossible, but in some there are hopes and intimations and in most a determination to go on trying. After the descent into destruction he goes forward a step, and a step, and a step. And, slowly, something begins to come clear. The faces of things are transformed and inner meanings revealed. The imagination begins to yield its secrets, and with this renewed vision, neither negotiation nor, indeed, reconciliation seems quite beyond the scope of man.

I am advancing no dogmas about what poetry should be. But it is surely necessary to have in every generation at least one poet who is at the limit, concentrating extraordinary intellectual psychic and linguistic resources on the effort to get clear of all contingencies and explore that territory which only the poetic imagination, in one form or another, can reach. And those who are exclusively concerned with the contingencies and with the civilized human world, and who deny the need for the larger awareness won by the visionaries, have no foundations more substantial than a heap of begged questions.

Man is always, all the time and for ever, on the brink of the unknown. The minute you realize this, you prick your ears in alarm. And the minute any man steps alone, with his whole naked self, emotional and mental, into the everlasting hinterland of consciousness, you hate him and you wonder over him. Why can't he stay cosily playing word games around the camp fire.

(D. H. Lawrence)

. . . Many reviewers and later critics have assumed that the territory Hughes was rapidly staking out was the world of animals. We have only to look down the titles of *Lupercal* [1960] to see horses, cats, a hawk, a bull, a mouse, a pig, an otter, thrushes, a bullfrog and a pike.

No poet has observed animals more accurately, never taking his eyes from the object, capturing every characteristic up to the limits of language. So vivid is his rendering, so startling and true his insights, that the way one looks at a hawk, a thrush or a pike (or, in later poems, a jaguar, a skylark or a swarm of gnats) is permanently altered. But the description generates metaphors, and the metaphors relate the creature to all other creatures and to human experiences and concepts.

In nearly all his poems Hughes strives to find metaphors for his own nature. And his own nature is of peculiar general interest not because it is unusual, but because it embodies in an unusually intense, stark form the most typical stresses and contradictions of human nature and of Nature itself. The poems are bulletins from the battleground within.

In the early poems the metaphors he found were so often animals because animals live out in such naked extremity the primary struggles, particularly that between vitality and death. They roar or bellow the evidence which men wrap in sophistry or turn a blind eye to. Their reality seems less questionable than ours.

In any discussion of Hughes as an animal poet it is not long before the name of Lawrence occurs, and rightly so. 'Bullfrog' is a particularly Lawrentian poem. There is the affectionate direct address to the bullfrog,

> But you bullfrog, you pump out
> Whole fogs full of horn – a threat
> As of a liner looming.

the easy colloquial style flexible enough to heighten instantly to

> Disgorging your gouts of darkness like a wounded god,

the unexpected, slightly comical, metaphors and exaggerations

> I expected . . .
> A broken-down bull up to its belly in mud,
> Sucking black swamp up, belching out black cloud
> And a squall of gudgeon and lilies

the freshness and liveliness, the touches of wit which have nothing to do with showing off but are a direct, amused, wondering and wholly serious response to a new awareness –

> all dumb silence
> In your little old woman hands.

'An Otter', too, has the creature there in a couple of perfect lines

> With webbed feet and long ruddering tail
> And a round head like an old tomcat.

So much for the appearance of an otter. Another two lines suffice for its distinctive movements:

> Gallops along land he no longer belongs to;
> Re-enters the water by melting.

Then, like Lawrence, into the little myth:

> Seeking
> Some world lost when first he dived, that he cannot come at since.

The otter is 'neither fish nor beast . . . Of neither water nor land'.

He wanders in search of the long-lost world he once ruled, where he knew himself and his kingdom.

The poem is less a description of an otter than an invocation of the spirit of an otter. The subject was suggested to Hughes by an Ouija board. The Ouija spirit liked poetry (particularly Shakespeare) and one hot day wrote a poem about 'a cool little spirit that wanted to live in the bottom of icebergs'. Hughes wrote Part I with great labour over a long period and was not really satisfied with it. The second part virtually wrote itself and seemed to Hughes to be the Ouija spirit's revision of the first part – and very much better. Here the otter is not just dispossessed, but hunted. As he hides under water, his dual nature forces him to breathe the air tainted by men and dogs. 'The otter belongs'

> In double robbery and concealment –
> From water that nourishes and drowns, and from land
> That gave him his length and the mouth of the hound.

So, in exile, the water's surface ('the limpid integument') is where he thrives. If he ventures on land he must not linger:

> Yanked above hounds, reverts to nothing at all,
> To this long pelt over the back of a chair.

The otter is the opposite of the hawk who rules his element imperiously, the kingdom of daylight. The otter is also a predator, giving short shrift to the trout, but, since man arrived on the scene with his trained dogs, is also prey, dual again in this.

No analogues are offered. But the otter, crying without answer for his long paradise, is surely, in part, an image of the duality of man, neither body nor spirit, neither beast nor angel, yearning for his Eden home where death was not.

In 'The Bull Moses', a boy leaning over the half-door of the byre can at first see nothing but a 'blaze' of darkness' – a darkness which strikes the eye as rich with dangerous potencies. Though he cannot see the bull, his other senses register very strongly the bull's presence:

> But the warm weight of his breathing,
> The ammoniac reek of his litter, the hotly-tongued
> Mash of his cud, steamed against me.

Then gradually, as if his mind's eye were giving the evidence of the other senses their appropriate embodiment, he begins to make out

> The brow like masonry, the deep-keeled neck:
> Something come up there onto the brink of the gulf,
> Hadn't heard of the world, too deep in itself to be called to . . .

Moses belongs to another world beyond the world of human consciousness, a gulf between. He looms up out of that potent darkness and now stands in a bovine twilight at the brink, the meeting point of the two worlds.

There was a time when bulls were undominated. Now

> Each dusk the farmer led him
> Down to the pond to drink and smell the air,
> And he took no pace but the farmer
> Led him to take it, as if he knew nothing
> Of the ages and continents of his fathers,
> Shut, while he wombed, to a dark shed
> And steps between his door and the duckpond;
> The weight of the sun and the moon and world hammered
> To a ring of brass through his nostrils.

The bull meekly submits to servitude. The boy is vaguely aware of what sleeps within the bull – 'the locked black of his powers' which no bolt or ring of brass could hold in check should he revolt. And why doesn't he? Has he forgotten his wild ancestors who roamed continents? Of the jaguar in *The Hawk in the Rain* we were told:

> His stride is wildernesses of freedom:
> The world rolls under the long thrust of his heel.
> Over the cage floor the horizons come.

Moses, too, is like a visionary in his cell:

> Some beheld future
> Founding in his quiet.

The animal lives in a world without time or death. The consciousness of Moses is a racial consciousness. What redeems his servitude is that he 'wombs', that is, he fills the wombs of many cows with his progeny, passing on what Lawrence, also writing of a bull, called the 'massive Providence of hot blood'. He is but a link in the unbroken continuity from his wild ancestors to his wild descendants, when man has ceased to rule. He is progenitor, Patriarch, and, like the other Moses, he beholds the Promised Land he will never himself enter, satisfied that simply by ensuring the continuity of the race, he has played his part. His descendants will escape from captivity

and inherit the earth. Providence will see to that – the powers which
inhabit the darkness of his dream.

The blackness beyond the gulf is not only the other world of the
bull, it is also 'depth beyond star', the outer darkness surrounding
the small area lit by the lamp of human consciousness, the source
of those imperatives by which non-human creatures live. There is a
corresponding darkness within ourselves, for the look into the
blackness of the byre is also 'a sudden shut-eyed look Backwards
into the head'. The gulf between man and animal is also the gulf
between civilized man and his animal self, which is also his angelic
self – the only self capable of recognizing a divinity in the darkness
and being at one with it.

'Pike' is another fine poem, with Lawrentian passages which are
yet pure Hughes:

> silhouette
> Of submarine delicacy and horror.
> A hundred feet long in their world.

The horror is in the pitch of specialization this fish has reached as
killer:

> The jaws' hooked clamp and fangs
> Not to be changed at this date;
> A life subdued to its instrument;

as though the whole creature existed purely to enable its jaws to
go about their business. Two marvellously economical anecdotes
substantiate the claim:

> Three we kept behind glass,
> Jungled in weed: three inches, four,
> And four and a half: fed fry to them –
> Suddenly there were two. Finally one
>
> With a sag belly and the grin it was born with.
> And indeed they spare nobody.
> Two, six pounds each, over two feet long,
> High and dry and dead in the willow-herb –
>
> One jammed past its gills down the other's gullet:
> The outside eye stared: as a vice locks –
> The same iron in this eye
> Though its film shrank in death.

When, at the end, the narrator fishes in terror at night

> For what might move, for what eye might move

he is no longer fishing for pike, but for the nameless horror which night's darkness frees to rise up from the legendary depth of his dream, his unconscious.

> Prehistoric bedragonned times
> Crawl that darkness with Latin names . . .

These lines are from 'To Paint a Water Lily' where again there are two worlds, that above and that below the surface, a world of daylight and a world of living darkness:

> Now paint the long-necked lily-flower
>
> Which, deep in both worlds, can be still
> As a painting, trembling hardly at all
>
> Though the dragonfly alight,
> Whatever horror nudge her root.

In 'Fish' Lawrence has a passage about a pike:

> But watching closer
> That motionless deadly motion,
> That unnatural barrel body, that long ghoul nose, . . .
> I left off hailing him.
>
> I had made a mistake, I didn't know him,
> This grey, monotonous soul in the water,
> This intense individual in shadow,
> Fish-alive.
>
> I didn't know his God.
> I didn't know his God.

But the thought of that unknown God does not make his hair freeze on his head with terror. Lawrence has not noticed 'the malevolent aged grin'. The other, smaller fish know fear, when the pike comes, but it is

> gay fear, that turns the tail springly, from a shadow.

None are eaten, and what their own bellies gulp we are not told.

> Food, and fear, and joie de vivre,
> Without love.
>
> The other way about:

> Joie de vivre, and fear, and food,
> All without love.

In Hughes's pond there is little room for joie de vivre. Lawrence not only insists on its presence, he insists on its primacy. It is essential to his metaphysic.

In his poems Lawrence seldom writes of predators (his mountain lion is seen as victim rather than killer) and shows little interest in the eating habits of the beasts he does describe. Yet in his prose he shows a full awareness:

Food, food, how strangely it relates man with the animal and vegetable world. How important it is! And how fierce is the fight that goes on around it. The same when one skins a rabbit, and takes out the inside, one realizes what an enormous part of the animal, comparatively, is intestinal, what a big part of him is just for food-apparatus; for *living on* other organisms. ('Reflections on the Death of a Porcupine')

This is also the main theme of Hughes's 'Mayday on Holderness':

> What a length of gut is growing and breathing –
> This mute eater, biting through the mind's
> Nursery floor, with eel and hyena and vulture,
> With creepy-crawly and the root,
> With the sea-worm, entering its birthright.

Hughes muses on Holderness as Joyce's Stephen Dedalus mused among the seawrack on Sandymount strand: 'A misbirth with a trailing navelcord, hushed in ruddy wool. The cords of all link back, strandentwining cable of all flesh. . . .' And the links are alimentary as well as naval: 'God becomes man becomes fish becomes barnacle goose becomes featherbed mountain. Dead breaths I living breathe, tread dead dust, devour a urinous offal from all dead' (*Ulysses*, 'Proteus').

Hughes evokes the same continuity. As the Humber feeds the North Sea with it dregs and refuse, including dung, corpses and misbirths, so his body, he feels, is a mere sheath for that 'mute eater' the intestine, designed, like an incinerator, like any scavenger, to receive all remains.

The same pattern is endlessly repeated.

> There are eye-guarded eggs in these hedgerows,
> Hot haynests under the roots in burrows.
> Couples at their pursuits are laughing in the lanes.

> The North Sea lies soundless. Beneath it
> Smoulder the wars: to heart-beats, bomb, bayonet.
> 'Mother, Mother!' cries the pierced helmet.

The eggs, so carefully watched over by the parent birds, are to produce new prey, if they are not sucked dry before they hatch. The laughing couples produce cannon-fodder for the next war. It is all like a madness, a frenzy. When Hughes writes of

> The expressionless gaze of the leopard,
> The coils of the sleeping anaconda,
> The nightlong frenzy of shrews . . .

he is writing not out of wonder and admiration, but out of horror, a horror he can evoke in a single line:

> The crow sleeps glutted and the stoat begins.

To call this pattern unredeemable would imply a concept of redemption. To call it mad would imply a concept of sanity. But here

> The stars make pietas. The owl announces its sanity.

There is nothing outside the pattern from which any other standard of holiness or sanity could be drawn.

When Lawrence was sickened by the war, he wrote: 'It isn't my disordered imagination. There is a wagtail sitting on the gatepost. I see how sweet and swift heaven is. But hell is slow and creeping and viscous and insect-teeming; as is this Europe now, this England' (*Collected Letters*, 338). The sanity announced by Lawrence's wagtail is 'sweet and swift' having nothing whatever in common with the madness and obscenity of men marching to war. But the 'sanity' of Hughes's owl is indistinguishable from its 'nightlong frenzy'. If the natural is the sane, then killing is sane. Wagtails also kill to live. Of course men need not kill each other to live. But slaughter is slaughter. If it is mad and obscene in men, why is it sweet and swift in a wagtail? In fact, one realizes, it is not the killing Lawrence finds mad and obscene so much as the regimentation. Killing as such he does not seem to mind: 'Leave me my tigers, leave me spangled leopards, leave me bright cobra snakes, and I wish I had poison fangs and talons as good. I *believe* in wrath and gnashing of teeth and crunching of cowards' bones. I believe in fear and pain and in oh, such a lot of sorrow' (*Collected Letters*, 651). Or again: 'The tiger,

the hawk, the weasel, are beautiful things to me; and as they strike
the dove and the hare, that is the will of God, it is a consummation,
a bringing together of two extremes, a making perfect one from the
duality' ('The Crown). This is very close to the position Hughes
comes through to in 'Crow's Table Talk':

> The tiger
> Kills like the fall of a cliff, one-sinewed with the earth,
> Himalayas under eyelid, Ganges under fur –
> Does not kill.
>
> Does not kill. The tiger blesses with a fang.
> The tiger does not kill but opens a path
> Neither of life nor of death:
> The tiger within the tiger:
> The tiger of the earth.
>
> O tiger!
> O brother of the viper! O beast in blossom!

But Hughes earns the right to this hard-won position as Lawrence
does not, by confronting and living through in his work the fear and
pain and sorrow. He hears the inaudible

> battle-shouts
> And death-cries everywhere hereabouts
> ('To Paint a Water Lily')

He shares the terror of the mouse 'staring out the chance it dared
not take' and knows that a man stands in God's eye no better than
the mouse in the cat's:

> Whether to two
> Feet or four, how are prayers contracted!
> Whether in God's eye or the eye of a cat.
> ('Cat and Mouse')

When Lawrence's cat torments a chipmunk 'it is a game, and it is
pretty'.

Lawrence is not only callous in comparison with Hughes, he is
also, in his animal poems, frequently sentimental. In 'A Living' for
example:

> A bird
> picks up its seeds or little snails
> between heedless earth and heaven
> in heedlessness.

> But, the plucky little sport, it gives to life
> Song, and chirruping, gay feathers, fluff-shadowed warmth
>
> and all the unspeakable charm of birds hopping and fluttering and
>   being birds.
> – And we, we get it all from them for nothing.

Hughes sees nothing heedless or sporting or charming about a bird
eating snails:

> Terrifying are the attent sleek thrushes on the lawn,
> More coiled steel than living – a poised
> Dark dead eye, those delicate legs
> Triggered to stirrings beyond sense – with a start, a bounce, a stab
> Overtake the instant and drag out some writhing thing.
>
> ('Thrushes')

The thrushes are terrifying not only for their ravening of writhing
things, but for the too streamlined efficiency with which they pursue
their unwavering purpose – the efficiency of a bullet (whose one
path is direct through the bones of the living). Whitman thought he
could 'turn and live with animals':

> They do not lie awake in the dark and weep for their sins.
>
> ('Song of Myself', 32)

Hughes draws the same distinction, but does not choose the animals
or even admire them. Their efficiency is too horribly automatic, like

> The shark's mouth
> That hungers down the blood-smell even to a leak of its own
> Side and devouring of itself . . .

What a man does neither defines nor deifies him, nor can he, unless
he is that hardly human thing, a genius, crash straight through
doubts, obstructions, temptations, sin, guilt and despair:

> how loud and above what
> Furious spaces of fire do the distracting devils
> Orgy and hosannah, under what wilderness
> Of black silent waters weep.

Beyond the little area lit by his consciousness, his desk-lamp, is a
vast darkness peopled by demons. The distracting devils which sin,
praise, or despair are those suppressed powers within any man
which will not let him be satisfied with the heroisms he invents at
his desk, or with any enclosed self-worshipping activity. A man
totally given over to those powers, genius or hero, is a madman or

automaton. A man totally cut off from them denies, trivializes or perverts the life that is in him, drops out of the divine circuit from which alone come the energies to destroy or create.

The poem which really established Hughes's reputation and got into all the anthologies was 'Hawk Roosting'. This poem, we were told, was a brilliant *tour de force* in entering the consciousness of a hawk. At one level it is certainly that. The whole poem is in the first person – a hawk's eye view of the world. The hawk, taking himself to be the exact centre, assumes that trees, air, sun and earth are there for his convenience; that the purpose of creation has been solely to produce him; that the world revolves at his bidding; that all other creatures exist only as prey; that his eye is stronger than change or death:

> It took the whole of Creation
> To produce my foot, my each feather:
> Now I hold Creation in my foot
>
> Or fly up, and revolve it all slowly –
>   . . .
> The sun is behind me.
> Nothing has changed since I began.
> My eye has permitted no change.
> I am going to keep things like this.

At a deeper level the hawk becomes a spokesman for Nature herself and speaks in accents close to those of Whitman when he permits Nature ('without check, with original energy') to speak through him:

> I know I am solid and sound,
> To me the converging objects of the universe perpetually flow . . .
> I know I am deathless . . .
> I see that the elementary laws never apologize . . .
> I exist as I am, that is enough . . .
> My foothold is tenon'd and mortis'd in granite . . .
>
> ('Song of Myself', 20)

> All forces have been steadily employ'd to complete and delight me,
> Now on this spot I stand with my robust soul
>
> (Ibid., 44)

Nature speaks through Tennyson too, a Nature 'red in tooth and claw', a loveless, careless, ravenous Nature:

> She cries 'A thousand types are gone:
>   I care for nothing, all shall go.
>
> Thou makest thine appeal to me:
>   I bring to life, I bring to death:
>   The spirit does but mean the breath:
> I know no more.'
>
> ('In Memoriam', LV)

Tennyson had built his faith on the assumption that love was Creation's final law. When Nature undeceived him he could only cry

> Are God and Nature then at strife?

In Hughes we find neither the admiration of Whitman nor the anguish of Tennyson. All these animal and nature poems get their characteristic tension from the attempt to fuse into a unified response both admiration and horror. The reconciling spirit might be described as one of awe. This was certainly the spirit in which the ancient Egyptians saw the hawk:

Under the name Hor – which in Egyptian sounds like a word meaning 'sky' – the Egyptians referred to the falcon which they saw soaring high above their heads, and many thought of the sky as a divine falcon whose two eyes were the sun and the moon. The worshippers of this bird must have been numerous and powerful; for it was carried as a totem on prehistoric standards and from the earliest times was considered the pre-eminent divine being. The hieroglyph which represents the idea of 'god' was a falcon on its perch. (Larousse *Encyclopaedia of Mythology*, 21)

In other words, a hawk roosting was 'god'. In his *London Magazine* interview (January 1971) Hughes said of his hawk:

That bird is accused of being a fascist . . . the symbol of some horrible totalitarian genocidal dictator. Actually what I had in mind was that in this hawk Nature is thinking. Simply Nature. It's not so simple maybe because Nature is no longer so simple. I intended some Creator like the Jehovah in Job but more feminine. When Christianity kicked the devil out of Job what they actually kicked out was Nature . . . and Nature became the devil. He doesn't sound like Isis, mother of the gods, which he is. He sounds like *Hitler's familiar spirit*. There is a line in the poem almost verbatim from Job.

Indeed Job's god is the god of hawks:

> Doth the hawk fly by thy wisdom, and stretch her wings
>   toward the south?

> Doth the eagle mount up at thy command, and make her nest
>   on high?
> She dwelleth and abideth on the rock, upon the crag of the
>   rock, and the strong place.
> From thence she seeketh the prey, and her eyes behold afar off,
> Her young ones also suck up blood: and where the slain are,
>   there is she.
>
> (Job: 39: 26—30)

And Job's God speaks like Hughes's hawk:

> Whatsoever is under the whole heaven is mine.
>
> (Job 41: 11)

> I kill where I please because it is all mine.
>
> ('Hawk Roosting')

That was before Jehovah became the God of Love; before he became Jehovah, for Job called him such primitive names as El, Eloah and Shaddai.

In Job we find God still acknowledges as his own the most crude and savage powers of nature – behemoth and leviathan. Behemoth is clearly phallic:

> Lo now, his strength is in his loins, and
>   his force is in the navel of his belly.
> He moveth his tail like a cedar: the
>   sinews of his stones are wrapped together.
> He is the chief of the ways of God.
>
> (Job 40: 16ff)

Leviathan represents the unkillable, untameable dragon (libido) of the sea (unconscious):

> Behold, the hope of him is in vain:
>   shall not one be cast down even at the
>   sight of him?
>
> (Job 41: 9)

Later the Hebrews, to accommodate their God to human morality, handed Nature over to the devil. For in terms of the Christian ethic, or of any sort of human morality, the hawk is evil or mad. An example the poem more directly evokes than Hitler is Shakespeare's Richard of Gloucester:

> For the one path of my flight is direct
> Through the bones of the living

is a paraphrase of Richard's

> For many lives stand between me and home.
>
> (3 *H.VI.* iii. iii. 173)

The hawk's solipsism is also Richard's:

> I am myself alone.   (v. vi. 83)

By attributing to the hawk a consciousness which can express itself in our language and concepts, the poem also invites us, though we envy the hawk his centrality, his freedom from the falsifying dreams, sophistries and arguments which distract and deflect men, to count the cost of letting such energies loose in a man.

Speaking of Job 38–41, the Voice out of the Whirlwind, I. A. Richards, says: 'Is it not well to reflect whether more than two thousand years' adoration of this utterance (however magnificent its phrases) might not have something to do with the sad state of the world and with the mad and abominable tyrannies which have so mercilessly infected it?' (*Beyond*, 73) Perhaps Job himself was suppressing similar doubts when he put his hand over his mouth.

> Though he slay me, yet will I trust in him:
> but I will maintain mine own ways before him.
>
> (Job 13: 15)

The chief of the ways of Job is his sense of justice. How can he hope to maintain that against a god of whom he has already said:

> For he is not a man, as I am, that I should answer him,
> and we should come together in judgment.
>
> (Job 9: 32)

This god is not interested in justice or morality. When Job tries to negotiate, God shouts him down, smashing straight through his arguments with sheer brute force. What is left for him? A choice of capitulation, futile rebellion, or putting his hand over his mouth?

(The same choice confronts Crow, who is both Job and hawk, and Prometheus on his crag whose unjust God daily sends his vulture out of the sun to torment him – a bird whose manners are tearing out livers.)

All efforts to understand Nature in terms of human morality are as doomed as Job's effort to understand his God. His successors decided to remake God in their own image, separating out and exalting the Logos, leaving the dark side of God, unacknowledged,

marauding destructively as Satan, serpent, dragon, Gog, unredeemable Nature and the ghosts of all the Pagan gods and goddesses.
And it is this process which Hughes sees as having more to do with
the sad state of the world than the adoration of Job's savage God
which Richards strangely imagines to have characterized the last
two thousand years.

In *Lupercal* Hughes gives us a few figures who escape the destructive
extremes. There is Dick Straightup 'strong as the earth', a living
legend because impervious to those forces to which Hughes feels
himself most vulnerable:

> But this one,
> With no more application than sitting,
> And drinking, and singing, fell in the sleet, late,
> Dammed the pouring gutter; and slept there; and, throughout
> A night searched by shouts and lamps, froze,
> Grew to the road with welts of ice. He was chipped out at dawn
>
> Warm as a pie and snoring.

The tramp in 'November' also withstands the worst that weather
can do. Then there are the 'Acrobats'. It is gravity they defy as they
fling

> Out onto nothing, snap, jerk
> Fulcrumed without fail
> On axes immaterial as
> Only geometry should use.

Hughes wonderfully mimes their 'hurtle and arc'

> somersaulting
> (As might hardly be dared in the head)
> Bodily out on space,
> Gibboning, bird-vaulting . . .

The verbs themselves launch out into space with their heavily
stressed first syllables. And that parenthesis achingly arrests the
somersault in mid-air. Such defiance of natural laws is 'unearthly',
miraculous. But the watching crowd have no share in it. It makes
them only the more conscious of their insecurity and vulnerability
and mortality

> bearing
> Plunge of that high risk without
> That flight; with only a dread

> Crouching to get away from these
> On its hands and knees.

The acrobats are the exception which proves the rule. The world of
nonchalant ease, freedom and grace which they inhabit ('a hundred
feet above ground') is as remote from ordinary men as heaven itself.
Ordinary men can but dream of such a world, or strive by means of
vigil, ordeal, prayer and spiritual disciplines at the body's expense,
towards it. But

> The acrobats flashed
> Above earth's ancient inertia,
> Faltering of the will,
> And the dullness of flesh –
> In the dream's orbit; shone, soared,
> Mocking vigil and ordeal,
> And the prayer of long attempting
> Body had endured
> To break from a hard-held trembling seat
> And soar at that height.

When Hughes was a boy, his brother told him the story of a tramp
sleeping in the heather, who stirred at an unlucky moment and was
shot dead for a fox by an alert farmer. Already the tramp, in his
imagination, was associated with those creatures we call vermin,
shoot at will and hang on gibbets 'pour encourager les autres'. Other
meanings of the tramp figure emerge in *Lupercal*. In 'Things Present'
the tramp in his sodden ditch is defined by what he lacks – fire, cat,
bread, shoes, honour and hope. His ancestors who gradually acquired
these appurtenances of civilized living 'honed their bodies away' in
the effort, that is, lost the stability and centrality that goes with a
sense of the bulk and weight, the instant and heat, of one's own
body. Most significantly he lacks 'a roof treed to deflect death'.
Imagine those characters in 'Wind' deprived of their roof and fire.

In 'November' we learn why the tramp is willing to forego these
things. The speaker is the same speaker as in 'The Hawk in the
Rain', desperately conscious of his own exposure, vulnerability and
mortality, running for shelter from the 'drilling rain'. The tramp
embodies a less spectacular, more passive form of the same mastery
of the elements which characterizes the hawk in the earlier poem.

> In a let of the ditch a tramp was bundled asleep:
> Face tucked down into beard, drawn in
> Under its hair like a hedgehog's. I took him for dead,

> But his stillness separated from the death
> Of the rotting grass and the ground. A wind chilled,
> And a fresh comfort tightened through him,
> Each hand stuffed deeper into the other sleeve.

His secret is his 'strong trust'.

> I thought what strong trust
> Slept in him – as the trickling furrows slept,
> And the thorn-roots in their grip on darkness;
>
> And the buried stones, taking the weight of winter;
> The hill where the hare crouched with clenched teeth.

What, exactly, does the tramp trust? That Nature will look after him, like the Babes in the Wood? That spring cannot be far behind, and better days? The speaker runs into a wood for shelter and there finds himself confronted by a gibbet:

> The keeper's gibbet had owls and hawks
> By the neck, weasels, a gang of cats, crows:
> Some, stiff, weightless, twirled like dry bark bits
>
> In the drilling rain. Some still had their shape,
> Had their pride with it; hung, chins on chests,
> Patient to outwait these worst days that beat
> Their crowns bare and dripped from their feet.

These creatures share the patience of the tramp, even his posture 'chins on chests'. Is their patience misplaced, since they are not, like the tramp, the furrows and the thorn-roots, merely asleep? Nature has no spring or better days in store for them.

The tramp, like them outcast, dispropertied, unaccommodated, has nothing to lose. He is willing to forego even a roof, because being without hope he is not prepared to devote his life to the doomed attempt to deflect death. His trust is in all life's purposes or processes, including death.

In 'Crag Jack's Apostasy' Crag Jack is another tramp or outsider. His name implies his toughness, the qualities he shares with Heathcliff: 'an unreclaimed creature, without refinement, without cultivation'. Apostasy is the abandonment of religious faith. The opening lines –

> The churches, lord, all the dark churches
> Stooped over my cradle once:

evoke an image of witches suffocating the new born child with sterile blessings, obscuring the light; also, perhaps of the Calder Valley, the cradle of a Methodism which often took an extremely repressive Calvinistic form. (Joseph and the Reverend Jabes Branderham in *Wuthering Heights* are caricatures of this.) Crag Jack has come clear of the world (power, wealth, comfort, security) and the churches with their dogmas, theologies and traditional imagery.

> I came clear, but my god's down
> Under the weight of all that stone:
> Both my power and my luck since
> Have kicked at the world and slept in ditches.

Though he has no desire to be reclaimed, Crag Jack fears to become, like Heathcliff, a 'wolfish man'. He has retained a deep need to worship, but not the god of the churches.

> I do not desire to change my ways,
> But now call continually
> On you, god or not god, who
> Come to my sleeping body through
> The world under the world; pray
> That I may see more than your eyes
>
> In an animal's dreamed head . . .

Exposed as he is to life at its most severe, his imagination can find no appropriate image for the forces which control life other than that of a wolf's head or eagle's feet. Crag Jack is like The Toughest in *Recklings* who also survives the collapse of church-towers and hears 'the laughter of great outer darkness' threatening 'to close its teeth on the skull'. The Great Outer Darkness is a name for God. It is also, in 'The Toughest', 'the same as the small inner darkness'. The images of organized religion do not match those of the violent world Crag Jack inhabits. They are supplanted by his dream images. The only god who reveals himself to Crag Jack is the god of predators, the god of ruthless killing; or, if this god has other aspects, it is only in this aspect that he ever reveals himself. 'Plum Blossom' III in *Recklings* might be one of Jack's dreams:

> Inside the head of a cat
> Under the bones, the brains, the blood-tissue,
> Bone of the bone and brain of the brain,
> Blood of the blood and tissue of the tissue,
> Is God's head, with eyes open.
> And under that my own head, with wide eyes.

> And under that the head of a cat, with eyes
> Smiling and closed.

These images, wolf's head, eagle's claws, shark's mouth, the curved jawbone which did not laugh

> But gripped, gripped and is now a cenotaph   ('Relic')

dominate *Lupercal*. Crag Jack's god is the god of death, of the underworld. If we must name him he is Pluto or Dis, or Februus, to whom the month of February was sacred. In 'February' the dominant image is again the wolf – winter gripping the world with vice-like jaws. The word 'wolf' throws up several images in the poet's mind – the wolves he remembers from those horrific nursery stories *Red Riding Hood* and *The Wolf and the Seven Little Kids*, the wolves of Norse legends, 'gibbet-hung wolves' he has seen in engravings, or the caged wolves he has seen at the zoo. But none of these images suffices to personify the spirit of February, none captures the pure spirit of wolf as it is captured in

> A photograph: the hairless, knuckled feet
> Of the last wolf killed in Britain . . .

These feet run and run in the darkness of his dream, and

> By day, too, pursue, siege all thought . . .

There are no wolves in Britain, no large predators at all to make the nights dangerous. And we like to think that we have got rid of the wolfishness in our own natures. But these feet run

> Through and throughout the true world

disdaining the storied, pictured or tamed world, searching

> For their vanished head, for the world
> Vanished with the head, the teeth, the quick eyes –

the world in which wolves roamed at will before man rifled the forests. And man, meanwhile, is terrified that these disembodied feet will choose his head, will occupy the brain they lay siege to, driving out his 'reasonable ways'.

> Now, lest they choose his head,
> Under severe moons he sits making
> Wolf-masks, mouths clamped well onto the world.

Making wolf-masks is the attempt to divert the wolf-spirit into the false world of art or fiction, where it can be dealt with. But that final image of the world held between the teeth of a wolf-mask through whose eye-holes the quick eyes of the savage god might look out is far from reassuring.

'Fire-Eater' is yet another variant on 'Egg-Head' (in *The Hawk in the Rain*). The poem falls into two halves (the second a mirror-image of the first). The first half is about the stars as fire-eaters, the second about the speaker's claim to be himself a fire-eater on a much vaster scale.

> Those stars are the fleshed forebears
> Of these dark hills, bowed like labourers,
>
> And of my blood.
>
> The death of a gnat is a star's mouth: its skin,
> Like Mary's or Semele's, thin
>
> As the skin of fire:
> A star fell on her, a sun devoured her.

The stars are like materialized fires, the gods making themselves visible to men. We give them the names of gods. These gods gave life, and they snuff it out as easily as swallowing the tiny spark which is the life of a gnat. Mere skin is no protection. Both Mary and Semele were pierced by stars, that is by gods. When Semele rashly persuaded Zeus to let her see him in all his glory, the vision killed her. But from her body Zeus took the unborn child and fostered him in his own body until he was born as Dionysus. Semele is a counterpart of Persephone, a virgin seduced by Pluto in the form of a snake and possibly with the aid of an apple. She also 'died' but gave birth in fire to a divine son, Dionysus again, who brought the gift of wine, as Demeter, mother and counterpart of Persephone, brought the gift of grain. Thus, in the pagan myth, the Fall, the crucifixion of the god and the birth of the god are one divine event. To be pierced by the god may be death, but it is also the guarantee of immortality. And in Jerusalem two thousand years after Christ as at Eleusis a thousand years before, the miracle is celebrated by the leaping of fire from the Holy Sepulchre.

There is a legend that the sacred fire at Eleusis once restored a blind man's sight, as Orion restored his by gazing at the sun. To expose oneself to 'the whelm of the sun' is to risk death, but also to let in restoration and fertility.

However, the speaker in the poem, far from showing a due reverence and humility before these powers, claims to be himself a fire-eater capable of managing whole constellations:

> My appetite is good
> Now to manage both Orion and Dog
>
> With a mouthful of earth, my staple.
> Worm-sort, root-sort, going where it is profitable.
>
> A star pierces the slug,
> The tree is caught up in the constellations.
> My skull burrows among antennae and fronds.

This is Faustus again, whose first request to Mephistophilis was for knowledge of astronomy. But before he can swallow stars, this man must eat earth as staple, burrowing downwards like any worm or root into inert matter. (We think of Blake's Newton at the bottom of the sea of materialism, his back to the sun and stars, putting the universe on paper.)

Even the slug is 'pierced' by the divine fire. Even the trees are 'caught up in the constellations', even the insects reach up their antennae, the plants their fronds towards the vivifying stars. But the last we see of our hero he is still underground, still eating earth not fire, and now a skull emptied of what fire it ever had. So much for his arrogant appetite to contain the universe. . . .

The god of the underworld may be the god of death, and February the month of the dead, but Persephone in the underworld is fertilized by Pluto and gives birth to Dionysus, who is Pluto himself in his creative, life-giving aspect. The wolf and the stoat cannot be exorcized from the human world, and if they could, along with the goat and all the other beasts of our being, there would be an end to the race.

One way to negotiate with these powers is through ritual. We call the animals fauna. Fauna was, in Roman mythology, the wife or daughter of Faunus, the fertility god, who corresponds closely to Pan or Dionysus. Under the name of Lupercus he was worshipped in Rome at a temple on the Palatine called the Lupercal. This temple was so called (*lupus* being Latin for wolf) because it was

believed to be on the site of the cave where the she-wolf (which is
the symbol of Rome) suckled Romulus and Remus, founders of the
city. The rituals, the Lupercalia, were celebrated on the 15th of
February. The purpose of the rituals was to restore fertility to barren
women. Goats and dogs were sacrificed. Young men, athletes, were
touched with blood and milk by the priests, then raced through the
streets striking the waiting women as they passed with whips of
goat-skin. Calphurnia, wife of Julius Caesar, once stood there, and
one of the runners was Mark Anthony:

> Forget not, in your speed, Antonius,
> To touch Calphurnia; for our elders say,
> The barren, touched in this holy chase,
> Shake off their sterile curse.   (*J. Caesar* i. ii)

The athletes run not to distingush themselves but to snatch the
lowliest, the barren women 'flung from the wheel of the living', back
into that wheel, into 'the figure of the racers'.

'Lupercalia' fittingly ends the volume, for it offers to resolve in
ritual the dilemma of Crag Jack and the horrors evoked in so many
of the poems. It is made up of four short poems, each describing
one of the participants – the dog, the barren woman, the goats and
the racers.

The dog, though its blood is declined from the days when it was
wolf, still 'held man's reasonable ways between its teeth'. There is
still the 'old spark of the blood-heat' in him. And it is this, 'the
brute's quick' which will be tinder, it is hoped, the touch of life on
the woman's barren body. What gave the bull Moses his foothold
in life, his sense of the continuity of his race, both heir and progenitor,
is what she lacks, what makes her a hostage to death:

> The past killed in her, the future plucked out.

The dog dies that she might live again.

The goat has always been thought of as an embodiment of
libidinousness, the lower half of the satyr, and of Pan the goat-god,
and of the devil.

> Goats, black, not angels, but
> Bellies round as filled wine-skins
> Slung under carcase bones.

That marvellous image is so right purely as a visual image,
descriptive, yet also suggests prodigality and licence, Dionysus and

the Bacchic rites. The god is even more evident in the goat's eyes:

> Yet that's no brute light
>
> And no merely mountain light –
> Their eyes' golden element.

The goat is also characterized by the 'stink of a rank thriving'. All these are to pass to the women through the goat-skin thongs.

In 'Acrobats' the performers are

> Fulcrummed without fail
> On axes immaterial as
> Only geometry should use.

The racers in their blessed fury achieve an unearthly access of power and become

> A theorem of flung effort, blades:
> Nothing mortal falters their poise.

But where the circus crowd were merely spectators excluded from the 'grace' of the acrobats, here the crowd are all participants as they urge on the athletes, their representatives. The racers become conductors of energy between earth and sky:

> The earth's crammed full,
> Its baked red bellying to the sky's
> Electric blue.

Through the ritual they are blessed by dog and goat, caught up in the intercourse of earth and sky, and as they strike a woman they draw her into their pattern, the divine circuit:

> And deliberate welts have snatched her in
> To the figure of racers.

So the poem and the book end with a prayer for life, for the miraculous fertilizing touch of the god:

> Maker of the world,
> Hurrying the lit ghost of man
> Age to age while the body hold,
> Touch this frozen one.

SOURCE: excerpted from the Introduction and the chapter on *Lupercal*, in *The Art of Ted Hughes* (Cambridge, 1975), pp. 2–5, 37–57, 58–60.

Geoffrey Thurley   Beyond Positive Values   (1974)

. . . 'Density'? 'Concreteness'? 'Body'? 'The strength of the English Language'? Surely, these lines have them, or the terms have no meaning. If Hughes, like Dylan Thomas before him, does not 'keep up' the English language, it is impossible to conceive what or who *could*. The failure of the academic world to acknowledge Hughes demonstrated that behind the concern for the 'body' of the language, lay the effectively dictatorial policy of 'positive values'; systematic self-denigration, and the ultimately corrupting concern for integrity. Against all these laws, Hughes offended grievously: neither interested in irony nor distrustful of himself, he did not seem aware of 'integrity' at all. He thereby raised in an uncomfortable form the doubts that must always have existed within the academic establishment: how much of significance can continue to be created by poets so obsessed with *showing* their awareness of their own intellectual transgressions, of the 'unease' they alone saw beneath the facade? The effect of power in Hughes's verse originated, clearly, in the poet's confrontation with experience of a far deeper and more intense order than was generally evident in contemporary poetry.

The strength of Hughes's verse made the ironist academics around him look the little poets they were. But what was most galling about Hughes was that he really justified swagger with achievement:

> The wind flung a magpie away and a black-
> back gull bent like an iron bar slowly.   ('Wind')

There are no massive words in these lines from 'Wind', no display of power. But the bending of the iron bar in the flight of the gull is felt physically, 'laced with instress': no poet since Hopkins had shown himself so capable of reinforcing the inert vocables of everyday words with such tension.

It cannot be too strongly emphasized that to speak of Hughes's strength and power is in no way to suggest any deficiency in fineness. Quite the contrary. 'Wind' itself demonstrates clearly enough that Hughes is possessed of an at times alarming combination of

tremulousness and force. This is manifest often in the strange
delicacy of the imagery. The house in 'Wind'

>   Rang like some fine green goblet in the note
>   That any second would shatter it.

The fine note is linked significantly with the idea of the destruction
of the house. Similarly, in 'October Dawn', the onset of winter's
fierceness is felt first in the 'premonition' of ice that forms on a glass
of wine left out all night. The film of ice on the wine suggests that
'The ice-age had begun its heave' – and it *does* heave! The language
sweats and strains under the load:

>   Soon plate and rivet on pond and brook;
>   Then tons of chain and massive lock
>   To hold rivers.   ('October Dawn')

Yet the massive armoury of *The Hawk in the Rain* – the Stegosaurus,
the Mammoth and sabre-tooth, the whole ark-load of pre-historic
monsters that inspire Hughes with such awe and admiration – all
this would be nothing without the inner energy, an energy of control
and containment, which enables him to hold the experience until it
has been forced to yield up its latent significances. This energy
governs and is governed by the dangerous responsiveness of sensibility that finds its most powerful symbols in the delicate and fragile
as often as in the immensely strong:

>   Now is the globe shrunk tight
>   Round the mouse's dulled wintering heart.
>   Weasel and crow, as if moulded in brass,
>   Move through an outer darkness
>   Not in their right minds,
>   With the other deaths. She, too, pursues her ends,
>   Brutal as the stars of this month,
>   Her pale head heavy as metal.   ('Snowdrop')

(The line, 'She, too, pursues her ends' . . . demonstrates how much
can be packed into the conscious play upon words: I find nothing
in Geoffrey Hill with the same impact.) 'To Paint a Waterlily' quite
deliberately contrasts the exquisitely refined with the savagely
unformed in which it has its ground. 'Still as a painting' the flower
hardly trembles,

>   Though the dragonfly alight,
>   Whatever horror nudge her root.

Hughes's feeling for the subtly poised as well as the brutally predatory emerges too in the superbly sustained rhythm of the following lines:

> . . . so the eyes praise
> To see the colours of these flies
>
> Rainbow their arcs, spark, or settle
> Cooling like beads of molten metal
>
> Through the spectrum.

The sinuous drawing-through of the image (we follow while the beads cool) demonstrates the penetrativeness of Hughes's mind. The effect derives here partly from the nouns used as verbs – 'raise', 'rainbow', 'spark' – but it is due above all to the steady pressure of intelligence Hughes always brings to bear upon his imagery.

At this distance in time, the amazing power and the close control that enabled Hughes to harness the huge energy of the verbiage seem less extraordinary than his penetrativeness – this ability to force through the motif of the poem to some further revelation of its inner nature. To effect what was effected in poems like 'The Horses' and 'The Hawk in the Rain' meant continuing the most serious struggle in the poem at the point where most poets, exhausted, leave off, a handful of verbal victories in their inert hands. It is this courage rather than the enormous energy and epic scale of his poetry that most significantly marks him off from his contemporaries, from Thom Gunn, for example, or Geoffrey Hill. For the penetration through to the final mangled stanza of 'The Hawk in the Rain' represents sustained spiritual strain, such strain as can only be endured when the poet is possessed of a seriousness bordering on the morbid, a seriousness that goes much deeper than the ironist concern for keeping an eye on the integrity-quotient. Indeed, it is a seriousness that cannot function unless the 'integrity' of the agent can be taken for granted. . . .

. . . the admiration for and kinship with a primitive and barbaric strain in the animal world has led Hughes to a contempt for 'mere' civilization and, even more, for the particular configuration of values and attitudes that has strangled man's native energy and perverted his force. He spoke with contempt of the 'rabble starlings of Trafalgar' at a time when it seemed obligatory for poets to chant and march in chorus; he can even 'see' the guts and character in the kind of Brigadier derided by John Osborne as 'pig-faced'. Hence, Hughes' radical disalignment with the attitudes of the current poetry goes deeper than a contempt for its namby-pamby techniques and automatic ironies: it reflects a profound philosophical negation of the complex of attitudes underlying it. It is a negation of the entire quiescent pattern of contemporary society, and a rejection of facile political orthodoxy in favour of a re-discovery of more fundamental layers of passion and experience.

This is why he is fascinated by the primitively strong, by the cohesive energy of undifferentiated consciouness. In 'The Horses' he moves directly from the consideration of the horses themselves, megalithic creatures with a primitive statuesqueness, 'draped manes and tilted hind hooves / Making no sound', to the eruption of a sunrise of a Beethovenian magnificence:

> Silently, and splitting to its core tore and flung cloud
> Shook the gulf open, showed blue,
> And the big planets hanging. . . .

There is nothing in English poetry of a comparable depth and power until we go back to the best of Dylan Thomas, or, further, to the Spender of 'Beethoven's Death Mask', and thence to Lawrence himself. Hughes is fascinated too by war, by the poetry of Wilfred Owen and Keith Douglas. His own poetry takes place as on a dead planet, on a planet whose animation has been suspended – or one whose time-scale has been dislocated, so that a split-second takes an age to pass, as if

> the approaching planet, a half-day off,
> Hangs huge above the thin skulls of the silenced birds.
>   ('Griefs for Dead Soldiers')

This sense of being the last man on earth reminds one strongly of the only other contemporary English writer who has displayed gifts of the same order, Alan Sillitoe. . . .

Like Lawrence, Hughes is impatient of the liberal mob-spirit which, substituting a collective Dutch courage for its fear, disguises the fear from itself. Hence, his respect for the pig-faced Brigadier; for the last English wolf; the jaguar; for the hawk roosting, that attacks out of the sun, and therefore has the sun and all evolution 'behind' him. The stripping of humanity down to the bare-forked animal is likely to run foul of *Lear* and Hughes doesn't always avoid the trap: 'Horses' ('We were born horses') substitutes a sententious literariness for archetypal relevance. But in 'Gog', Hughes strikes through to a primal violence existing within the civilized man that is at the same time an intimation of a new awareness, a mutation almost, ready for the future. On the purely verbal level, it is one of Hughes's most carefully lithe achievements, its words vibrant with ambiguity, yet coming as though at the behest of a dream-consciousness:

> The dog's god is a scrap dropped from the table,
> The mouse's saviour is a ripe wheat grain.
> Hearing the Messiah cry
> My mouth widens in adoration.   ('Gog')

The definitional finesse of the stanza quoted matches the semantic thoughtfulness of Geoffrey Hill, but shot through with the weird insight of Christopher Smart. As an act of spiritual archaeology, 'Gog' can be compared only with the finest moments of *The Waste Land*. Like Eliot, Hughes succeeds in returning to an ancient past which is at the same time a future barbarianism:

> My feetbones beat on the earth,
> Over the sound of motherly weeping. . . .

Like Lawrence, on the other hand, Hughes suggests the need for a new kind of man, a kind of mentality superior to the self-doubt of the liberal tradition, one which will extricate man before he is boxed up and herded by totalitarianism. These two processes – the archaeological analysis and the overreaching synthesis – provide the dynamism to Hughes's poetry. Indeed, the one is essential to the other: it is as the first English poet successfully to absorb the fact of D. H. Lawrence's thought that Hughes is so significant. Until the poet does something bigger than himself; that is, in some sense renounces the world of the schemes of emotion as Rimbaud did; he will be unable to achieve any significant composition. Hughes has expressed the need for this renunciation with chilling precision: 'Flowerlike' he wrote of his childhood,

> I loved nothing.   ('May Day in Holderness')

Ignoring the distractions of self-awareness and positive values, and also the disabused modesty the English had resigned themselves to in their decline, D. H. Lawrence pierced to the region at which new values, new consciousness, could exist. This meant having the strength to ignore the self in order to find it. Hughes too had this strength. . . .

Hughes's poetry is . . . essentially a continuation of the native English tradition. He informed the existential sobriety of the English rural idiom with a new intensity, and a new sense of role and purpose. *Crow* makes it clear how far he was prepared to push this idiom: it is an often frenzied affirmation of the sense of existence that informs the greatest works of the tradition to which it is something of an end-game: what, we may imagine Hughes asking himself, must I do now? Where can I go – in what direction? The answer was downwards, downwards and inwards. Unable to change, but aware of the new climate in which he was working, Hughes simply thrust down into the earth at his feet. He pursued himself from an awareness of existence – the sense in 'Gog' of man having just that very second alighted on this earth – to an exploration of the foundations of this existence. *The Hawk in the Rain* has lost none of its force and freshness, but what appeared in the Cambridge of 1956 an alarming display of violence now seems a rustic idyll. By the late 'sixties Hughes was fighting for his creative survival, as his own 'Famous Poet' had refused to fight. *Crow* is a logical continuance of the direction insisted by the earlier books, but it is also a fairly desperate manoeuvre by a poet feeling himself out-flanked.

Yet the general direction of the book seems to have escaped notice, and along with it the imaginative mechanism of the individual lyrics themselves. They represent a final concentration of Hughes's masculine energy: they smash through the fibres of personal psychology (though nobody but Hughes could have written them, these poems are completely de-personalized), and of language itself. Their characteristic effort is to shatter the appurtenances of consciousness, their characteristic movement from obscurity through density to clarity. Each lyric is a drill trying to burst through to the other side. The other side of what? The terms do not really matter – the other side of consciousness, of matter, of pain, of ecstacy – the other side! To emerge is the aim of the Crow poems. The whole book wants to say with Lawrence, look, we have come through. The poet tries to reach a peace in annihilation, and occasionally succeeds. 'Robin Song' ends with the world rolling 'to crush and silence knowledge'. 'Conjuring in Heaven' ends with Crow 'cataleptic'. 'Crow Goes Hunting' sees him finally 'speechless' with admiration. He hears 'the wingbeat of rock, and his own singing'. Another conclusion

finds him 'lonelier than ever'. The catalogue could be extended to
include practically every poem in the volume. Starting in horror
and mess, the lyrics seek to force their way through to silence, to
peace, to non-being, to isolation – to horror, perhaps, but a horror
clean and without distraction from itself. It is in this way that *Crow*
finally destroys the existential tradition. Like Beckett – a writer who
has interested Hughes much over the past decade – Hughes too
wants to be left just with the consciousness of existence, even if this
is Absurd.

In the *London Magazine* interview with Ekbert Faas . . . Hughes
refers to Eliot and Beckett more than to any other writers. The
importance of *Crow* in relation to Western literature in the mid-
twentieth century cannot be over-estimated: it annihilates – and
transcends in annihilating – a whole phase of European consciousness. It does so by the exercise of that enormous masculine energy
I have already referred to. To refer to it again, is to do more than
to praise once more the poet's endless metaphoric dynamism (the
images zip off the page in *Crow* with more demonic intensity than
ever); it is rather to try and focus the peculiar significance he has
for poetry now. There is nothing left to chance in Hughes's verse,
nothing uncontrolled, nothing random. To a fault, his language is
tightly reined, and let out very much at the poet's discretion. The
force of his writing in fact derives precisely from this. An effusion, a
release of violence, such as we see in most of Dali's painting, and in
the novels of Ian Fleming and the later films of Hitchcock, does not
create anything like the sort of impression made by Hughes's poetry.
The power of Ted Hughes's verse derives substantially from the
containment of force, not from the release or indulgence of it.
Hughes's masculinity is Faustian, Orphic – a refusal to allow the
feminine its due. It is an asseveration of the Will, like Beethoven's
music and Dürer's painting, or Milton's poetry. In the *London
Magazine* interview, Hughes offers a historical hypothesis – owing
much to Lawrence and Robert Graves – which goes far to explain
his own mechanisms. He suggests that modern England has rejected
the presence of the great goddess of the ancient world which Catholic
countries have managed to retain in the figure of Mary. He uses
Shakespeare's *Venus and Adonis* to stand for a basic conflict between
reason and libido . . . .

He might have gone instead to Euripides, for the *Bacchae* dramati-
zes just this quarrel. What is interesting, however, is less the theory

itself (Graves's *White Goddess* has put the case already) than Hughes's relations to its fundamental premises. Hughes equates Adonis with 'logical rationalism', and as it were sides with Venus in rejecting *his* rejection of her passionate unreason. Throughout the *London Magazine* interview, in fact, the poet puts all the weight of his massive personality behind the veneric principle, behind Dionysus behind fertile and wise anti-rationalism. He sees his own role as bringing to light some of the otherwise fouling force of the id, and justifies his own 'poetry of violence' in terms of the much more evil violence wrought in the name of conscious restraint and logical rationalism. . . .

SOURCE: extracts from the chapter 'Beyond Positive Values: Ted Hughes', in *The Ironic Harvest, English Poetry in the Twentieth Century* (Arnold, 1974), pp. 174–7, 181–2, 182–4, 185–6, 186–7.

Ekbert Faas   On *Crow*   (1980)

1. Pseudo-Biblical and Mythical Poems

At first sight the mythological allusiveness of *Crow* seems to belie Hughes's claim that there was no planning in the poems themselves. Not only does the protagonist, in a variety of apocryphal narratives, share the stage with the Biblical Creator, the Serpent or Adam and Eve. He also encounters Proteus, Ulysses, Hercules and Beowulf, poses as Oedipus or parodies the latter's fortunes in 'Song for a Phallus'. The sequence, in short, recalls Joyce's *Ulysses* which, in Eliot's well-known phrase, manipulates 'a continuous parallel between contemporaneity and antiquity' with the effect 'of controlling, of ordering, of giving a shape and a significance to the immense panorama of futility and anarchy which is contemporary history.'

Yet a closer look at *Crow* shows that the poet's use of traditional mythology contravenes Eliot's comment in every single point. Instead of developing a parallel between present and past, the poem evokes a supratemporal world of global religious dimensions in which Western myths figure side by side with the Tibetan Buddhist Womb Door or an Eskimo Genesis. And far from giving order to the chaos of modern life, classical and Biblical myths for the most part appear as the very roots of this chaos.

Naturally for a sequence about Crow 'created by God's nightmare's attempt to improve on man', the poems with pseudo-Biblical content follow the pioneer example of 'Theology' (1961) by inverting the orthodox Christian doctrine. 'In the beginning was Scream' instead of the Word ('Lineage'). The Serpent, originator of sin and death, is changed back into a phallic symbol of life ('A Childish Prank'). Resting on the seventh day, it appears as the true lord of creation which is disrupted by God, an interloper who instead of the apple uses cider to cause the fall of man in a bout of drunken debauchery ('Apple Tragedy'). Causing a similar disruption, God tries to teach Crow the meaning of 'love' but 'Crow's First Lesson' is at every turn refuted by the 'horror of Creation'. God, as usual, 'exhausted with Creation' and convulsed in nightmare, cannot answer Crow's questions, leaving the protagonist in a stupor of defiant silence –

> humped, impenetrable.
> Half-illumined. Speechless.   ('Crow Communes')

Eventually, the quester realizes that beyond the traditional God – 'the man-created, broken down, corrupt despot of a ramshackle religion' who 'accompanies Crow through the world in many guises, mis-teaching, deluding, tempting, opposing and at every point trying to discourage or destroy him' – there must be another God,

> bigger than the other
> Loving his enemies
> And having all the weapons.   ('Crow's Theology')

His subsequent quest 'aims to locate and release' this true creator who has become 'God's nameless hidden prisoner'. Crow encounters him 'repeatedly but always in some unrecognisable form'. For Crow himself is imprisoned in an ego which declares his every act a crime ('Crow's Nerve Fails') and darkens his vision with its civilized concerns ('Crows Vanity'). Hence he can perceive little more than the destructive aspect of this other God: in the 'King of Carrion' with his palace of skulls, in the Sun which he challenges in mock heroic combat ('Crow's Fall') or in another bird whose song resounds like an oracle of Juggernaut destructiveness:

> I am the maker
> Of the world

> *That rolls to crush*
> *And silence my knowledge.*   ('Robin Song')

Even the mythic female whom Crow at first fails ('Crow Tries the
Media') but subsequently half manages to sing about, is mainly
revealed in her negative elementary character ('Crow's Undersong').

However limited these insights, they give the tricksterish bird
sufficient self-confidence to contravene God at every turn in 'over-
correct[ing]' his faulty creation. Even God's ever more gruelling
retaliation in trying to crush Crow, tear him to pieces or bury him,
effects little more than to strengthen the protagonist in his arrogant
attitude while bringing despair to the torturer ('Crow's Song of
Himself'). When the Serpent, in the guise of a nuclear bomb-like
ecological monstrosity, threatens to take over God's creation, Crow
'Beat the hell out of it, and ate it' ('A Horrible Religious Error'). Or
when God's creation finally falls apart, 'Crow nailed . . . heaven and
earth together', causing a 'horror beyond redemption . . . Crying:
"This is my Creation", / Flying the black flag of himself' ('Crow
Blacker Than Ever').

A truer counter-image to God's creation than Crow's tricksterish
over-corrective is implied in 'Snake Hymn', the last of the pseudo-
Biblical fables. Both in content and tone the poem harks back to
'Theology'. Quietly yet unerringly it dismantles the Christian doctrines
of the fall, the crucifixion and God's infinite love until nothing remains
but a few basic facts about sex, birth, life and death:

> Nothing else has happened.
> The love that cannot die
> Sheds the million faces
> And skin of agony.
>
> To hang, an empty husk.
> Still no suffering
> Darkens the garden
> Or the snake's song   ('Snake Hymn')

Like these pseudo-Biblical fables to which 'Snake Hymn' is the
appropriate summing up, the poems involving classical myths usually
follow a highly dramatic 'dialectics of mockery and apotheosis' reminiscent of Jerzy Grotowski's similar efforts in the theatre. Unlike his Greek
namesake, 'Oedipus Crow' chooses to flee rather than search out his
destiny and is mutilated by circumstances rather than by his own
hand. The untragic protagonist remains unredeemed. 'One-legged,

gutless and brainless, the rag of himself', he is tripped by up Death, who holds him up with a laugh, Crow dangling 'from his one claw' – corrected for some unknown crime, a Kafkaesque 'warning' to others whose mere existence is their hereditary sin. Instead of climaxing in the tragic deed of horror, his agonies follow a shamanistic pattern of repeated dismemberment, which for all its gruesomeness is 'full of buffoonery, mimicry . . . and magical contortions'. The line about Crow who after losing a leg is 'cheered by the sound of his foot and its echo', would suit a satyr play rather than the more rarified mood of classical tragedy.

Hughes's reversal of the same myth in 'Song for a Phallus', originally to be part of his adaptation of Seneca's *Oedipus*, maintains this savage black humor throughout. Instead of curing the plague-ridden Thebes by answering the Sphinx's riddle, Hughes's Oedipus searches for the solution by splitting the monster from top to toe, but only releases a host of further monsters. The riddle's final answer is rendered in one of Hughes's recurrent nightmare hieroglyphs: a deliberate or unconscious destruction of the female revealing the guilt-laden interrelatedness of nature. Man in 'Revenge Fable' kills his mother with the result that 'His head fell off like a leaf'. Crow, repeating man's technological abuse of Mother Nature, finally

> Crashed on the moon awoke and crawled out
>
> Under his mother's buttocks.   ('Crow and Mama')

Similarly, Oedipus hatchets his mammy, who had emerged from the gory intestines of the Sphinx, only to find

> himself curled up inside
> As if he had never been born   ('Song for a Phallus')

A similar inversion of the Proteus myth results in another parable about man's destructive search for knowledge ('Truth Kills Everybody'), while Crow's pursuit of Ulysses and Hercules turns the ancient heroes into victims to be assimilated by the protagonist's deadpan imperturbable 'Crowego'. Ovid's principle of metamorphosis, which some of these poems use as their structural pattern, serves to show that destiny is both elusive and ineluctable. In pursuit of Ulysses, Crow only manages to catch a worm; grappling with Hercules' two puff-adders, he strangles in error Dejanira ('Crowego'); trying to grasp Proteus, Crow finds that he has caught Achilles who in turn assumes multiple other shapes from a 2000 volts naked powerline to Christ's hot pounding heart. Yet unlike the secrets which the classical Proteus finally yields to his questioner, the truth totally eludes and even kills Crow ('Truth Kills Everybody').

2. The Influence of Primitive Poetry

Although *Crow*, like *The Waste Land*, is bound to send critics on a wild goose chase after crows and the Holy Grail, the author's intention was 'to produce something with the minimum cultural accretions of the museum sort . . . as it might be invented after the holocaust and demolition of all libraries'. Naturally this pursuit found its prime model in primitive song which Hughes, in his 1962 review of C. M. Bowra's study on the subject, discovered to be full of the qualities of 'ideal poetry' – 'full of zest, clairvoyantly sensitive, realistic, whole, natural, and passionate'. More specifically, he noted a tendency toward parallelism and couplets, the 'artful use of repetition and variation, and possibly rhyme'. An example like the following may well have helped inspire the basic structure of 'A Disaster', 'Truth Kills Everybody' and several other Crow poems.

> The great Koonak mountain in the south yonder,
> I see it
> The great Koonak mountain in the south yonder,
> I behold it,
> The gleaming light in the south yonder,
> I look at it.
> Beyond the Koonak it stretches,
> The same light that wraps
> Koonak towards the sea.
> See how in the south the clouds
> Swell and change;
> See how in the south
> They make one another beautiful.

Another of Bowra's examples is characteristic of a more advanced stage of primitive poetry, where, again as in several Crow poems, 'repetitions are fewer and the variations more adventurous':

> Ostrich, rising and flying,
> Long-necked and big-toed,
> Belly full of rock-flint, great bird,
> Wide-mouthed male ostrich,

> Flying, running, great bird,
> Give me one of your grey feathers.
>
> . . . .
>
> Male ostrich, looking up,
> Belly that says *khari, khari,*
> Ostrich, whose bowels alone are not fit to eat,
> Give me one of your leg-bones, ostrich!
>
> He who has two bones, which say *hui-hui,*
> Male ostrich, who has wonderful marrow,
> Who with his face says *gou-gou,*
> Might I possess you, my ostrich!

The poem's structure vividly recalls Hughes's 'Littleblood' although its content for understandable reasons does not. For ostriches and bears may have their rightful place in the neo-primitive poetry of a Snyder or Rothenberg. In the work of an English poet, who instead may invoke 'the last wolf killed in Britain' (*Lupercal*), they would look out of context. No wonder that native European rather than non-Western primitive poetry came to exert the major influence on *Crow*. Hughes was fortunate to hit upon one of its rare treasures, a six volume anthology of *Carmina Gadelica* in which one can find examples of all the primitive poetic strategies analysed by Bowra. As he told me in August 1977,

Alexander Carmichael's collection contains a lot of old Gaelic spells, chants, healing songs, invocations and so on. It's a long time since I saw it but that really is the source of it as much as anything. Some of these poems were really extraordinary and at the same time gave me a feeling that this was a source I could really lay claim to. Whereas with ordinary primitive literature you always feel like being a bit of a tourist if you use it. There is obviously a lot of ways in which you *can* use it but you can't suddenly seize that as a style.

Again recalling 'Littleblood', the following poem, entitled 'Little Bird', strikingly confirms what is said here:

> Little Bird! O Little Bird!
>   I wonder at what thou doest,
> Thou singing merry far from me,
>   I in sadness all alone!
>
> Little Bird! O Little Bird!
>   I wonder at how thou art,
> Thou high on the tips of branching boughs,
>   I on the ground a-creeping!

> Little Bird! O Little Bird!
> Thou art music far away,
> Like the tender croon of the m
> In the kindly sleep of death.

Hughes's comparison between literary and
in his 1967 essay on Vasko Popa, indirectly
development under the influence of primitiv
the *Wodwo* poems seem to 'hide behind per
had 'abandoned the struggle with circumstan
the unifying focus that comes of that'; they ap   ...ave lost 'morale
and surrendered to the arbitrary imagery of the dream flow'. All such
surrealist vagaries disappeared from *Crow* whose 'folktale surrealism'

is always urgently connected with the business of trying to manage practical
difficulties so great that they have forced the sufferer temporarily out of the
dimension of coherent reality into that depth of imagination where understanding has its roots and stores its X-rays. There is no sense of surrender to the
dream flow for its own sake or of relaxation from the outer battle. In the world
of metamorphoses and flights the problems are dismantled and solved, and
the solution is always a practical one. This type of surrealism, if it can be
called surrealism at all, goes naturally with a down-to-earth, alert tone of free
enquiry.

These more recent stylistic influences reinforced two earlier ones which
the poet, as late as 1970, described as the most forceful in his entire
career. In Hughes's view, the techniques of parallelism, repetition and
variation etc., which Bowra had located in primitive song, left a
powerful legacy in Hebrew poetry and Shakespeare. It was this multiple
heritage compounded of Biblical, Shakespearean, modernist and primitive elements rather than any single source which Hughes managed to
reclaim in the little fables, visionary anecdotes, apocryphal lectures
and totem songs of *Crow*.

3. The Story of Crow

Hardly born from his 'egg of blackness', 'Trembling featherless elbows
in the nest's filth', Crow is subjected to a first encounter with Death
in 'Examination at the Womb-Door' and made to experience the basic
cruelty of existence as victim ('A Kill') and destroyer ('Crow and
Mama') even before he struts forth into the actual world through a
black doorway described as the eye's pupil in the world's earthen wall

. Here, his childish pranks with God or the latter's inane
about love are quickly muted by the horrors of nuclear
tion ('Crow Alights', 'That Moment'). Where God's teachings
ve Crow with nothing but a sense of guilt, his own search for
instruction only results in forlorn helplessness ('Crow Hears Fate
Knock on the Door'). In no time Crow has moved from childlike
laughter to guilt-ridden despondency. And though he is quick to choose
self-preservation as a way out of this moral dilemma, Crow eats his
grub weeping ('Crow Tyrannosaurus') or experiences how his inner
'prophecy' of a will to power is 'Slowly rending [his] vital fibres'
('Crow Hears Fate Knock on the Door').

Crow's explorations of the world often proceed in a backward
journey through history. Thus the nightmare visions of nuclear
destruction are followed by 'Crow's Account of [a] Battle' in traditional
strategic warfare. The protagonist's growing sense of evil, destruction
and guilt crystallizes in 'The Black Beast', which Crow tries to track
down with the ferocity of Ahab chasing the White Whale. Life in the
world has already corrupted him to the point where he repeats most
of man's errors, so that this hunt gradually assumes the proportions of
man's recent ecological devastation of Mother Nature.

> Crow roasted the earth to a clinker, he charged into space –
> Where is the Black Beast?

Crow is unaware that the Black Beast may after all be found in his
own being.

In terms of its title, *From the Life and Songs of the Crow*, the sequence's
opening poems up to 'The Black Beast' primarily deal with Crow's
life. 'A Grin', an enigmatic folktale allegory whose meaning seems to
transcend the quester's limited insights at this point, could be seen as
the first of his actual songs. As against the unremitting 'horror of
Creation', the 'cortege / Of mourning and lament', 'sorrow on sorrow'
which we have witnessed so far, it allows the first glimmer of
real hope to emerge from visions of further passion, agony and
destruction. Thanatos's derisive grin fails to find a 'permanent home'
of 'tenure / In eternal death' however hard he tries for it in the
grimaces of a murderer, a woman in labor, a firing machine-gunner
or lovers at the moment of death-like self-annihilation. For 'none of
it lasted'. Even the 'face / In the electric chair' finally relaxed. After
Crow's schoolboy-like triumph over death in 'Examination at the

Womb-Door', the poem reaffirms the refusal of death's dominion in
oblique yet at the same time more realistic terms.

> The grin
> Sank back, temporarily nonplussed
> Into the skull.

Crow, in his idiosyncratic interpretation of St George, proceeds to
unmask England's patron saint as the key figure in the 'neurotic-
making dynamics of Christianity'. As shown earlier, his account is a
direct comment on why the legend of St George, 'the symbolic story of
creating a neurosis', should, in Hughes's view, be a forbidden story
for children. For like Crow himself, St George is a creature who in his
craze for order, 'truth' and dominion over nature, has denied the Black
Beast in himself. And it is doubly ironic that one of the shapes of this
Beast which, in inversion of the original legend, outwits St George,
making him murder his family instead of a monster, is that of a bird
like Crow:

> A bird-head,
> Bald, lizard-eyed, the size of a football, on two staggering bird-legs.
> ('Crow's Account of St George')

Crow's growing experience teaches him how the world has been
devastated and atrophied by the Word as by a magical monster:

> The word oozed its way, all mouth,
> Earless, eyeless.
> . . . sucking the cities
> Like the nipples of a sow.
> ('A Disaster'; cf. 'The Battle of Osfrontalis')

Yet the Word's ultimate impotence leads Crow to surmise a creator
beyond Logos ('Crow's Theology'). His subsequent 'fall' from the
heights of all these half-assimilated insights is one of tricksterish hubris.
But always quick to have recourse to his basic strengths, Crow, charred
black by his attack on the sun, 'spraddled head-down in the beach-
garbage, guzzling a dropped ice-cream' while most birds escape from
everyday reality into more rarified realms ('Crow and the Birds').

While following an implied surrealistic folktale narrative of sorts,
the sequence accumulates much of its deeper meaning from an ever
more densely woven texture of interrelating themes such as the basic
cruelty of life, man's ineluctable guilt and the closeness between ecstasy
and agony. 'Criminal Ballad' picks up several of the strands. Man, the

unconscious 'Abattoir/Of innocents' from 'Crow Tyrannosaurus', is given a semi-biographical portrait. At every point, from birth to adulthood, his life is the death of somebody else, until suddenly, in an image recalling *Macbeth*, his hands are covered with blood, perhaps after he has unwittingly murdered his wife and children. Like Crow he starts crying, but the despair has reached a hysterical pitch where tears turn into laughter. In a later poem, the same laughter in despite of life's agonies, has, like 'A Grin' and 'The Smile', grown into another phantom allegory in the surrealistic fantasy world of *Crow*—

> laughter scampers around on centipede boots
> Still runs all over on caterpillar tread
> And rolls back onto the mattress, legs in the air
>
> ('In Laughter')

'Crow on the Beach' resumes the story of the protagonist. He has become more and more alientated from a world which turns a cold shoulder on all his crowomorphic needs and desires. But at least Crow has learnt that hearing 'the sea's ogreish outcry and convulsion'

> he was the wrong listener unwanted
> To understand or help –

Not so 'The Contender' in whose self-inflicted suffering a Grin seems to have found the 'permanent home' it couldn't find elsewhere.

> He lay crucified with all his strength
> On the earth
> Grinning towards the sun
> .   .   .   .
> Grinning through his atoms and decay
> Grinning into the black.

In his sacrifice for mankind the hero not only performs a 'senseless trial of strength' but finds the whole of humanity and nature ranged against himself. Man's misery, which Christ's and Prometheus's suffering helped relieve, merely increases the Contender's agony:

> their tears salted his nail-holes
> Only adding their embitterment
> To his effort.

In the following poem, progress and technology, as championed by the original Prometheus, have become mere chimeric projections of 'Crow's Vanity' –

> Mistings of civilisation   towers   gardens
> . . . .
> Mistings of skyscrapers   webs of cities –

the protagonist looking for 'a glimpse of the usual grinning face' in 'the evil mirror' and breathing heavily with excitement. Yet Crow continues indefatigably, playing further pranks with God's creation or trying out the media in order to sing about a nameless 'her' and finding the entire world united in wanting to smother his attempt. No wonder that for a moment 'Crow's Nerve Fails'. Guilt-ridden since his 'First Lesson' in which God tries to make him pronounce the word 'love', Crow has learned that, like man who is 'a walking/Abbatoir/Of innocents' he is a creature whose 'every feather [is] the fossil of a murder'. And pondering this universal guilt he gains the conviction that there is neither atonement nor heaven.

The world's only response to its disasters are noises which reverberate like cosmic roars of laughter. Bemused 'Crow Frowns', wondering about the signatures of his own strength. Rather than in a Promethean striving for human progress or the Christian expectation of a better hereafter gained through grace or right moral conduct, he finds the answer in a koan-like paradox:

> We are here, we are here.
> He is the long waiting for something
> To use him for some everything
> Having so carefully made him
>
> Of nothing.   ('Crow Frowns')

In Crow's world every thought, no less than every act, leads to unmitigated disaster. Even the attempt to escape this vicious circle in a thought of quietude only results in further action reducing the protagonist to the inertia of self-destructive pusillanimity ('Magical Dangers').

Crow's own songs, or those he listens to, often read like cryptic answers to the protagonist's bewilderments. 'Robin Song' seems to tell him that as creator and destroyer in one, the true God is the very image of life's natural cruelty. Along with 'Owl's Song', 'Dawn's Rose', 'Notes for a Little Play', 'King of Carrion', 'Two Eskimo Songs' and 'Littleblood', the poem is one of a series of lyrical masterpieces that focus the collection's multiple shades of meaning. As hunted victim, helpless sufferer and maker

> Of the world
> *That rolls to crush*
> *And silence* [its] *knowledge,*   ('Robin Song')

the Robin, like its creator, embodies the various facets of life in a mythograph that may be disturbing to Christians but could elicit little more than an approving nod from readers nurtured, say, on the *Bhagavad Gita* or much of primitive literature. The parallel concept of a creation emanating from a final 'emptiness of inexhaustible contents' or *śūnyatā*, of which 'Conjuring in Heaven' gives a semi-burlesque account, causes similar consternation to Crow, although an earlier poem already spoke of how the creator had 'so carefully made him / Of Nothing' ('Crow Frowns').

But Crow is slow to learn and often makes errors which he had earlier managed to avoid. After calmly surveying the devastations caused by words ('A Disaster') and even warding off their attempts to encroach upon his life ('The Battle of Osfrontalis'), he finally cannot resist the temptation of trying out words himself. Yet all they teach him, in a sequence of metamorphoses following the pattern of several other poems, is the ultimate elusiveness of phenomena. Crow undergoes an experience which Hughes describes as his own in *Poetry in the Making* [1967]:

It is when we set out to find words for some seemingly quite simple experience that we begin to realize what a huge gap there is between our understanding of what happens around us and inside us, and the words we have at our command to say something about it. (p. 119)

The hare Crow chases with a 'lovely pack' of words permanently eludes him by assuming ever new shapes even though the hunter changes his words according to these various metamorphoses. Finally, the hare reappears leaping for the hill,

> Having eaten Crow's words.

> Crow gazed after the bounding hare
> Speechless with admiration.   ('Crow Goes Hunting')

An appropriate afterword to Crow's unsuccessful experiments with words, 'Owl's Song' celebrates an art which like Hughes's own will neither flinch from the unredeemable suffering of man nor be muted by the ultimate silence.

> He sang
> How everything had nothing more to lose

                    Then sat still with fear

                    Seeing the clawtrack of star
                    Hearing the windbeat of rock

                    And his own singing.   ('Owl's Song')

And again Crow seems to learn. For his 'Undersong' is an example of
just such poetry which makes 'audible meanings without disturbing
the silence, an art of homing in tentatively on vital scarcely perceptible
signals, making no mistakes, but with no hope for finality, continuing
to explore' [*Poetry in the Making*, p. 202].

  'Crow's Undersong' offers an important landmark in Hughes's
general development. For here the White Goddess lost since the
nineteen year old poet's address to the Lady of 'Song' (*Hawk*) and
buried under 'all that stone' of the dark churches which already
'Stooped over [his] cradle' ('Crag Jack's Apostasy' (*Lupercal*)) makes
her first reappearance in his work. In 1970, shortly before publishing
'Crow's Undersong', Hughes described the historical development
of which his own is both a result and foreshortened mirror image:
'Christianity deposes Mother Nature and begets, on her prostrate
body, Science, which proceeds to destroy Nature.' But since the
early sixties this process has been reversed. 'Nature as the Great
Goddess of mankind, and the Mother of all life' has re-emerged as
a dominant force in our culture. Unlike this programmatic statement,
the poem explores the possibilities of this rebirth rather than stating
it as a fact. Its very opening line is a negation:

                    She cannot come all the way.

But from then on, the voice which went dumb after dictating 'Song'
not only seems to recover speech but to deliver its message of hope in
direct contrast to the earlier poem. There the lady turned away from
the poet; though destined to survive, she was not to come home. Now
she is coming back. The precious despair of 'Song' has yielded in
'Crow's Undersong' to a vitalism of hope, an elaborate, almost
Petrarchan refinement replaced by 'a super-simple and super-ugly
language' which 'shed[s] everything except what [it] wanted to say':

      She has come amorous it is all she has come for

      If there had been no hope she would not have come

And there would have been no crying in the city

(There would have been no city)

The life, of which the female in 'Crow's Undersong' is the guarantor, also means suffering, an insight further developed in 'Crow's Elephant Totem song'. The hyenas devour the graceful little elephant for giving them illusions about a 'Land of Peaceful'. In Crow's universe there is no such paradisaic beyond, and even though the elephant after his resurrection keeps on singing 'About a star of deathless and painless peace / . . . no astronomer can find where it is'. What the reader finds instead, is that the resurrected elephant with his

> Deadfall feet and toothproof body and bulldozing bones
> And completely altered brains
> Behind aged eyes, that were wicked and wise

has come surprisingly close to his murderers whose behavior has remained consistent even in afterlife. Their song, proclaiming that their life –

> In hourly battle with a death
> The size of the earth
> Having the strength of the earth –

is the only 'Land of Peaceful' there is, is the poem's central message.

Along with 'Crow's Undersong' and 'Crow's Elephant Totem Song', 'Dawn's Song' seems to stem from the sequence's earlier conception in *Eat Crow*. While the two songs expand upon the figure of Morgan's female guide and the choral dialogue of Morgan's bones 'all chattering together', 'Dawn's Rose' reads like a versified version of the earlier work's conclusion. Here again we encounter the crow which as 'a sign of life', 'has come up from the maker of the world' before dawn, sitting 'in the early gray light', watching a 'gray desert of tumbled stone[s] . . . in their usual trance, rapt to the circles of galactic dust' and singing 'the song of silence', its mind 'resigned to the superior stamina of the empty horizon (*Eat Crow*).

'Dawn's Rose' is the collection's only poem about a crow rather than about Crow himself who reappears in 'Crow's Playmates'. Once more repeating a mistake which man has made before him, the protagonist, in an effort to escape loneliness, invents all kinds of gods. But such wishful imaginings backfire, disassociating Crow from direct contact with the elements and making him realize, after yet another vaudeville-like learning process, that existence essentially means loneliness.

In 'Crowego' the protagonist, gazing 'Like a leopard into a fat land', after he has devoured Ulysses, strangled Dejanira and drunk Beowulf's blood, seems to have turned into one of his totem animals. Like Hughes himself who considers the 'comparative religion / mythology background' to be irrelevant to *Crow*, its protagonist is indifferent to the heroes of our past.

> His wings are the stiff back of his only book,
> Himself the only page – of solid ink.   ('Crowego')

Replacing the mythic figures of this erudite tradition are semi-allegorical phantasmata like 'A Grin', 'Laughter' or 'The Smile'. The last in this series of poems, which in regular intervals map the wider cosmic background to Crow's adventures, 'The Smile' prepares us for the conclusion of the entire sequence. The poem, like this conclusion, is far from a happy one. It is more like the end of Shakespeare's Gloucester whose heart

> 'Twixt two extremes of passion, joy and grief,
> Burst smilingly.   (*K. Lear* v. iii. 200–1)

'The Smile' reads as if Hughes had set out to translate these lines into cosmic terms. Searching unsuccessfully for a home in people's faces which elude it with their own deceitful smiles, the Smile, unlike its parallel allegory, the Grin, finally manages to find a tenure in death. Touching a dying man's lips, it succeeds in

>   altering his eyes
> And for a moment
> Mending everything
>
> Before it swept out and away across the earth.

As if to forestall the poem's misinterpretation in terms of our traditional tragic humanism, we are made to see a more ominous smile in the following poem. A person who in various ways tries to take destiny into his own hands is frustrated at every turn and finally, in a process of piecemeal destruction, reduced to his own ashes –

> And so the smile not even Leonardo
> Could have fathomed
> Flew off into the air, the rubbish heap of laughter
> Screams, discretions, indiscretions etcetera
>   ('Crow Improvises')

Even the smile of relaxation in death only lasts for a moment before life and suffering continue. And while Crow is alive, he is prepared to answer the guffaws of fate with his own defiant laughter to the point of emulating the cosmic phantasmata in their very antics. Just as Laughter 'scampers around on centipede boots / . . . And rolls back onto the mattress, legs in the air', Crow

>   rolls on the ground helpless,

>   And he sees his remote feet and he chokes he
>   Holds his aching sides –   ('Crow's Battle Fury')

'Crow's Battle Fury' or defiant laughter in the face of life's agonies suddenly turns into a shamanistic ritual of self-disintegration and renewal. This shattering of the self in laughter and the subsequent 'labour of fitting it together again' is described in imagery Hughes shares with Plath:

>   (With his glared off face glued back into position
>   A dead man's eyes plugged back into his sockets
>   A dead man's heart screwed in under his ribs
>   His tattered guts stitched back into position
>   His shattered brains covered with a steel cowl)

>   He steps forward a step,
>   and a step,
>   and a step –

Donning a grin in the attempt to counter God's sham world of love with a counter-creation of agony, 'Crow Blacker Than Ever' again overcorrects things in trying to change them. Even so, he acts no worse than his humanitarian fellow brethren who, like the 'person' in a 'Revenge Fable', commit suicide in killing off Mother Nature or, like his counterpart in 'A Bedtime Story', lose all contact with body and soul.

Creation has failed again. We are back to the original Crow narrative about God's nightmare's attempt to improve upon God's creation by creating Crow, and God's own attempt to frustrate this second Genesis. As Crow's 'Song of Himself' informs us, God, despite repeated attempts, has little success in destroying Crow. Yet although the protagonist's defiance has matured into genuine strength, he still reacts in panic when confronted with the ultimate mystery of his life. He has yet to learn that wherever he may turn he will always be confronted with his own self. Like Oedipus in 'Song for a Phallus', he instead goes on trying to hew his way towards the 'truth'. The real truth is finally revealed to him when he is faced with 'fear', tries to strike it down but in doing so only knocks himself down ('Crow Sickened').

Neither 'Song for a Phallus' nor 'Apple Tragedy' mention Crow, but they both have their place in the thematic and stylistic texture of *Crow* as a whole. By contrast, 'Crow Paints Himself Into a Chinese Mural', a piece rescued from the unpublished 1964 verse play *Difficulties of a Bridegroom*, is as alien to the sequence as the melodramatically overstated 'The Lovepet' seems superfluous to it. Along with 'Crow Hears Fate Knock on the Door', 'Crow's Fall', 'The Contender', 'Crow Tries the Media' and 'Crow's Elephant Totem Song', both poems were added to the American edition of *Crow*, and there was good reason for eliminating 'The Lovepet' from the second Faber edition (1972) which otherwise retains the American additions. It would have been equally appropriate to eliminate 'Crow Paints Himself Into a Chinese Mural'. With its surrealistic diffuseness this poem would fit into *Wodwo* but is at variance with the didactic, imagistic and mythopoeic precision of *Crow*. True enough, the two poems cannot be said to disrupt an Aristotelian unity with beginning, middle and end. But even within the open texture of *Crow* their inappropriateness is sufficiently felt, and particularly so at a point where they distract from an ever increasing thematic density as the sequence draws towards its conclusion.

'Crow's Last Stand' is an appropriate introduction to this last section. Whatever hope there is, is based upon survival despite utter reduction. Burnt to a charred stump by his old antagonist the sun,

> Crow's eye-pupil, in the tower of its scorched fort,

is all that remains of the protagonist. The world is indifferent to his needs and emotions, yet holds him imprisoned in its everlasting torture chamber. There is no way of ignoring what a previous poem evokes as the 'sea's ogreish outcry and convulsion' ('Crow on the Beach):

> He turned his back and he marched away from the sea

> As a crucified man cannot move.   ('Crow and the Sea')

All his attempts to come to grips with the world only lead to his utter destruction ('Truth Kills Everybody'), and whatever strength he develops in this battle is a fiendish 'arrogance of blood and bone' (*Lupercal*). In no time Crow has turned into a monster, 'Holding the

very globe in terror' ('Crow and Stone'). And little is going to change
even if Crow should survive forever. For the Eternal-Feminine which
gave him birth is herself an image of the destructiveness and suffering
he has come to embody. Her brow, the 'notable casket of gems', shows
'many a painful frown'; 'her perfect teeth' have a 'hint of a fang at the
corner'; not to mention her vagina which as 'the ticking bomb of the
future' is a source not only of life but of apocalyptic doom ('Fragment
of an Ancient Tablet'). A follow-up to 'Apple Tragedy', 'Notes for a
Little Play' with its ironically understated title, deals with one such
apocalypse, a total nuclear holocaust and its survivors, 'Mutations –
at home in the nuclear glare,' dancing a strange nuptial dance 'in the
darkness of the sun, / Without guest or God'. Whether these strange
items are the successors of man or even of Crow, there is one force
alone which can guarantee the survival of either, the force which Plato
misinterpreted as Eros and Christianity as agape.

> The blood in Adam's body
> That slid into Eve
> Was the everlasting thing
> Adam swore was love.   ('Snake Hymn')

Love's true image is more like that of the crawling beast with two
backs reminiscent of Francis Bacon's paintings.

> His kisses sucked out her whole past and future or tried to
> He had no other appetite
> She bit him she gnawed him she sucked
>
> .   .   .   .   .   .
>
> And their deep cries crawled over the floors
> Like an animal dragging a great trap.

And yet there is more to it than the mere coupling of two animals.
Sex may not be the first step in an ascent towards ideational values,
but its death-like ecstacies can be a means of spiritual rebirth in which
sponsa and *sponsus* become each other's saviors. In shamanistic terms,
a mutual dismemberment is followed by mutual reintegration. After
their aggressive sexual acts,

> Their heads fell apart into sleep like the two halves
> Of a lopped melon, but love is hard to stop
>
> In their entwined sleep they exchanged arms and legs
> In their dreams their brains took each other hostage
>
> In the morning they wore each other's face.   ('Lovesong')

Again Crow is the last one to get the message, so once more he tries
to make the world answer his need for affection. But

> The touch of a leaf's edge at his throat
> Guillotined further comment.   ('Glimpse')

As many a previous lesson could have taught him, speechless wonder
is the only appropriate response to a world of apocalyptic doom in
which 'King of Carrion' rules over silence.

'Fleeing From Eternity' reaffirms these experiences in an inverse
sequence. The rise of man's consciousness is a process of self-reduction.
Originally faceless, eyeless and mouthless, man becomes aware of
things by being deprived of them. Unlike Oedipus, he learns to
experience the world through suffering until, finally he 'gashed holes
in his face' with a sharp rock and

> Through the blood and pain he looked at the earth.

The only solace afforded him in his 'cemetery earth' comes from his
contacts with his shamanistic Earth Mother representative or *ayami*, 'a
woman singing out of her belly', who assumes part of the burden of
his own suffering.

> He gave her eyes and a mouth, in exchange for the song.
> She wept blood, she cried pain.

A song in exchange for learning to taste the bitterness of life sounds
like a fitting description of Hughes' own art, and the second 'Eskimo
Song' as well as 'Littleblood', the collection's culminating achievement,
provide us with the appropriate illustrations. Like the book as a whole,
'How Water Began to Play' suggests a conclusion beyond its actual
end, and 'Littleblood' gives us a glimpse of that beyond. Genuine
playfulness or līlā only begins after all hope has vanished, when Water
'had no weeping left' and 'lay at the bottom of all things / Utterly worn
out utterly clear'. Littleblood, a surrealistic fairy tale creature, has
experienced this total vulnerability and absurdity of existence –

> hiding from the mountains in the mountains.
> Wounded by stars and leaking shadow
> .   .   .   .
> Reaping the wind and threshing the stones.

Like the survivors of nuclear holocaust in 'Notes for a Little Play', it
has begun to dance a strange dance 'in the darkness of the sun, / Without
guest or God' – 'drumming in a cow's skull / Dancing with a gnat's

feet / With an elephant's nose with a crocodile's tail'. And to this creature, as his future Muse, the poet addresses his final appeal.

> Grown so wise grown so terrible
> Sucking death's mouldy tits.
>
> Sit on my finger, sing in my ear, O Littleblood.

4. From *Crow* to *Orghast*

But for the event remembered in its dedication, *Crow* without doubt would be a different book. The deaths of Assia and Shura in March 1969 not only brought the actual writing of the poems to a sudden standstill; the sequence as it was put together about a year later also seems to differ markedly from the original impulse behind *Crow*. Even when Hughes, early in 1970, talked to me about the typescript he was then about to send off to Faber, his almost obsessive focus was on Crow's descent into the underworld where the quester rescues a desecrated female through his own disintegration before both become bride and bridegroom. Yet of this the published sequence reflects as little as of the actual Crow story as a whole. Poems that bear a direct relation to either were apparently excluded from both the British and American editions of *Crow* and only a few of these were allowed to surface in small editions after 1970.

One such poem, 'Crow's Song About God', is about the first part of the Crow story. Man sitting under the gatepost of heaven and trying to hand his life back to God has suffered the disintegration familiar from similar descriptions in both Hughes's and Plath's poetry.

> Eyesockets empty
> Stomach laid open
> To the inspection of the stars
> The operation unfinished
> (The doctors ran off, there was some other emergency).

Another poem deals with a female victim of similar desecration, perhaps the one destined to become Crow's bride, –

> She tried to keep her breasts
> They were cut from her and canned
> She tried to keep her cunt
> It was produced in open court she was sentenced –
>
> ('Crow's Song About England')

A third describes God's unsuccessful attempt to provide Crow with a substitute bride made out of the burnt carcasses of hags of which cartloads are shipped into the furnaces of heaven ('Crow's Courtship'). Yet none of these poems published shortly after *Crow* covers the rescue of the desecrated female by her bridegroom, a happy end which the tragic events of March 1969 removed from the poet's reach.

If Hughes, nonetheless, persisted in his quest, it was by retracing his steps and resuming his mythopoeic journey from its beginnings. Hughes's 1973 description of the Crow story, in which the protagonist's creator, originally God's nightmare, has turned into 'the mysterious, powerful, invisible prisoner of the being men called God', indicates the most general direction which this recasting of the story was to take. The result was *Orghast* [produced in 1971] whose interior mythology, as the poet has commented, was 'of a piece with parts of [his] earlier writing'. To readers of Hughes who witnessed the actual spectacle amongst the royal tombs at Persepolis, *Orghast* must have appeared like a sudden floodlit revelation of the secret quarry from which Hughes's poems had been hewn for several years. But just as the poems were half undecipherable messages from some distant mythic battlefield, so its direct dramatisation in *Orghast* remained inarticulate in a language of mere sounds.

SOURCE: from chapter on *Crow* in *Ted Hughes: The Unaccommodated Universe* (Santa Barbara, California, 1980), pp. 98–117.

Terry Gifford & Neil Roberts   On *Cave Birds*   (1981)

Cave Birds [1975]* is, we believe, Hughes's finest book to date. . . .

* [Ed.] Poems in *Cave Birds* were read in May 1975 at the Ilkley Literature Festival, and soon afterwards on BBC Radio Three. Ten of them were published then in a limited edition, with illustrations by Leonard Baskin. Others of them were published in magazines in 1974–76. The edition published by Faber in October 1978 omits two of the poems in the broadcast version, and also the narrative links provided for that by the poet. All save one of the poems in the Faber edition of 1978 are accompanied by a Baskin illustration.

Several poems – certainly 'The Executioner', 'The Knight', 'Bride and Groom' and 'The Risen' – are among Hughes's greatest achievements. The terror that is essential to its subject, the hero's transformation, is never far removed from a sense of splendour, and a promised or actual joy. Hughes permits himself a much greater richness and sensuousness of language than in *Crow*, yet the poems are more disciplined than many in the earlier sequence. The 'living, suffering spirit, capable of happiness' (Introduction to Vasko Popa's *Selected Poems*) emerges from the reductive questioning of *Crow* as a subject of celebration, and the metaphysical discovery hinted at in *Crow*'s final poems, such as 'How Water Began to Play' – the discovery of the universal in the self – is the basis of *Cave Birds*. The authenticity of this celebration is the fruit of the rigours of Hughes's earlier 'adventure'. . .

The sequence begins with a kind of psychic trauma in which the hero's complacent view of the world and his place in it is shattered by the visitations of various terrifying bird-beings who confront him with the evidence of his material nature and mortality. His own ego is symbolized (in the drawing of 'The Accused') by a cockerel. He is taken on a journey into himself, the first stage of which is a classic process of death and rebirth. This death is both the destruction of the complacent ego and a full conscious realization of his own actual physical death. He is changed from a cockerel to a 'flayed crow in the hall of judgement'. After an interlude in which he is offered and rejects various illusory heavens he enters the second major stage, the symbolic marriage with a female who is both his hitherto imprisoned daimon or inner self and the spirit of material nature. The last poem, an apotheosis of the transformed hero as a falcon, is followed by a brief Finale which undermines any complacent sense of finality the reader may have about the process he has been taken through.

The *Cave Birds* sequence opens with a striking poem which immediately confirms that this book is an extension of the central concerns of Hughes's work.

The scream

There was the sun on the wall – my childhood's
Nursery picture. And there was my gravestone
Which shared my dreams, and ate and drank with me happily.

All day the hawk perfected its craftsmanship
And even through the night the miracle persisted.

Mountains lazed in their smoky camp.
Worms in the ground were doing a good job.

Flesh of bronze, stirred with a bronze thirst,
Like a newborn baby at the breast,
Slept in the sun's mercy.

And the inane weights of iron
That come suddenly crashing into people, out of nowhere,
Only made me feel brave and creaturely.

When I saw little rabbits with their heads crushed on roads
I knew I rode the wheel of the galaxy.

Calves' heads all dew-bristled with blood on counters
Grinned like masks, and sun and moon danced.

And my mate with his face sewn up
Where they'd opened it to take something out
Raised a hand –

He smiled, in half-coma,
A stone temple smile.

Then I, too, opened my mouth to praise –

But a silence wedged my gullet.

Like an obsidian dagger, dry, jag-edged,
A silent lump of volcanic glass,

The scream
Vomited itself.

The tone of the opening lines suggests that the first-person voice of the
poem is a persona. What is caught in that tone is a too-easy acceptance
of the nature of things that amounts to a glib complacency in its
expression. The happy acceptance of the hero's own death is childishly
expressed, indicating no distinction between his response to this and
his response to what he sees as the world at work without tensions.
Lines like 'All day the hawk perfected its craftsmanship', and 'Worms
in the ground were doing a good job' might appear to be close to the
spirit of unironical celebration found in a *Season Songs* poem such as
'Swifts':

> And they've made it again,
> Which means the globe's still working.

In fact a sense of the universe at work in all its complementary
processes is at the heart of *Cave Birds*, but these early expressions of
the hero betray a complacency of inaction implying that there is no
need to look further. The detail of 'Swifts' demands that the reader
achieve a sense of the world working by looking attentively at the
evidence of a swift. . . .

In comparison with such discipline the blind faith of the hero in
'The Scream' is clearly naïve. What begins as naïvety becomes
callousness at the point when the hero's response to violent death is a
self-satisfied cosmic generalization. His easy praise is prevented by that
part of his nature that he has failed to take account of and which
therefore appears to be autonomous:

> The scream
> Vomited itself.

What is released by the scream in this first poem is to be the evidence
and the focus of the accusation in the trial which is heralded by the
appearance of the summoner in the following poem. The confidence
that Hughes has in this first poem, which we feel to be entirely justified,
is indicated by the omission of the narrative introduction to the
broadcast of *Cave Birds*: 'The hero's cockerel innocence, it turns out,
becomes his guilt. His own self, finally, the innate nature of his flesh
and blood, brings him to court.' . . .

Obviously judgement is what the hero is now waiting for, and the
judge is appropriately the next figure in the sequence. But who is to
sit in judgement and what can the concept of judgement mean in the
material universe? Hughes's meditation on Baskin's fine drawing sets
up a dense maze of paradoxes ['The Judge' is then quoted – Ed.].

. . .

This poem must present something of a shock for the reader, in that
it is clearly different from the other legal figures. This figure is an
abstraction ('The pondering body of the law') who is at the same time
a physical denial of abstractions. Previous figures have represented
aspects of the natural world that demand fear and awe, but this parody
appears to challenge the narrative. It is not until one recognizes the
voice of the hero in 'The Scream' that this poem's place in the narrative
can be seen. This figure results from an attempt to reconcile two
conceptions of nature. First there is the idea that a figure presiding

over the universe is preserving equilibrium. The concept of pure balance lies behind the sort of expression the hero used in 'The Scream' ('I knew I rode the wheel of the galaxy'), just as it underlies 'web-glistening geometry' and 'cosmic equipoise' [in 'The Judge']. Against this conception is the voracious view of nature represented by the judge's gluttony. The judge seems to think that his fat buttocks will sit with dignity on the throne of the Absolute. The capital letter betrays the grand illusion at the centre of the parody.

The wit of the poem draws attention to the fact that these two conceptions of nature cannot be reconciled. A concise phrase like 'Nero of the unalterable' sums up the poem's parody of a presiding figure maintaining balance over what are in fact the unalterable works of physical processes. In effect the poem is saying that there can be no judge since 'judgement' is irrelevant to a description of material processes. The poem acts as a warning early in the sequence that the figures be seen, not as independent controlling forces but as representatives of the hero's own physical nature. . . .

. . . If the hero's finding weapons in his own grave suggests that he must discover his own subjection to death and that this knowledge strengthens his life, it is the quality of that subjection and completeness of that power which constitute the achievement of 'The Knight'.

The discipline of the poem's central metaphor permeates the tone of the poem so that complete submission to the process of death achieves a still knowledge of unity with the material universe:

> *The knight*
>
> Has conquered. He has surrendered everything.
>
> Now he kneels. He is offering up his victory
> And unlacing his steel.
>
> In front of him are the common wild stones of the earth –
>
> The first and last altar
> Onto which he lowers his spoils.
>
> And that is right. He has conquered in earth's name.

The 'conquest' of the knight (actually a dead bird) is without irony: the simple statement and its dignity of 'rightness' expresses the achievement of accepting his own death as an actual contribution to the earth itself. The quiet celebration of his own body's physical decay

is here the product of a discipline of consciousness. It is in this sense
that the knight's bones are his weapons. In the final stanzas the
implications of this achieved state of consciousness are indicated in the
completeness of the self and the sense of oneness with the processes of
the universe:

> the skull's beauty

> Wrapped in the rags of his banner.
> He is himself his banner and its rags.

> While hour by hour the sun
> Strengthens its revelation.

To the knight the sun's revelation is that he is unified with the material
universe. In the alchemical sequence such a revelation will become
embodied in a new persona for the hero. Perhaps this is what is
glimpsed in the form of the eagle-hunter at the end of the next poem
. . . 'Something Was Happening' [quoted in full – Ed.].
  . . .

The process of rebirth is . . . begun in the poem 'The Gatekeepers',
which repeats in a series of generalizations the points established in a
less dogmatic way in earlier poems. In the next poem the hero is
flayed, a transformation motif that Jung remarks on in his commentary
on the visions of the alchemist Zosimos the Divine. In the words of
Lawrence's Birkin: the hero must 'cease to be, for that which is perfectly
himself to take place in him'. The opening of this poem 'A flayed crow
in the hall of judgment', superbly re-creates the sensations suggested
by Baskin's drawing:

> Darkness has all come together, making an egg.
> Darkness in which there is now nothing.

> A blot has knocked me down. It clogs me.
> A globe of blot, a drop of unbeing.

> Nothingness came close and breathed on me – a frost
> A shawl of annihilation has curled me up like a few foetus.

> I rise beyond height – I fall past falling.
> I float on an air
> As mist-balls float, and as stars.

> A condensation, a gleam simplification
> Of all that pertained.

The complete integration of images of non-being with the spark of re-creation they contain is perfectly suggested by the womb-darkness, the bloodclot that is also the 'globe' of life, the frost that curls leaves and creatures into a foetal shape, and the water-drop image of reduction and source. The questions which the hero then starts to ask develop the consciousness which is at the mercy of processes outside itself.

> Where am I going? What will come to me here?
> Is this everlasting? Is it
> Stoppage and the start of nothing?
>
> Or am I under attention?
> Do purposeful cares incubate me?
> Am I the self of some spore?
>
> In this white of death blackness,
> This yoke of afterlife?
> What feathers shall I have? What is my weakness good for?

The final questions of the poem strongly recall Hamlet's famous speech:

> If it be now, 'tis not to come; if it be not to come, it will be now; if it be not now, yet it will come. The readiness is all. Since no man has aught of what he leaves, what is 't to leave betimes? Let be.   (*Hamlet* v. ii)

Hamlet's condition in the final act of the play is perhaps a useful analogue to this stage in the cockerel's transformation. If we can see the condition of Shakespeare's hero not as a paralysed fatalism but as a recovered and enlarged sense of self, deriving from an acknowledgement of his subjection to forces outside himself, it should be possible to respond similarly to the fatalistic implications in this stage of Hughes's sequence. . . .

In these poems [the poems of rebirth and union which dominate the second part of the volume – Ed.], it is impossible and unnecessary to make a rigid distinction between the levels of meaning. Sexual union is a metaphor for wholeness of being and oneness with the world; it is also both a cause and a consequence of wholeness and unity. Interlocking, as it were, with this group of poems is another group that deal directly, in individual terms, with the transformed nature of the protagonist. The reader's attention is made to alternate between these complementary groups so that the way one reads 'The Guide', for example, is influenced by the marriage group, and influences our reading of that group in turn. This poem was earlier titled 'A True

Guide', emphasizing the contrast with the false guide of 'A Green Mother'.

> When everything that can fall has fallen
> Something rises.
> And leaving here, and evading there
> And that, and this, is my headway.
>
> Where the snow glare blinded you
> I start.
> Where the snow mama cuddled you warm
> I fly up. I lift you.
>
> Tumbling worlds
> Open my way
>
> And you cling.
>
> And we go
>
> Into the wind. The flame-wind – a red wind
> And a black wind. The red wind comes
> To empty you. And the black wind, the longest wind
> The headwind
>
> To scour you.
>
> Then the non-wind, a least breath,
> Fills you from easy sources.
>
> I am the needle
>
> Magnetic
> A tremor
>
> The searcher
> The finder

This is the first of the bird-figures that has nothing terrifying, absurd or equivocal about it. Its straightforwardly beneficent nature indicates, of course, the change that has taken place in the hero. The guide seems to represent the achievement of an intuition, a sure instinct of living, that starts from subjection to the elements. We are reminded of the hero's delivery, by the speaker of 'A Riddle', into 'a changed, unchangeable world / Of wind and of sun, of rock and water' and, from much earlier in the sequence, the plaintiff's words, 'Right from

the start, my life / Has been a cold business of mountains and their
snow / Of rivers and their mud.' This transformed condition is further
expressed in 'Walking Bare':

> What is left is just what my life bought me
> The gem of myself.
> A bare certainty, without confection.
> Through this blowtorch light little enough
>
> But enough.

He is integrated into the world in the sense that he does not interrupt
its processes; he is a channel for messages that have nothing to do with
him; he no longer egotistically considers himself the privileged recipient
of every sign:

> Hurrying worlds of voices, on other errands,
> Traffic through me, ignore me.

The poem also seems to be trying to express a patient waiting for
predetermined moments of revival by forces outside the self, but there
is an obscurity in the way 'corolla' has also to suggest 'corona' in the
astronomical metaphor in the final lines:

> A one gravity keeps touching me.
>
> For I am the appointed planet
> Extinct in an emptiness
>
> But a spark in the breath
> Of the corolla that sweeps me.

'Walking Bare' seems to be straining to find images for a condition
that is both human and fully at one with the non-human. A much
more satisfactory poem is 'The Risen', but its success as a poem entails
an ironic reflection on the way the sequence has seemed to develop.

> He stands, filling the doorway
> In the shell of earth.
>
> He lifts wings, he leaves the remains of something,
> A mess of offal, muddled as an afterbirth.
>
> His each wingbeat – a convict's release.
> What he carries will be plenty.
>
> He slips behind the world's brow
> As music escapes its skull, its clock and its skyline.

Under his sudden shadow, flames cry out among thickets.
When he soars, his shape

Is a cross, eaten by light,
On the Creator's face.

He shifts world weirdly as sunspots
Emerge as earthquakes.

A burning unconsumed,
A whirling tree –

Where he alights
A skin sloughs from a leafless apocalypse.

On his lens
Each atom engraves with a diamond.

In the wind-fondled crucible of his spendour
The dirt becomes God.

But when will he land
On a man's wrist.

The effect of this superb poem depends on the most subtle relation between levels of meaning to be found anywhere in the sequence. Like so many of the best poems, it starts out as a response to the Baskin, which is also one of the best in the book. A falcon stands on broad talons and trunk-like legs, his wings raised but not spread. Behind him, less broad than himself, is a black background, like a doorway, that he seems to have come through. In isolation the poem's subject would seem to be simply the falcon, with the shift at the end to the question, whether the bird's splendour and control can ever be attained by a human being. The poem captures, in an almost naturalistic way, the bird's speed, his sudden inexplicable disappearance and emergence somewhere else, and above all the electrifying alteration that takes place in everything within his range of vision, so that he really does resemble a God, altering nature by simply being there. . . .

Source: extracts from ch. 7, on *Cave Birds*, in Terry Gifford and Neil Roberts, *Ted Hughes: A Critical Study* (London, 1981), pp. 199, 202–4, 205, 208, 209, 213–14, 216–18, 226–9.

Stuart Hirschberg   'From *Gaudete*: A Retrospect'   (1981)

After reading the poetry Hughes has written over the past twenty years we have the overwhelming impression of having accompanied him on a very personal spiritual journey. From the assertion of strength in the guise of the shaman to the acceptance of a permanent spiritual crisis, through the image of the scapegoat, which paradoxically calls for even greater courage, Hughes's poetry inexorably reaches this point of crisis and holds it. Loneliness, submission to the violence in oneself and moments of stark silent terror are the signposts and milestones that tell us of the complexity and depth of struggle Hughes has engaged in with himself to achieve poetry expressing the greatest mental, spiritual and emotional tension conceivable. With the poetry written in the epilogue of *Gaudete* Hughes achieves a vulnerability, an openness so complete and profound that these poems are like crystal on which a bittersweet complex design has been etched in the acid of remorse and self-accusation. The flow of Hughes's poetry moves from a shamanistic identification with powerful, violent and destructive predators like the hawk, the bear, the jaguar and the pike expressed in a style at once self-controlled, self-possessed and vehement, through a series of changes to become the poetry of the suffering victim, the self offered to the self as sacrifice, crucified, motionless, in the grip of anguish and self-purgation. Between shaman and scapegoat, trickster plays a crucial role. He is the one figure in myth and legend who is alternately both predator and victim. In the cycle of Crow poems Hughes holds the balance for a few years and writes poetry that is objective, realistic and grotesquely comic. The Crow poems are the turning point in Hughes's spiritual journey from his unspoken allegiance with the mythical life of devouring predators to the poetry of the scapegoat, a poetry of humilities that celebrates and embraces the symbolic death of his former self.

Significantly, each work after *Crow*, including *Prometheus on his Crag*, *Cave Birds* and *Gaudete*, re-enacts the moment of crisis in different guises, that exact moment when the intellect and the ego become aware that they must die, premonitions of which we have seen emerge intermittently in 'Snow', 'Wodwo' and *The Wound*. In these works an intellect that is accustomed to dominating events receives the first intimation of the call to submission, the breaking of the ego's stronghold. Understandably, this is felt as indescribably threatening, as if the ground has opened up beneath one's feet. Yet, this must be how the prospect of a complete psychological and spiritual transformation first appears – as the threat of extinction. We can trace this developing schism in Hughes's poetry quite clearly, from the complete identification of the self with the natural, the animal, the literal processes of nature, perceived of as the only reality, through poems like 'Wodwo' where the self and body are not split but are not in synchronization with each other to those poems beginning with 'Song of a Rat' where the schism is fully dramatized. The split first appears as the polarization between the self as victim and nature, in the guise of a demonic vengeful feminine force, as predator. Aware that it is caught in a trap from which it cannot escape Hughes's victim protagonist, replicated in many disguises, begins to attempt to locate the nature of the crime against womanhood for which it is being punished.

At this point the battle or more properly, the trial of strength, begins in earnest. One of the most unusual features of Hughes's poetry is that the nature of the enemy, the antagonist who is capable of bringing him to his knees, is obviously not apparent in the first stages of the struggle even to Hughes himself. His consciousness of who his antagonist truly is to lag behind his awareness that a challenge has been thrown down, his fear of the implications of what the nature of that challenge will mean for him and how much he will have to change and what he will have to give up. At first, the struggle appears senseless, as in 'The Contender' but this is simply because Hughes has not discovered its use for himself. He identifies the antagonist with the Erinyes, the vengeful pursuing Furies, the vulture in her various guises and with outraged womanhood in *Gaudete*.

Yet, behind these disguises is Hughes's ultimate opponent: himself. Only in *Gaudete*, by presenting the spiritual journey in parable form as the life of Reverend Lumb do we sense that Hughes is becoming aware that the Furies are but the occasion through which the soul meets itself. The experience is similar to that projected in the 'Song of a Rat' where the rat in the trap knows that henceforward his fate is to be enmeshed in conditions not created by himself and so inescapably horrendous that it will not be possible for him to live without constant reference to them; he knows he has been overtaken by his fate, a fate he attempts to come to terms with in successive stages. In *Prometheus on his Crag* Hughes's protagonist bears his suffering for an eternity while he reviews the meaning of his suffering, point by point. Then Hercules and Dionysus, in turn, appear, each more susceptible towards self-transformation, each more successively violent and correspondingly more persecuted by those their madness and savagery have injured. In *Gaudete* we see self-confrontation returning to the world of modern day England, returning the struggle to the sphere of the everyday world, after a temporary retreat to inaccessible regions of crag or cave and after a temporary withdrawal, in *Cave Birds*, using animal forms to mirror the subhumanity of his protagonist. By no slight coincidence do Hughes's protagonists in both *Cave Birds* and *Gaudete* now see their lives as inseparable from the fate that encompasses them.

Now there arises that peculiar quality of silence in Hughes's poetry, as if his words have travelled enormous distances until they appear before us, like refugees from some far off war, surviving not because of their force of will but because they are utterly open and utterly vulnerable with the weakness of saints. All those forces with which Hughes's predators had been accustomed to dominate, demand and receive complete submission, have been inverted and the dominant emotion in Hughes's scapegoat protagonists is one of complete submission. In Hughes's shaman poems powerful creatures administer death and destruction to others, yet are themselves sealed off from any consequences. In the trickster poems we see a figure who both plays tricks on others and has the tables turned on himself. But in works centred around the scapegoat archetype we witness Hughes's protagonists's fate as existential victims, suffering in their own persons and lives, both cause and effect, as they are compelled to experience what they send into the world. We move, as it were, from the moral universe of Francis Bacon, a world of efficiency regardless of consequences, to the moral universe of Shakespeare, a world of victims undone by their own passions.

Significantly, Hughes begins to use the cycle of poems, in *Crow*, as the most viable poetic form, precisely at that moment when the universe appears to be one of both causes and effects, where one can be either predator or prey and, horrifyingly, often both in the same lifetime. Hughes is attracted to the cyclical pattern of developing poems as the closest formal equivalent to the ongoing spiritual battle. Once generated he lets the elements within each work, whether *Crow* or *Cave Birds* or *Prometheus on his Crag*, exhaust themselves to produce that final silence, the unspoken afterbeat, beyond which the rational intellect is helpless. His critics have seen Hughes as simply being anti-intellectual, anti-rational and anti-Socratic. This is not so, it is simply that for him, the intellect is no longer a serviceable or even desirable means for grasping an ultimate reality grown so distant, so unidentifiable with the usual conceptions of God that it must seem like a deity composed of silences, of emptiness. Yet, this is but the last stage of the struggle by an extremely powerful intellect that has surveyed and has an excellent grasp of literature, history and philosophy. Indeed one has the very strong impression of a mind that increasingly must improvise, almost with every phrase or word, to capture and express a reality that is sensed but ungraspable. One feels the presence of a mind that has exhausted everything within reach, legends, myths, folklore of many nations, literature itself, a mind that now gropes, distrusting anything not under its control and strong enough to control everything except itself. This in turn produces that peculiar quality of moral alertness, the stylistic equivalent of perpetual vigilance that is so much a part of the heart-rending simplicity of Hughes's poetry, bespeaking a mind turning at great speed, but in neutral, unable to go forward, unable to return, burning itself out, exhausting itself, submitting itself to a savage self-transformation.

We see it in the plight of Prometheus torn between eternity and death, heaven and earth, unable to live, unable to die, a figure of superhuman endurance suffering his wound to be torn open by the vulture. Prometheus embodies the metaphor of self-inquisition, the need to redeem his suffering by understanding it and to be forced to endure his suffering until its meaning is burned into him. We see it in *Cave Birds* with Hughes's choice of Hercules on which to base his protagonist, the necessary breaking of strength of the strongest of all men. His image is one of self-immolation, Hercules on the pyre, a mind and consciousness stripped bare in the throes of self-recrimination. In all three major works since the Crow cycle, that is, in *Prometheus on his Crag*, *Cave Birds* and *Gaudete*, Hughes painstakingly creates in different contexts the conditions under which self-confrontation can take place, conditions where each motive can be weighed, analysed and where a dominating intellect can see itself broken and where self-purification and ultimately self-forgiveness can occur. In the figure of Reverend Lumb we see Hughes's ultimate victim, modelled on Dionysus who has long stood as a symbol of the necessary dismemberment the self must experience before spiritual rebirth can take place.

The story of *Gaudete* re-enacts a fateful choice made, so to speak, before life itself began. The prologue describes the conditions of this contract, and the story shows how circumstances are inexorably created through which many women, and one woman in particular, are destroyed because of Reverend Lumb's unwitting, ruthless Dionysus-like cruelty. In turn, their destruction leads to his persecution and death. In the epilogue a new Lumb re-emerges with different values, those of humility not violence, submission of the will, not blind self-assertion. Yet, plainly this changed Reverend Lumb would not have come into existence if the preceding events in which the destructive side of his personality was projected had not occurred. Lumb, like Dionysus, ultimately shares the fate of the women who have been victims in his cause. In *Gaudete* we see Hughes's awareness, rising momentarily from the unconscious, into parable form, that the circumstances of his life have been created by prior agreement between himself and a figure he represents as the ultimate goddess of nature. The nature of the agreement suggests that the only set of events in the world which could provoke him to promote a change of his nature must grow out of his being entangled in a net of circumstances so pervasive, so inescapable, that he will be forced to change. This change seen in the light of his ongoing spiritual journey is an absolute necessity since in the scheme of things the number of changes that are allowed to one diminish as one throws them away. This is what gives *Gaudete* its enormously resonant depth of meaning. In Hughes's choice of Dionysus on which to model the Reverend Lumb we see him choosing a figure who unwittingly causes the destruction of those women who share his fate and, at the end, the madness he embodies hunts him down as well. Like Dionysus, Lumb shares the fate of his women victims. He becomes the hunter who is himself hunted, the devourer of normality who is himself rent apart. He is the ultimate victim of the destroying madness he brings to others.

We must realize that Hughes seizes upon these elements of tragic savagery within his protagonists as a way of making himself aware that they are indeed their own worst enemies. Evidently, this thought would never rise to consciousness if it were not dramatized in such a terrifying extreme form. Without the full scale projection of the aggressive, violent, fanatic and unwittingly cruel traits in Reverend Lumb's nature, the new Reverend Lumb who appears in the epilogue as an embodiment of submission and humility could not have come into existence. Yet we must not forget that ultimately, the Reverend

Lumb's submission is only in relation to himself, to the way he was. Seen in this light, we understand that the desire for vengeance directed against the Reverend Lumb is a disguised form of self-confrontation. The conscious intellect, the ego, the very stronghold of the personality must be assailed and brought down. Through an inexorable logic, Hughes projects situations in which his protagonists must submit to precisely that destructive violence which, in his shaman poems, he had earlier seen as the dominant feature of nature. So, too, in the work of Janos Pilinszky and Vasko Popa, East European writers to whose poetry Hughes is instinctively drawn and who have achieved a vision of victimhood analogous to Hughes's own, although for very different reasons, we see the soul *in extremis*, no longer seeking to change anything and for this reason, paradoxically, invulnerable to all temptations to transcend the conditions of its suffering.

SOURCE: 'Conclusion' of *Myth in the Poetry of Ted Hughes: A Guide to the Poems* (Portmarnock, Co. Dublin, 1981), pp. 211–16.

PART THREE

R. S. Thomas

1. THOMAS ON HIMSELF AND POETRY

I   THE RESILENCE OF WORDS

... One must take the words as one finds them, and make them sing. And here arises another question: Are words the poet's servant or master? We are familiar, no doubt, with Mr Elliot's pessimistic conclusion in 'East Coker', although he wins through to some sort of détente in 'Little Gidding', where he speaks of 'the complete consort dancing together'. I think that any practising poet would agree that there can be no hard and fast rule in this matter. Most poets compose with great difficulty, choosing and rejecting and altering their words, until often the finished draft bears little relation to what they began with. In this way, the poet would seem to be the master, forcing the words to do the bidding of the conscious mind. Yet this, also, is a travesty of the position. Words have surprising resilience, and get their own way often by appearing to yield. The idea of the poet's eye 'in a fine frenzy rolling' and of the words flowing ready mixed with the ink of the tip of his pen is, of course, a fiction. Yet here again most poets could tell of periods of inspiration of varying length, when the words and lines did appear to come with agreeable ease. And although we have Yeats's words as a warning against being deceived by an appearance of ease, we also have it on Mr Vernon Watkins's authority that he said, too, that a poem is a piece of luck. This is a pregnant statement, but certainly one aspect of it has to do with words themselves – a lucky finding or perception of the right word, the felicitous phrase or brilliant metaphor. ...

II   POETIC THEORY AND PRACTICE

... It seems that it has always been easier for poets to evolve theories of language than to stick to them. Wordsworth was a case in point; Yeats another. It was Coleridge who remarked that the lofty and sustained diction which characterised Wordsworth as a poet was a complete contradiction of his theory about the speech of natural man. And although Yeats had a temporary spasm for deleting from his verse all words which were not understood by Irish washerwomen, fortunately for the state of English poetry the lunacy passed. I would be inclined to doubt whether much poetry of top rank has ever been written in accordance with a theory. Wordsworth at his most puling lends me support. It is better far to observe, not necessarily consciously, what you are able to do with words, and what they can do to you, and on that basis, *post hoc*, as it were, to evolve your theory of poetry. Personally I have often agreed that there is something feminine about words, and, of course, the muse herself is female. It is as though the more one woos words, the more desperately in love with them one grows, the more coquettish and refractory they become; whereas a certain insouciance or aloofness in the writer will often bring them fawning about his feet. But I realise that such an attitude is based more on the craftsman's, the maker's approach to poetry. . . .

SOURCE: excerpts I and II are drawn from Thomas's 'Words and the Poet' (1964), reproduced in Sandra Anstey (ed.), *R. S. Thomas: Selected Prose* (Cardiff, 1983), pp. 81 and 82.

III 'IN DEBT TO EVERY OTHER POET'

. . . A poet has to learn his craft from the study of all other people who have written. People write to me and say, 'Who is it that has influenced you?', and I always say, 'This is a question I don't answer because it is up to everyone else to find out what influences are visible in one's writing', but I always add that I am in debt to every other poet who has ever written and whom I have ever read.

This is how we learn to write poetry, by studying the achievement of the great masters; and not only the great masters, because as Yeats once said, he learned his technique from a man who was a very bad poet. Often a person who is not a good poet has none-the-less hit upon a certain way of saying things which is interesting, and then a superior mind – a better poet – will take this up, and where the other man failed the better poet succeeds. I believe that the public guided by discerning critics, are never really wrong in responding to what is good in poetry . . . .

SOURCE: extract from 'The Making of a Poem' (1969), reproduced in *Selected Prose* (1983), op. ct., p. 82.

IV   'A POEM'S MESSAGE IS IN ITSELF'

. . . Finally a word about Wordsworth's message for today, which
in a way is a non-subject, for a poem's message is in itself. One can
no more tear apart form and content in a poem than body and soul
in a human being. The medium is the message! The sustained and
lofty diction, the sense of form, the aura of the poems are their own
justification. They convey to us the thoughts and feelings of a literary
genius living in a particular place at a particular time. That place
was England; the time, around 1800. They speak of the peace that
is to be found in solitude, the sublimity of earthly moments, the
movement of the spirit of man. They extol beauty and love and
natural wisdom at the expense of a shallow meddlesomeness. They
set a 'wise passiveness' to nature above the need to put her to the
question. They decry too great an indulgence of the scientific spirit,
which 'murders to dissect' and which would 'botanise upon a
mother's grave'.

As Wordsworth reclined in a grove sometime in 1798, it grieved
his heart to think 'what man has made of man'. To many in these
islands nearly two hundred years later, it may be grievous to think
what man has made of nature. . . .

SOURCE: extract from the Introduction to *A Choice of Wordsworth's Verse*
(1971), reproduced in *Selected Prose* (1983), op. cit., pp. 126–7.

V   REVEALING GOD

. . . There is no God but God. The very use of the word answers all
questions. The ability to create life automatically posits the ability
to re-create it. We die utterly, completely. Our bones are consumed
in the crematoria. Shall the Creator, who composed this solid, fertile
earth out of incendiary gases, find more difficulty in forming a new
life around the nucleus of a human soul? The question is rhetorical.
It can be framed in a hundred different ways. It was a cardinal
doctrine of Aquinas that God reveals himself in accordance with the
mind's ability to receive him. I have already scoffed at democracy.
To one person, God may reveal himself as a loving shepherd leading
to green pastures; to another as a consuming fire. I must end this
talk, surely, by telling you how he has revealed himself to me, if

that is the right way to describe the knowledge – half hope, half intuition – by which I live.

'When the sun rises, do you not see a round disc of fire somewhat like a guinea?' 'O no no, I see an innumerable company of the heavenly host crying, "Holy, Holy, Holy is the Lord God Almighty!" I question not my corporeal or vegetative eye any more than I would question a window concerning sight. I look through it and not with it.' So said William Blake and, similarly, in my humbler way, say I. With our greatest modern telescope we look out into the depths of space, but there is no heaven there. With our supersonic aircraft we annihilate time, but are no nearer eternity. May it not be that alongside us, made invisible by the thinnest of veils, is the heaven we seek? The immortality we must put on? Some of us, like Francis Thompson, know moments when 'Those shaken mists a space unsettle'. To a countryman it is the small field suddenly lit up by a ray of sunlight. It is T. S. Eliot's 'still point, there the dance is', Wordsworth's 'central peace, subsisting at the heart of endless agitation'. It is even closer. It is within us, as Jesus said. That is why there is no need to go anywhere from here.

SOURCE: extract from 'Where do we go from here?' (1974), reproduced in *Selected Prose* (1983), op. cit., pp. 151–2.

VI   PRESSURE ON THE CREATIVE WRITER

... This brings us to the question of pressure on the creative writer, pressure which has been experienced down the centuries. Kierkegaard defined a poet as one who suffers. It is in his anguish that he opens his mouth, but the sound which comes out is so sweet to the ears of his listeners that they press him to sing again, that is to suffer still further.

Here we see the first temptation for the creative writer to commit suicide, namely by writing those things which tickle the public's fancy, in order to secure reward or praise, rather than those things he really wants to write. Who is not aware of the tricks in which a writer is prepared to indulge for the sake of public applause, until he loses every mite of originality that once belonged to him? And yet this too is debatable, because if he is a great enough writer he can compose a masterpiece yet please the public at the same time, as Shakespeare did in his plays and as the Welsh *cwyddwyr* did in their *cwyddau gofyn*. It is a matter of how intelligent and cultured the public itself is. Where a public proves itself to be such, a writer may make a living and still retain his literary stature. Where these conditions are not fulfilled, his only choice is to make his money in another way, trying to follow the muse in his spare time, or to commit suicide as a writer. . . .

SOURCE: extract from 'The Creative Writer's Suicide' (1978), reproduced in *Selected Prose* (1983), op. cit., pp. 170–1.

2. CRITICAL STUDIES

Calvin Bedient 'Natural Magic and
Moral Profundity' (1974)

. . . Thomas's poetry is like a briskly descending brook. Everything about it is bent to a single aim, namely the swift, happy arrivals at a mainstream realisation.

The same holds true of Thomas's words. They, too, are naked daylight. They have none of the pregnant darkness of things. They refer, they throw up blinds before their subjects. Though eloquently modulated, pleasingly united, they seem scarcely conscious of themselves as sounds. Nor do they jostle their traditional meanings. Sometimes, indeed, especially in figures, they are all too common. When Thomas is not brilliant at metaphor, he is dully conventional; . . . . Yet for the most part Thomas's language is taut. It is form following function. In 'Let me smell / My youth again in your hair', for instance, the words are simple and straightforward. Only the thought is extraordinary. Reading Thomas, we seldom miss newly peeled words, or for that matter formal music, compulsive rhythms, or stanzas and rhymes, because we are too much under the power of his phrase. To seem at once lean and sensuous, transparent and deeply crimsoned, is part of his distinction.

Lean as they are, Thomas's words conduct both strength and subtlety. If he is swift it is not because he has lightened his load; he is swift without leaving anything behind. 'Ninetieth Birthday', for example, delicately rings several contrasts between living history and various eternities that elude it – stone, prolonged isolation, the distant sea, an old mind gone to seed: profound contrasts that are immediate to feeling. Nor is Thomas's tone, as a rule, unshaded. In the same poem, for instance, he is as impatient as he is tender. In fact, almost all his poetry, as we shall see, is a compassionate scolding. How this Anglican priest despairs of leading the old peasant's soul to the great sacramental unity. The sea flashes, but the stone farm is up around the bend, provincial. He is patient, generous, but despondent as he leans across the abyss – she has fallen into the wrong eternity, this lost old child, she is lodged in a crevasse of time. So the poem, for all its swiftness, is deep and full.

Thomas's poetry almost always faces outward. It has just seen someone or something that has brought it to a passionate pause. Often the first lines are hooks thrown out to fetch us to a soul in trouble: 'This man swaying dully before us'; 'Consider this man in the field beneath'; 'Farmer, you were young once'; 'My name is Lowri Dafydd . . .'. '. . . As I go through my day at my desk', Thomas writes in his essay 'Words and the Poet', 'in my contact with others, or out in the world of nature, I see something, begin to turn it over in my mind and decide that it has poetic possibilities. The main concern will be not to kill it. . . .' Poetry such as Thomas's – a poetry of 'the order and beauty of the world', in Simone Weil's phrase – thus begins when the world seizes a passing man and plants itself within him like a seed. This annunciation is a sacrament: Thomas must not 'kill' it. He must look upon himself as a medium.

Of course he must be active, too, an author, the balancing half of the poetic equation. 'The men took the corn, the beautiful goddess, / By the long hair and threw her on the ground': memory or perception proposes, imagination disposes, and such a line comes to be. Poetry is a co-operation between the world and the spirit in the creation of magical appearances. The world draws around, releases from itself and lightened, the spirit at last gains density, having put on the world like flesh, and existence is for the moment complete. The poet's imagination grapples with the world in an ecstasy that could be reverence but that could equally be a terrible rivalry to see which will seem the more real.

What helps make Thomas's poetry *poetic* is the grateful dependence of his senses on the world. He needs matter temperamentally as poetry needs it aesthetically: as the blood of his spirit. 'Every true artist', writes Simone Weil, 'has had real, direct, and immediate contact with the beauty of the world, contact that is of the nature of a sacrament.' This sacrament is Thomas's goad. (If often his attention is fixed on the black question mark at the centre of the view, the stooped peasant at his plough, it is in grief that it mars the contact, is marred, mars itself.) The beauty of the world rushes into Thomas's poetry because he leaves himself open as he rushes

out to meet it. The universe is, for this artist, itself the supreme
work of art. I quote 'The view from the Window':

> Like a painting it is set before one,
> But less brittle, ageless; these colours
> Are renewed daily with variations
> Of light and distance that no painter
> Achieves or suggests. Then there is movement,
> Change, as slowly the cloud bruises
> Are healed by sunlight, or snow caps
> A black mood; but gold at evening
> To cheer the heart. All through history
> The great brush has not rested,
> Nor the paint dried; yet what eye,
> Looking coolly, or, as we now,
> Through the tears' lenses, ever saw
> This work and it was not finished?

So it is that this poet's subject teaches him his end.

A related reason that Thomas's poetry is strong and authentic is
that it is inspirited by memory – memory being spirit in its most
basic and helpless attachment to the world. 'The humblest function
of spirit', Bergson notes in *Matter and Memory*, 'is to bind together
the successive moments of the duration of things.' Spirit, then,
begins in memory. Nor, much though it is a temporal flowering on
the fixed laws of space, can it ever quite escape from 'things' and
remain vigorous as spirit. It evolves by looking back. Rising out of
matter, as the perception of its duration, it returns to it at length, in
works of art, as love.

For a natural poet such as Thomas, memory is the morning air
of imagination. Indeed, Thomas is homeward to a fault. He never
tires of speaking of what is around him, though we sometimes do,
for he has told us about it before. We seem often to be passing the
same tree, or seeing the same hills 'buttressed with cloud'. On the
other hand, take him out of his Welsh hills, put him in Spain or
start him reflecting on manned flights to the moon, and his
imagination pales. We must take his excess with his best, nor is this
hard, for it is an excess of love.

One fruit of this love is a magnificent talent for metaphor. In this
Thomas perhaps excels all English poets since Hopkins, bringing to
mind the great, wild outcrop of figurative genius in the seventeenth
century. Here is a Thomas sampler:

There were larks, too, like a fresh chorus
Of dew . . .

        . . . O, hers is all
This strong body, the safe island
Where men may come, sons and lovers,
Daring the cold seas of her eyes.

You who never venture from under your roof
Once the night's come; the blinds all down
For fear of the moon's bum rubbing the window.

        . . . I blame the earth,
This brown bitch fawning about my feet.

I remember also the trapped wind
Tearing the curtains, and the wild light's
Frequent hysteria upon the floor . . .

Prytherch, man, can you forgive
From your stone altar on which the light's
Bread is broken at dusk and dawn . . . ?

Mother, he said, from the wet streets
The clouds are removed and the sun walks
Without shoes on the warm pavements.

      No, no, you must face the fact
Of his long life alone in that crumbling house
With winds rending the joints, and the grey rain's claws
Sharp in the thatch; of his work up on the moors
With the moon for candle, and the shrill rabble of stars
Crowding his shoulders.

        . . . sin was the honey
Bright as sunlight in death's hive.

The fox drags its wounded belly
Over the snow, the crimson seeds
Of blood burst with a mild explosion,
Soft as excrement, bold as roses.

Clean-edged, hard, bright, Thomas's tropes are an enameller's art. They are all firmness, there is never any smear. Yet they are resplendent with the light of actual things; the world seems to press itself into them. What is more, for all their tidiness they have an acrobat's daring. Their forms start from as far away as they can

and still meet in the centre without strain. Little miracles of
implosion, they hurl two particles of the world so hard upon each
other that, for the imagination, they become one. Yet the meeting
appears as gentle as the sudden, balance-defying close of a butterfly's
wings.

   Though metaphor is not essential to poetry, it constitutes nodes,
at least in poetry on the beauty of the world, where the purpose of
the poem is raised to an electric intensity. Most poetry and most
metaphors have the same end: in Frost's words, 'the philosophical
attempt to set matter in terms of spirit, or spirit in terms of matter,
to make the final unity'. Thomas's poems, pomegranates full of
kernels, pack in as much of the infinite beauty of the universe as
they can; and metaphors, among other things, are a device for
infolding beauty. They form the foothills of the spirit – of spirit that,
as Jaspers says, always pushes on towards the whole of Being,
seeking relation and the totality of relations. Metaphors are the love
forms have for one another. They seduce the unity of things. I
quoted from 'Farm Wife':

>   Hers is a clean apron, good for fire
>   Or lamp to embroider, as we talk slowly
>   In the long kitchen, while the white dough
>   Turns to pastry in the great oven,
>   Sweetly and surely as hay making
>   In a June meadow . . .

The fire becomes an embroidering farm wife; the farm wife makes,
as it were, a meadow; all hint at a common being. Thomas's figures
are often signals flashed from a far sea of unity. Of course they have
more limited functions too: clarification, vivification, happy release
from the literal. Whatever their purpose, they bespeak a powerful
empathy with forms. They give Thomas's poems a rich, impacted
beauty.

   In truth, however, metaphor is somewhat too prominent in the
poems. . . .

   . . . Thomas could throw away half the figures in his volumes and
still beglamour us. Yet he does well, I think, to make the most of
his gift. Modern British poetry needs it, rather as the eye needs
greens and blues. . . .

The moral quality of Thomas's poems is as remarkable as their
aesthetic quality – as sharp and unexpected. Nowhere else in English

etter to be a 'people' than an anonymous heap by the roadside.
etter to be in time than in nothing at all:

> History goes on;
> On the rock the lichen
> Records it: no mention
> . . . of us.

And what a people the Welsh were: the 'warriors / Of a free people'
are the sole cause 'the sun still goes down red'. 'You cannot live in
the present, / At least not in Wales': 'Above the noisy tractor', hear
the old 'strife in the strung woods'. Folding up his priest's gear,
walking back through the centuries, Thomas enters the 'vixen-
footed / Firelight' a bard, a worshipper of barbarous splendour:

> The stars were hooded and the moon afraid
> To vex the darkness with her yellow braid.
>
> Then he spoke, and anger kindled . . .

But the Welsh do indeed forget the past:

> Four centuries now
> We have been leaving
> The hills and the high moors
> For the jewelled pavements
> Easing our veins of their dark peat
> By slow transfusions.
>
> We have forgotten
> The far lakes,
> Aled and Eiddwen, whose blue litmus
> Alone could detect
> The mind's acid.

In fact – twisting, bandaging, never giving the arm of his country a
rest – Thomas at times *wants* the past forgotten. 'An impotent
people, / Sick with inbreeding, / Worrying the carcase of an old
song' – this is to be neither a people nor present in history. When
'we have finished quarrelling for crumbs / Under a table', he writes
in 'Welsh History', 'or gnawing the bones / Of a dead culture, we
will arise, / Armed, but not in the old way.'

On the other hand, Thomas wants the peasants to remain up a
side path, outside of history. For what is history beside eternity?
And what if their inertness is only another name for the peace of
God? So, reconstructing them, giving them the benefit of the doubt,

poetry do we find poem after poem directed, in love and anger, at
an entire people. There is something of Whitman in Thomas, but a
severe, severely tender, hardened, narrowed, and disillusioned
Whitman. Thomas is to Wales a kind of Good Samaritan, Mary
Magdalen and fearsome Jahweh in one. Turning to his next poem
we scarcely know whether to expect a poet blessing or scorning, or
steeped in an acid of despair. What we do know is that we will find
him as terribly open to his country as a wound.

Often, conscious of his collar, Thomas writes from the implicit
position of God's deputy in Wales. And yet, having entered his
bloodstream, his Anglicanism emerges, in great part, not as dogma
but as a badgering compassion. 'Creative attention', writes Simone
Weil, 'means really giving our attention to what does not exist.
Humanity does not exist in the anonymous flesh lying inert by the
roadside.' Such is the quality of Thomas's concern. Of course, as a
poet Thomas is a Good Samaritan only in the sphere of imagination:
it is himself and his readers whom he makes human by his attention.
But the atmosphere of generosity is the same as if he had lifted a
peasant bodily from the road. It may glare:

> I am the farmer, stripped of love
> And thought and grace by the land's hardness;
> But what I am saying over the fields'
> Desolate acres, rough with dew,
> Is, Listen, listen, I am a man like you . . .

It may be subdued:

> You would think sometimes that summer never comes
> To the farmer in his fields, stripped by the wind
> To the blue bone, or impotent with snow.
> You have become used to his ascetic form
> Moving within its cell of leafless trees.
> Not so; his blood uncurls with the slow sap,
> Stretching itself among its sinuous boughs;
> His blood grows hot, the singing cloak of flies,
> Worn each day, bears witness; the stones ring
> Fierce echoes of his heat; he meets himself
> Everywhere in the smell of the ripe earth.

It may crackle with the hail of disapproval:

> And she was fertile; four strong sons
> Stood up like corn in June about you.
> But, farmer, did you cherish, tend her

As your own flesh, this dry stalk
Where the past murmurs its sad tune?
Is this the harvest of your blithe sowing?

If you had spared from your long store
Of days lavished upon the land
But one for her where she lay fallow,
Drying, hardening, withering to waste.
But now – too late! You're an old tree,
Your roots groping in her in vain.

But the atmosphere of compassion is continually present – asserting the human, brightening when it finds it, darkening when it does not, but always itself a warmth and an illumination.

In Thomas the love of our neighbour (in Simone Weil's phrase) seems to be an offshoot of the love of the beauty and order of the world. Thomas wants the peasants to bestir themselves until, like him, they see the big stars shaking, wildly signalling.

You failed me, farmer, I was afraid you would
The day I saw you loitering with the cows,
Yourself one of them but for the smile,
Vague as moonlight, cast upon your face
From the dim source, whose nature I mistook.
The hills had grace, the light clothed them
With wild beauty, so that I thought,
Watching the pattern of your slow wake
Through seas of dew, that you yourself
Wore that same beauty by the right of birth . . .

This is from a poem called 'Valediction', which ends:

For this I leave you
Alone in your harsh acres, herding pennies
Into a sock to serve you for a pillow
Through the long night that waits upon your span.

But in fact Thomas cannot leave the peasants alone. They obsess him; his threats and valedictions are but bravura. He cannot really delight in the wood until he has healed, has tried to heal, the wounded deer within it. Let him name in hard words the peasants' faults; they only endear themselves to him the more. After all, everything about them says, Make allowance: 'The mixen sours the dawn's gold'. So he comes upon their gaunt kitchens, the hens going in and out of the door, the 'stale smell / Of death in league with . . . dank walls', their stinking clothes, eyes 'Fuddled with coldness',

'slow lips' opening 'like a snail', their vacancy
the fire, the 'beast's gait', their coats like sack
corners / With the rain's drops' – as he comes upo
sinks, as if through a hole in the beauty of the worl

Often in these poems Thomas is the Word, as i
helpless before a rock. For what can he do, howe
change a life that can be summed up like this?

Walter Llywarch – the words were a nam
On a lost letter that never came
For one who waited in the long queue
Of life that wound through a Welsh valley.
I took instead, as others had done
Before, a wife from the back pews
In chapel, rather to share the rain
Of winter evenings, than to intrude
On her pale body; and yet we lay
For warmth together and laughed to hear
Each new child's cry of despair.

Here, 'subject to necessity', in Bergson's description
everyone 'repeats the past unceasingly', each generation
to the 'accepted pattern', each day emptying the labo
sack. Their shepherd in the 'bad Welsh hills', Thoma
they are too far gone in their age-old necessities to hear.
them there, the 'nameless and dear', some remote on a
like a rag on 'a bush of cloud', others nearby in the lan
their cattle's breath 'like a cloak' to hide from him.
Sundays,

. . . As the melody rises
From nothing, their mouths take up the tune,
And the roof listens. I call on God
In the after silence, and my shadow
Wrestles with him upon a wall
Of plaster, that has all the nation's
Hardness in it. They see me thrown
Without movement of their oblique eyes.

A few call him in, when dying, to boast of their blood's forme
For the rest, they are indifferent, 'Caring not whether I pr
blame'. 'I do not fight / You; it is you who fight / Me', he may
'wounding yourself / With blows that I will not give'. . . .

If he cannot give them God, he offers Wales; for, found
memory, nationalism is at least a rudimentary form of the s

making them the resting point of his mind, Thomas sometimes approaches his mute, unchanging, unprotesting parishioners, not with asperity, but with awe, as one moves out on a still lake.

> Prytherch, man, can you forgive
> From your stone altar on which the light's
> Bread is broken at dusk and dawn
> One who strafed you with thin scorn
> From the cheap gallery of his mind?
> It was you who were right the whole time;
> Right in this that the day's end
> Finds you still in the same field
> In which you started, your soul made strong
> By the earth's incense, the wind's song.
> While I have worn my soul bare
> On the world's roads, seeking what lay
> Too close for the mind's lenses to see,
> And come now with the first stars
> Big on my lids westward to find
> With the slow lifting up of your hand
> No welcome, only forgiveness.

'Which is the greater blessing', asks Teilhard de Chardin, 'to have the sublime unity of God to centre and save the universe? or to have the concrete immensity of the universe by which to undergo and touch God?' Suffering, as he does, the grateful shortsightedness of the artist, Thomas answers, through his poems: Give me the world to undergo. All the same, and for all its 'concrete immensity', it does not weigh him down enough. His mind skitters with the times. He feels impelled to 'seek', as if what he sought had not pinned him down. Or the swelling surface sensuality of the earth distracts him:

> . . . Have I been wise
> In the past, letting my nostrils
> Plan my day? That salt scrubbing
> Left me unclean. Am I wise now,
> With all this pain in the air,
> To keep my room, reading perhaps
> Of that Being whose will is our peace?

So it is that he comes to envy the peasants their awful privilege of self-annihilation. The stoop of their backs is the sign of a stolid but blessed consent. There about the angry, shamefaced priest seething with words are the meekest of Christians, nailed without murmur to the brute necessities of the Creation.

But the pagan in Thomas vies with the ascetic in emulating the

peasants. To the ascetic they have a 'tree's / Knotted endurance',
they are 'stern like the soil'; their only knowledge is of God and is
the ache in their bones. To the pagan, by contrast, they are a shell
in which, could he put an ear to them, he might hear the sea of
forgotten lore. After all, their hands have dabbled 'in the world's
blood'. Were the peasant to speak, 'would not the glib tongue
boast / A lore denied our neoteric sense, / Being handed down from
the age of innocence?' And has not every right word on the tongue
'a green taste'?

Or it may be Thomas in his very character as poet who envies
the peasants their 'thoughts of no date'. Stanley Burnshaw is one of
the latest and best to argue that poetry is an expression of man's
'drive to regain . . . his primary organic unity with the rest of
creation: his "seamlessness", which endured through his millions of
years, whose heritage is inscribed in his myths, his religions, his
arts, his rituals.' Verse, which turns back on itself, as the name
suggests, and back on the poet's past, may turn all the way back as
well to the 'seamless web' of pre-rational creature knowledge. And,
creatures of elemental recurrence as the peasants are, servants of
the turning earth, 'scholars / Of the fields' pages', what natural poets
they must be – spider-souled, before time. '. . . I know, as I listen',
says Thomas, 'that your speech has in it / The source of all
poetry . . .' . . .

When Thomas is not attempting to change the peasants, he is
thus aspiring to be what they are. The truth is that he does not
know what to make of them. Indeed, they are almost always present
in his poems as what forces supposition, interpretation, judgement:
they are afield as the problematical.

> . . . I passed and saw you
> Labouring there, your dark figure
> Marring the simple geometry
> Of the square fields with its gaunt question.
> My poems were made in its long shadow
> Falling coldly across the page.

The farmers, notes another poem, are busy 'In ways never to be
divulged / To the still watcher beyond the glass / Of their thin
breath'. . . .

Yet if poetry is a consciousness of Being that, however complete
for the moment, aspires to final permanence only in its form of
expression, then Thomas's frustration before the mute men of Wales

may be counted a poetic asset, since it keeps his consciousness of
life restless and pressing. It has led, at any rate, to poetry finally
balanced and alive in its contrary moods and uncertainties.

It is in their common pacing quality that Thomas's manner and
matter blend to form a strong and harmonious mood. The lines will
not, cannot slow down enough to delight in their own rhythms; nor
can the mind at work in them finally rest in any one view of its
subject. The open, passionate manner, catching at the world by
tufts of metaphor, swiftly climbing, is the aesthetic manifestation of
the poet's philosophical quandary, his interpretative eagerness, his
need for certainty and its continual frustration. . . .

. . . Unsettled in themselves as his poems may be, they are yet –
perhaps partly for that very reason – quick with life, and certain to
live.

Besides being internally harmonious, Thomas's poems are also
balanced in what Arnold called poetry's two 'interpretations':
natural magic and moral profundity. Both qualites are vigorous in
his work – the first in the rank strength and quite amazing beauty
of his sensuous imagination, the second in his reflection on the lives
of the poor and bare, and on his own.

No wonder that in reading Thomas at his best – for instance
in 'Green Categories', 'Ninetieth Birthday', 'Walter Llywarch',
'Absolution', 'Portrait', 'The Gap in the Hedge', 'A Peasant', 'The
Airy Tomb', 'Death of a Peasant' – one feels a high excitement. In
Thomas one can rejoice that another rare poet has come, though as
yet scarcely heard of, to the English-speaking world.

Source: extracts from the chapter on R. S. Thomas in *Eight Contemporary
Poets* (Oxford, 1974), pp. 54–9, 59, 60–3, 63–6, 66–7, 67–8.
[Ed. note: Calvin Bedient quotes widely, without attribution – to convey
the territory of these earlier poems, and their continuity with Thomas's
lifelong religious quest. I have left this aspect unedited.]

John Mole   On the Recent Poetry
of R. S. Thomas   (1978)

. . . As Yeats observed, we make poetry out of the quarrel with

ourselves. When that quarrel ceases and we become *convinced*, we
start attending conferences and are ready to ambush the kneeling
poet. So there is a great divide between the arid, unquestioning
territory of dogmatism and the imaginative landscapes of honest
doubt or tenuous belief.

It is as the kneeling poet that R. S. Thomas – albeit rather
oversimply – may be characterised. In an obvious, external, sense
this is apt, since he is a priest of the Church of England and from
an early poem like 'In A Country Church' to the recent 'The Empty
Church' he has dramatised the contemplations of the individual
alone with himself and God, giving them a recognisable parochial
setting; but more importantly, over the past few years and with
an increasingly urgent immediacy matched by a corresponding
refinement of diction, he has achieved a striking pitch of intimate
debate and interrogation. The anthologists' labels – Poet of the
Welsh Hill Country, Bleak Pastoralist, Compassionate Recorder of
Peasant Life etc. – will no longer serve. He has overtaken them to
become much more the companion of Herbert and Hopkins, an
awkward, contentious believer who struggles through paradox after
paradox with a saviour who has all the odds.

Typical of his recent work, with its emblematic title, its theme of
spiritual engagement and the measured solemnity of its tone, is this
poem 'The Combat' from *Laboratories of the Spirit* (1975):

> You have no name.
> We have wrestled with you all
> day, and now night approaches,
> the darkness from which we emerged
> seeking; and anonymous
> you withdraw, leaving us nursing
> our bruises, our dislocations.
>
> For the failure of language
> there is no redress. The physicists
> tell us your size, the chemists
> the ingredients of your
> thinking. But who you are
> does not appear, nor why
> on the innocent marches
> of vocabulary you should choose
> to engage us, belabouring us
> with your silence. We die, we die
> with the knowledge that your resistance
> is endless at the frontier of the great poem.

In 'In A Country Church', 'the one kneeling down' to whom 'no word came' was *balked* by silence. In 'The Combat', we are *belaboured*. It is the same silence, but more ubiquitously, more portentously, baffling. We have moved, as it were, from the parish which for a long time gave the cursory reader of Thomas's poetry the illusion of a limited parochialism – with its etched landscapes and enduring inhabitants – into the galaxy. The journey has been by way of the radar screen, the laboratory, the operating theatre, and all the annexes where the virus, the mystery of existence, is explored. And yet, at the same time, we remain waiting in the cold stone church. Thomas's territory has become cosmic, but his poetry is still profoundly rooted in human experience:

> Why, then, do I kneel still
> striking my prayers on a stone
> heart? Is it in hope one
> of them will ignite yet and throw
> on its illumined walls the shadow
> of someone greater than I can understand?

Chase, combat, truce, evasion. Every one of Thomas's poems now, it seems, is a *resumption* of what he has called the 'linguistic confrontation with ultimate reality', although at a closer look this can be seen to have always been the case. In 'No Through Road' (from *A Song at the Year's Turning*), for example, he declares 'All is vain, I will cease now / My long absorption with the plough' yet by the time he reaches the sestet of his sonnet he is acknowledging that for him there is really, despite all, only *one* theme to be pursued again and again, one story only worth the telling:

> But where to turn? Earth endures
> After the passing, necessary shame
> Of winter, and the old lie
> Of green places beckons me still
> From the new world, ugly and evil,
> That men pry for in truth's name.

In the recent work, however, that 'new world, ugly and evil' has become central. Its representative, in Thomas's characteristic metaphysical short-hand, is *the machine*. In 'Once' which opens the watershed collection *H'm* (1972) there is the clear suggestion that no spiritual rebirth can be achieved without facing the machine and all that it stands for. It is a symptom, part of the virus, and must be an element in the cure:

> I took your hand,
> Remembering you, and together,
> Confederates of the natural day,
> We went forth to meet the Machine.

Now, six years later in the poem 'Directions' . . . the smile of the 'wiseacre' is described as being 'glossy as the machine that thinks it has outpaced belief'. The closed systems of material progress are linked in the imagination with the flashed smile of unmitigated self-confidence. The particular power of the Machine, though, as an emblem, lies in the fact that it is at once contemporary and the repository of a tradition which goes back to Bunyan and beyond. The *wiseacre* is a direct descendent of Mr Wordly-Wiseman and the Machine is Apollyon. In fact it is interesting that, by many, the genre of Science-Fiction is viewed as being the most popular and successful vehicle for the development of allegory in the modern age, and that Thomas's poems seem to be fusing the traditional furniture of Christian allegory with the vocabulary of the scientists: 'It is / how you play, we cry, *scanning* the future for an account / of our performance' . . . 'The *dismantling* / by the self of a self it / could not resemble' . . . 'The silence a process in the *metabolism* / of the being of Love'. It is even at times, the emergence of *The Pilgrim's Progress* from a landscape by Arthur C. Clarke or Isaac Asimov:

> Circular as our way
> is, it leads not back to that snake-haunted
> garden, but onward to the tall city
> of glass that is the laboratory of the spirit.

In 'Words and the Poet' (delivered as a lecture in 1963), R. S. Thomas suggested that 'fairly close attention to a number of poets would, from the recurrence of certain words, be revelatory of their chief concerns and obsessions, as well as of the sort of persons they were' and he went on to observe that:

the potential audience of a poet is one of town dwellers, who are mostly out of touch, if not sympathy, with nature. Their contact with it is modified by the machine. This is tending to deprive country-rooted words of their relevance . . . A vast amount of new knowledge is accumulating with its accompanying vocabulary. One of the great questions facing the poet is: Can significant poetry be made with these new words and terms? People say: 'I don't see why not'. They quote words such as chromosomes as being actually attractive. My own position is usually to allow this as a legitimate theory, but to ask in practice, 'Where are the poems?'

This was fifteen years ago, and it is interesting to place these observations beside the opening of a poem, 'Bravo!' from Thomas's most recent collection, *Frequencies* [1978]:

> Oh, I know it and don't
> care. I know there is nothing in me
> but cells and chromosomes
> waiting to beget chromosomes
> and cells . . .

Perhaps the answer to his own question would have to be 'I am writing them'.

It is in the light of this development, of his work having outpaced the anthologists and having overtaken his own previous reservations concerning an appropriate language for poetry, that we should now be reading R. S. Thomas. Can we see his move away from the more naturalistic settings of the earlier books as an *artistic* growth arising from an intensification of the debate with 'ultimate reality'?

> . . . the emerging
> from the adolescence of nature
> into the adult geometry
> of the mind. I begin to recognise
> you anew, God of form and number.

To some, this has seemed a disappointment, a disintegration into fragments of abstraction. They recall the graphic particularities of strong, local poems like 'Hill Farmer', and the dramatic monologues of 'The Minister'. There is already a nostalgia for Iago Prytherch which would seek to confine Thomas forever to that 'one furrow'. There is relief when, as in a poem such as 'Woman Combing, Degas' from *Laboratories of the Spirit*, he shows that he can write an occasional, observant piece of great lyrical beauty, but a reluctance to accept the voice of a poet who can utter such relentlessly explicit lines as lines 11–17 from 'Gradual' . . . .

Where is the poetry in that? I should say, perhaps a little deviously, that it is being prepared for. These lines are a necessary stage in a characteristic Thomas move towards a resonant conclusion. 'The achievements of poets do not depend on their use of language alone. There is that peculiar rhythm and tone, which immediately distinguishes certain poets' (*Words and the Poet*). Just as we should not, for example, attempt to separate the contrived, demotic idiom of the opening of Philip Larkin's 'High Windows' from the terrible

chill beauty of its ending, so we should always let R. S. Thomas
finish. The development of 'Gradual' is, in itself, gradual. With gentle
yet deliberate echoes of Edward Thomas (whose *Selected Poems* he
has edited), he begins 'I have come to the borders / of the understanding', then in the text-book vocabulary of that 'understanding' – of
the *lesson* – he makes the statement which is the poem's centre, but not
its justification: this comes with the conclusion, the *prayer* / beginning:
'Call your horizons / in'.

The range of allusion and dramatic effect, here, is what makes
the poem. The horizons, like the hounds of heaven, must be *called
in* – and the urgency of the demand is dramatised by the placing of
in immediately after the stanza break, making a cry of it. (There
are similar effects, though admittedly more splendidly strenuous, in
Hopkins.) At the same time, the calling in of horizons is a plea for
the narrowing of God's territory, a limiting of the expanse to be
contemplated from those 'borders of understanding'. 'Call them in';
i.e. bring them closer to home, make yourself more local, more
approachable. Then there is the placing, at the end of the first two
lines of the last stanza, of the apparently abstract words *domestication*
and *ferocities*. What counts, here, is the force they register, isolating
the phrase 'for a moment' (which *is* only for a moment) between
them. Their weight and opposition dramatises the spiritual struggle –
the desire for peace and security *vs.* the acknowledgement of a fierce,
universal law – with the word *suffer* (allow) also subtly anticipating
and reinforcing (in its other sense of experiencing pain) the impact
of *ferocities*. Then finally, though by no means exhaustively, we have
the lion becoming the lamb – echoes of Blake, and Isaiah's Peaceable
Kingdom – and another breathing space, a temporary Eden, a
sacred love bower where ignorance (in its true meaning) is bliss.

Of . . . other poems . . . – 'Postscript' for example, from *H'm*,
provides a gloss on the 'desert of language' – and as for 'the
simpleton / with his mouth open crying: / How far is it to God' it is
moving to regard him in company with the idiot at 'The Fair', from
the same volume:

> The idiot goes round and around
> With his brother in a bumping-car
> At the fair. The famous idiot
> Smile hangs over the car's edge,
> Illuminating nothing. This is mankind
> Being taken for a ride by a rich

> Relation. The responses are fixed:
> Bump, smile; bump, smile. And the current
> Is generated by the smooth flow
> Of the shillings. This is an orchestra
> Of steel with the constant percussion
> Of laughter. But where he should be laughing
> Too, his features are split open, and look!
> Out of the cracks come warm, human tears.

Herbert's God asks 'Who made the eyes but I?'. Thomas's wiseacre, in 'Directions', proud to be associated with the 'smooth flow of the shillings', might certainly ask, 'Who built the Fair but I?'. From Vanity Fair to multi-storey Shopping Precinct . . . and when the shadow of the cross falls on 'the smoothest of surfaces' we cannot dissociate that smoothness from the glossy mechanistic smile which preceded it a few lines earlier in 'Directions' or, indeed, from the 'smooth flow of the shillings' in 'The Fair'; all are linked as part of Thomas's vision of that forest of metal amongst which the warm, human tears continue to be wept if not adequately observed. It is a profound, fundamentally contemporary polarity.

. . . It may be perverse, even a little sentimental, to insist upon making the connection with R. S. Thomas in the figure of the kneeling poet,[1] but, for me, Thomas is a poet remarkable in his patience and gravity surrounded by the trappings of a frantic, headlong society founded upon a vacuous rationalism. In a world of systems, signifying nothing, he has not escaped to the pastures of gentle illusion or based his work on mere passing satire; instead, he has addressed himself to the heart of the matter – 'this struggle to balance off the urgency of one's need for revelation with the need for patience. God, reality, whatever it is, is not going to be forced, it's not going to be put to the question, it works in its own time.'[2] . . . And this in a time when, as he sees it, the Word on the signpost has been worn away. It is an unfashionable, uncomfortable position – all the glamour is elsewhere – but it has produced a poetry of uncompromising strength and frequent beauty.

SOURCE: the substance of the article 'On the Recent Poetry of R. S. Thomas', in *New Poetry*, 43 (1978), pp. 6–11.

NOTES

1. [Ed.] John Mole begins his article with the story, 'possibly apocryphal', of Hardy's giving a lecture at a conference of rationalists, and afterwards being found 'alone, on his knees, in the local parish church'; 'he was not invited again . . .'.

2. R. S. Thomas, *Priest and Poet*; from a transcript of John Ormond's film for BBC television (2 April 1972), published in *Poetry Wales* (Spring 1972).

Kevin Nichols (1978)   Untenanted Cross

. . . R. S. Thomas was born in Wales. He is vicar of a country parish there, and lives, works and writes in the hill-country of the North. That countryside and the national consciousness (the former more than the latter) have deeply coloured his poetry and his experience of faith. It is a bleak, spare country, the bones showing through

> That bare hill with the man ploughing
> Corrugating that brown roof
> Under a hard sky.

Sometimes he hated its earthiness and the narrowness of spirit it begets. It seems sometimes a ghost country washed up by the past, a dying race and culture, a dying language.

> There is no present in Wales
> And no future:
> There is only the past,
> Brittle with relics
> Wind-bitten towers and castles
> With sham ghosts.

The English come over the border and stop their cars by the roadside to inspect these strange foreigners. He feels like the curator of a vast national museum as they come

> Scavenging among the remains
> Of our culture . . .
>   . . . elbowing our language
> Into the grave we have dug for it.

Yet there is beauty in it, this landscape, as it comes out in the poems, 'Beauty is truth, truth beauty.' A critic once wrote that the acid test (and the falsification) of this principle is a look at a hippopotamus. Yet Keats rarely wrote anything without some deep 'truth of the imagination' in it. In Thomas's case, this is the way in which his experience is embodied. The language is simple and austere, no superfluous words, no jam on the bread, only an occasional exotic word, carefully placed, a risk worth taking. The verse-form also, though free, is usually carefully shaped. If it almost always seems right, this is not because of the external discipline of sonnet or Spenserian stanza. It is because the form takes the discipline of the inner movement of the experience being built into a poem. The imagery has the same character of finding its beauty in its truth. We find tiny images that explode and die in the middle of a poem like squibs:

> thick ambush of shadows
> Hushed at the field's corners.

Thomas also has the true poet's ability to start an image going, tease it all through sound and sense and rhythm, stretch its tentacles into all the corners of his poem. 'The Belfry' begins just with the sight of one, grey and gaunt. Then there are times when

> a bleak frost is upon
> One's whole being, and the heart
> In its bone belfry hangs and is dumb.

But perhaps someone continues to answer the call to prayer even through

> the hard spell
> Of weather that is between God
> And himself.

And perseverance in prayer brings life again and warmth

> the sun and afterwards flowers
> On the raw graves and the throbbing of bells.

The people who inhabit this landscape do not stand far apart from it. They grow out of it rather of the earth, earthy. The soil is all. The peasant mechanically docks swedes,

> the knife errs
> Burying itself in the shocked flesh,

> Then out of the wound, the blood seeps home
> To the warm soil from which it came.

In this life, understanding, refinement, flicker only feebly. It is a life whose true realities are the resistant soil, the weather, the elemental rhythms from birth to dying. It leaves little room for the expansion of the spirit in the strait confines of the land and its society. The hill people come at Christmas to

> the bread's
> Purer snow, fumble it in their huge
> Hands, put their lips to it
> Like beasts.

But they return without much illumination to comprehensible realities

> Their horizon contracted
> To the one small stone-riddled field.

Occasionally 'narrow but saved', more often stunted sometimes to imbecility, they are certainly not witnesses of a liberal enlightened Christianity, or even humanity. Yet there is about them an enduring toughness, a permanence, an atavistic courage in the teeth of seasons and circumstances. The peasant Iago Prytherch stands for them all. He moves blindly through the routines of farming, sits in the evening with his frighteningly vacant mind,

> His clothes sour with years of sweat
> And animal contact, shock the refined
> But affected sense with their stark naturalness.
> Yet this is your prototype who, season by season
> Against siege of rain and the wind's attrition
> Preserves his stock.

He lasts with a kind of inarticulate existential courage.

> His hands are broken
> But not his spirit. He is like the bark
> Weathering on the tree of his kind.

Yet you may say, this primitive permanence – the solidity of ancient granite – can give little comfort to a priest. His task is to blow up some flame of the spirit from these unpromising embers. Does it seem an altogether hopeless task, words falling on deaf ears, head battered against a stone wall?

> I am Prytherch, forgive me, I don't know
> What you are talking about; your thoughts flow

> Too quickly for me; I cannot dawdle
> Along their banks.

Sometimes, the poetry comes close to that; like Hopkins, on the edge of despair but never quite over it.

> Go
> To that lean parish; let them tread
> On your dreams . . .
>   Test your belief
> In spirit on their faces staring
> At you, on beauty's surrender
> To truth, on the soul's selling
> Of itself for a corner
> By the body's fire.

What hauls the poetry back from the edge of despair is its truth, its reality. Physical needs, the immediacy of nature will always predominate. The world, that of the stone-riddled field or that of the 'dumb cogs and tireless camshafts' will always be difficult to penetrate, to illuminate with word and spirit. Yet

> Is there blessing? Light's peculiar grave
> In cold splendour, robes this tortured place
> For strange marriage.

It is a light which breaks in occasional moments of vision and radiance, as in the country church

> the air a staircase
> For silence; the sun's light
> Ringing me

or on the moor where

> I walked on
> Simple and poor, while the air crumbled
> And broke on me generously as bread.

There is also a muted and hidden light; a perception that the resistant intransigence of reality has not destroyed the secret force of grace

> Don't think even the dirt
> And the brute ugliness reigned
> Unchallenged. Among the fields
> Sometimes the spirit enchained

So long by the gross flesh raised
Suddenly there its wild note of praise.

Humanity is not a *massa damnata*. The dough may not seem to rise but the leaven is alive there. The faith-vision which R. S. Thomas embodies in his poems is certainly a bleak one. It is hard to imagine him joining in, still less writing, a charismatic chorus.

If he is surprised by joy it is occasionally, unexpectedly and against the odds. It is true that he remembers with a little nostalgia how once in a country church

a preacher caught fire
and burned steadily before them
with a strange light

so that his hearers

sang their amens
fiercely, narrow but saved
in a way that men are not now.

Still, in general, the fields, the seasons, the beasts, the heaviness of life in the flesh erodes the spirit, damps down enthusiasm.

nature's truth
Is primary and her changing seasons
Correct out of a vaster reason
The vague errors of the flesh.

Redemption is seen in a long vista; not in an immediate transformation of reality, but in a distant vision, a long-term acceptance and trust. How does this stand within a Christian faith which, it is often said, should result in ecstasy and joy? There is in Christian spirituality, a tradition, recessive but persevering, of realism verging on pessimism. It is not a long-term pessimism.

But it sees our life on earth as one in which the forces which weigh us down and prevent the expansion of spirit are usually dominant. Man moves towards eternal happiness and ultimately his life is enfolded in God's unfailing love. But in this sublunary world his days are most commonly nasty, brutish and short. We find this view of reality in the Book of Ecclesiastes. It is also there in St Augustine, in Pascal, in Kierkegaard, about whom Thomas writes so movingly:

> wounded he crawled
> To the monastery of his chaste thought
> To offer up his crumpled amen.

R. S. Thomas sees and embodies the value and beauty of this ultimate amen offered out of a life of which we seem to have made little but disaster and confusion. We do well to ponder his poems. Christians stand in some danger at present, of falling into a superficial cult of success; mental health, rich relationships, fulfilment and maturity are the watchwords. Thomas's vision is that humanity doesn't change very much. The marvellous qualities of genius, beauty and holiness make only occasional appearances on the human stage. We are for the most part, redeemed as and where we are. The tangle and dough of our lives is itself the substance of redemption. God becoming man takes this intractable human world and suffers it. God doubtfully creates the hand, symbol of human action and freedom. It cries out to him:

> Tell
> me your name and I will write it
> in bright gold. Are there not deeds
> to be done, children to make, poems
> to be written . . .
>   But God feeling the nails
> in his side . . .
>   fought on in
> silence.

In this world, the believer must suffer, strive yet press forward. He must not hope to arrive quickly at the celestial Jerusalem. His road

> runs on
> With many turnings towards the tall
> Tree to which the believer is nailed.

The priest, especially, whose sole task it is to blow the embers of spirit into flame, seems in this world an odd, enigmatic, sometimes ridiculous figure; both to the peasants from the hill farms and also to the owners of the dumb cogs and tireless camshafts

> 'Crippled soul' do you say? looking at him
> From the mind's height; 'limping through life
> On his prayers. There are other people
> In the world, sitting at table
> Contented, though the broken body
> And the shed blood are not on the menu'.
> 'Let it be so', I say, 'Amen and amen'.

Another crumpled amen; but not one of defeat or passive acceptance. It is the amen of a faith which survives and thrives despite
appearances; which has been tested against the bleak realities of
everyday life. The churches are largely empty, musty, mildewed.
The priest must continue to kneel there when

> There is no other sound
> In the darkness but the sound of a man
> Breathing, testing his faith
> On emptiness, nailing his questions
> One by one to an untenanted cross.

The Cross is the central, recurring symbol. It is the sign of God's
acceptance of the bleak human lot. Occasionally – in a shaft of
sunlight – it appears as the tree of life, *arbor decora et fulgida.*

> love in a dark crown
> Of thorns blazing, and a winter tree
> Golden with fruit of a man's body.

Usually it is empty, 'untenanted', barren of golden fruit, shedding
no light across the winter landscape; the place of faith where the
believer himself must hold, questioning but steady.

In these poems, the symbol of the Cross becomes the source of a
strange kind of grace. They make no pretences. No adjectival glamour
plasters over the austerity of the poet's experience. Yet he succeeds
without detectable effort in enfolding the bleak human condition in a
blanket of compassion and prayerfulness. There his true (though not
obvious) success as a man, a priest and a poet flow together.

> Deliver me from the long drought
>   of the mind. Let leaves
> from the deciduous Cross
>   fall on us, washing
> us clean, turning our autumn
>   to gold by the affluence of their fountain.

SOURCE: the substance of article, 'The Untenanted Cross: The Poetry of
R. S. Thomas', in *Clergy Review*, 63 (1978), pp. 83–5.
[Ed. note: Kevin Nichols, like Calvin Bedient, quotes widely without
attribution – using early and 'middle' poems, with the same focus on
Thomas's religious quest. I leave this aspect unedited.]

Antony Conran (1979)   'Poet of Vision'

Abersoch

There was that headland, asleep on the sea,
The air full of thunder and the far air
Brittle with lightning; there was that girl
Riding her cycle, hair at half-mast,
And the men smoking, the dinghies at rest
On the calm tide. There were people going
About their business, while the storm grew
Louder and nearer and did not break.

Why do I remember these few things,
That were rumours of life, not life itself
That was being lived fiercely, where the storm raged?
Was it just that the girl smiled,
Though not at me, and the men smoking
Had the look of those who have come safely home?

[from *Tares* (1961)]

'There was that headland', 'there was that girl', 'There were people':
the casual, half-colloquial, half-demonstrative form gives the verb *to
be* an almost Wordsworthian significance and emphasis. Nothing is
happening, everything just is. Looked at closely, the poem shows
itself to have considerable emblematic significance. The headland
is asleep on the sea, though all around it, in the distance, the storm
which is later identified with life makes the air 'brittle with lightning'.
Transporting from the symbolic language of dream-imagery, that
is, the conscious mind is asleep on the depths of the subconscious
'out of the swing of the tide', on a promontory that the storms of
history, while they continually get nearer, do not reach. The girl is
riding her cycle – controlling her *karma* – with her hair at 'half-
mast', like a flag of a people in mourning and yet contented: she
smiles, though not at me. Men are smoking, boats are at rest, people
are going about their business, even though they are not involved
in the passions of history. They are 'rumours of life, not life itself'.
The poet, fresh from the clear-cut concerns of the Active Life, is,

typically, baffled by his poem: 'Why do I remember these few things?' Its visionary quality seems to have nothing to do with him, like the girl's smile. But the importance is unmistakable, once you set it in a contemplative context: it is the first, tentative vision of something like a 'field full of folk', seen without prejudice of action, with 'the look of those who have come safely home'. . . .

. . . The poems that give *Laboratories of the Spirit* [1975] its uniqueness are the poems of 'Illumination', filled with the sense of God's presence or near-presence, utter transparencies of the spirit: poems like 'Suddenly', 'The Flower', 'Alive', 'The Bright Field', the marvellous 'Sea-watching', and (in a slightly different vein) 'Good'.

In these the sensation of God's presence is conveyed in many different ways, some traditional, others new-minted. In 'Suddenly', for example, it is an experience of the Resurrected Christ, as in the 'Shewings' of Dame Julian of Norwich –

> Yet was he
> no more there than before,
> his area occupied
> by the unhallowed presences,

He is seen by Thomas

> not with the eye
> only, but with the whole
> of my being, overflowing with
> him as a chalice would
> with the sea.

In 'The Flower', again, we have two traditional images: the poet asks for riches, and God gives him the whole world, earth, sea and sky –

> I looked at them
> and learned I must withdraw
> to possess them. I gave my eyes
> and my ears, and dwelt
> in a soundless darkness
> in the shadow
> of your regard.

He that would have his life must lose it. The other image is that of the flower itself, the 'rosa mystica' perhaps, the flower of true contemplation, that grows in him and fills him with its fragrance. Men come to him from the four winds to hear him talk of this unseen flower.

> whose roots were not
> in the soil, nor its petals the colour
> of the wide sea; that was
>   its own species with its own
>   sky over it, shot
> with the rainbow of your coming and going.

In 'Alive' we again have a traditional way of expressing the experience of eternity – this time the vision of the universe as a living being, instinct with the life of God:

> I listen
> and it is you speaking.
> I find the place where you lay
> warm. At night, if I waken,
> there are the sleepless conurbations
> of the stars. The darkness
> is the deepening shadow
> of your presence; the silence a
> process in the metabolism
> of the being of love.

In other poems we have the water that turned to wine at the marriage-feast at Cana ('Ann Griffith'); the 'holy nothing' from which all things come ('Phew!' from *The Way of It*, 1977); the moment of sunlight that was the pearl of great price, the one field that had the treasure in it ('The Bright Field'). These are all traditional images of the life of Contemplation, and of the presence of God that illuminates it.

I suppose, though, that of all these poems it is 'Sea-watching' that is most memorable, and the most original image . . . . The poet makes the comparison with prayer explicit in the first lines of the poem:

> Grey waters, vast
>   as an area of prayer
> that one enters. Daily
>   over a period of years
> I have let the eye rest on them.
> Was I waiting for something?
>   Nothing
> but that continuous waving
>   that is without meaning
> occurred.

The rare bird, the mystical experience, *is* rare – that is its nature. It came when he wasn't looking for it, when he wasn't there to see it. The language begins to flicker with ambiguities. When he wasn't there – does it mean quite what it says, in fact? Obviously so, with the bird. But with God! The mystic seeks by self-surrender to know God: the only time God can be known by you is when you (in the ordinary sense) aren't there to know him.

The discipline of sea-watching is stressed:

> You must wear your eyes out,
> as others their knees.
>   I became the hermit
> of the rocks, habited with the wind
> and the mist.

'Habited' both refers to the dress of a monk or hermit and to his contemplative work. He has the habit of it, he does it without novelty or strain. One remembers that this poem was probably written at Aberdaron, on the headland that looks over to Bardsey, Enlli of the saints, where the old Celtic monks spent their lives of fasting and prayer among the rocks. R. S. Thomas speaks of days when the emptiness that the rare bird might have filled was so beautiful that 'its absence was as its presence': as precise a description of contemplative illumination as you are likely to find. The poet's mind was so single, after its long fast, so at one, that his watching was indistinguishable from prayer. . . .

SOURCE: extracts from article, 'R. S. Thomas as a Mystical Poet', in *Poetry Wales*, 14, no. 4 (Spring 1979), pp. 14–15, 21–3, 23–4.

Brian Morris   Mr Thomas's Present Concerns   (1979)

On the front endpaper of his copy of George Barker's *Calamiterror* (1937) Mr Thomas copied out extracts from a translation of Brecht's *An Die Nachgeborenen*:

> Indeed I live in the dark ages.
> A guileless word is an absurdity. A smooth forehead betokens

A hard heart. He who laughs
Has not yet heard
The terrible tidings . . .

I came to the cities in a time of disorder
When hunger ruled.
I came among men in a time of uprising
And I revolted with them.
So the time passed away
Which on earth was given me.

I ate my food between massacres.
The shadow of murder lay upon my sleep.
And when I loved, I loved with indifference.
I looked upon nature with impatience.
So the time passed away
Which on earth was given me.

In my time streets led to the quicksand.
Speech betrayed me to the slaughterer.
There was little I could do. But without me
The rulers would have been more secure. This was my hope.

The copy is not dated, but was probably made in the early 1940s, and it illustrates the continuity and organic integrity of his work, because many of the qualities which inform Brecht's vision appear (concentrated, refined, and transmuted) in Mr Thomas's last three volumes, *H'm* [1972], *Laboratories of the Spirit* [1975] and *Frequencies* [1978].

He is very conscious that he lives 'in the dark ages', and such laughter as there is in these three volumes is not more than the flicker of a grim and mordant wit. He knows of the disorder of the cities, and, more and more, he has withdrawn from them. In his time, streets have led to 'where the pound Sings and the doors open To its music', the cities 'have outgrown their promise', and 'at the switchboard of the exchanges of the people of all time' he learns that 'the news from the city is not good'. But, most notably, these three volumes show him sharing Brecht's sense of the absurdity of the guileless word, the treacherous quicksands of language which lie before the poet's feet. His utterance, always guarded and restrained, has become even more controlled, winnowed and transpicuous; the poems, always short, win their effects out of an even greater fastidiousness in the handling of words. The point is made, trenchantly, in 'After Jericho':

> There is an aggression of fact
> to be resisted successfully
> only in verse, that fights language
> with its own tools. Smile, poet,
>
> among the ruins of a vocabulary
> you blew your trumpet against.
> It was a conscript army; your words,
> every one of them, are volunteers.

The tone, the stance, is recognisably that of Mr Thomas's earlier volumes, but the succinctness, the precision, the frugality even (there is only one adjective in that poem, 'conscript'), create an assurance and an authority that is new.

Such conciseness is only one thread in the cloth of Mr Thomas's poetic language, which is still deeply imbued by the religious register of our tongue. This is clear to any semantic investigation, but most evident in his technique of allusion. The experiences of Elijah between Carmel and Horeb (1 Kings, 18–19) are a frequent source of reference, but they are used obliquely, not descriptively. In 'Parry' he writes:

> Shout then,
> I cry; waken
> The unseen sleeper; let
> Him come forth . . .

But in the context of the poem the words are those of the rebellious sceptic, not the mocking prophet; the allusion is inverted. Similarly, in 'Once', the words 'God spoke. I hid myself in the side / of the mountain' connect Horeb with the poet's unusual view of Genesis, and in 'The Prayer' the phrase 'after the weather of his asking, no still, small voice . . .' alerts the reader to 1 Kings, 19. 12, but requires a knowledge of the full context in which the despair of the prophet under the juniper tree images the dryness of the Christian labouring at prayer. The technique is deployed on different material at the end of 'Ann Griffith':

> I am the live God,
> nailed fast to the old tree
> of a nation by its unreal
> tears. I thirst, I thirst
> for the spring water. Draw it up
> for me from your heart's well and I will change
> it to wine upon your unkissed lips.

Here the 'live God' is the 'living water' (John, 4. 10), and the lines
require the reader to connect the Johannine account of the crucifixion
with the story of the Woman of Samaria (John, 4) and the miracle
at Cana in Galilee (John, 2). And the irony of comparing the Woman
of Samaria with Ann Griffith is not fortuitous. The language which
depends so upon hints and suggestions cannot be accused of lacking
a most defensive guile.

   The deepening of this 'deciduous language', where the poet is
'breaking my speech from the perennial tree of my people', is a more
fundamental development in Mr Thomas's art than the immediately
obvious shift in vocabulary. The poems in these volumes are studded
with genes, molecules, atoms, nodes, metabolisms, computers,
bombs, explosives and equations, and the liberal use of scientific
and technological terms and concepts has deceived many into
thinking that the poet has now chosen to put away the childish
things of orthodox religion in favour of the adult toys of the
laboratory. It is not so; it is nothing so simple. The unwary should
be warned by the words (written before 1972) in 'Earth':

> We are misled
> By perspective; the microscope
> Is our sin, we tower enormous
> Above it, the stronger it
> Grows.

The machine has replaced the hands that crucified God, but (he
insists) the machine cannot absolve us, and the resonances of that
word 'absolve' indicate the mind's struggle to balance the traditional
insights inherent in religious language with the religious insights of
scientific terminology. In one of the most recent poems he says:

> I modernise the anachronism
>
> of my language, but he is no more here
> than before . . .   ('Absence', *Frequencies*)

And in 'The Times' he might be held guilty of subtle self-advertise-
ment when he discerns against 'a background of guns and bombs
. . . One voice, quieter than the rest' (again, the subdued reference
to Elijah at Horeb), and of ironic advice to his readers:

> Men put it on tape
> For the future, a lesson in style.

You cannot argue with that. The poet has created an intricate,
invincible language with very godly guile.

The central concern in these three volumes is the poet's exploration of the nature of the Deity. . . . This concentration, this narrowing-down, is, in a way, not unlike the progress of Beckett's work with its reductive urge, its insistence on 'lessness'. But where Beckett's obsession with ultimate nothingness has so distilled his vision and limited his options that every new work seems like an escapology from silence, Mr Thomas's relentless pursuit of the vanishing God seems to have liberated his imagination. His most characteristic procedure is by the use of what we may call 'created myths', inventing narrative or dramatic situations to embody a perception. Some develop existing myths, like the story of Jacob wrestling at Peniel (Genesis, 32), which is approached from a different angle in 'The Hand':

> It was a hand. God looked at it
> and looked away . . .
>
> But the hand wrestled with him. 'Tell
> me your name,' it cried, 'and I will write it
> in bright gold . . .

This is essentially a narrative development of the poet's technique of complex and connected Biblical allusion, but it requires invention, and the poem's theme (mankind's 'coming of age') does not obviously arise from the Biblical original. A more distant example, but still in touch with an Old Testament model, occurs in 'Dialogue', where the poet, like Job, argues with his Maker:

> 'I had to do it that way.'
> 'A god, then, is under constraint?'
> 'Put it like that, but the material –'
> 'Whose material?'
>   'You don't understand.
> It was always here, a matter
> of refinement.' . . .

The poem goes on to explain the dinosaurs as God's plough, and mankind as his waste of breath, 'the casualty of my imagination'. Like many another poem in these collections it struggles to account for the existence of evil and the problem of pain, but does so by a creative hypothesis about the nature of God. In 'Dialogue' as elsewhere God is presented as an applied scientist (Mr Thomas is modernising the anachronism of the landscape gardener in Genesis) who needs not bone but 'the chemistry of the spirit', and who takes

the human heart in order to 'experiment with it a little longer in
the crucible of the adult mind'. Job's problem is attempted from
God's point of view.

Some of the created myths are pure invention. 'Echoes' investigates
God's anger at the apathy of his creatures:

> What is this? said God. The obstinacy
> Of its refusal to answer
> Enraged him . . .

He strikes the earth, and Nature bandages its wounds. It becomes
beautiful, and God looks at it again. He creates trees, birds and
animals to provide earth's answer, and eventually 'the shapes' come
to his call, curious to build:

> On the altars
> They made him the red blood
> Told what he wished to hear.

The God of the poet's myths is no omnipotent, omniscient, transcendent, inscrutable creator whose name is Love. He often appears as
a 'deus irae', as irritable as the God of André Obey's *Noah*, as in
the opening of Soliloquy':

> And God thought: Pray away,
> Creatures; I'm going to destroy
> It. The mistake's mine,
> If you like. I have blundered
> Before; the glaciers erased
> My error . . .

He is the God of the invisible viruses, 'the personnel Of the darkness
that do my will'. Mr Thomas is concerned with what kind of God
could be responsible for the universe as humanity experiences it, and
his anthropomorphic projections are challenging in their attempts to
provide solutions to the theodicean problem. Perhaps the most
abrupt confrontation with the traditional image of a charitable
Creator is provided by the almost Swiftian flight of invention in
'The Island':

> And God said, I will build a church here
> And cause this people to worship me,
> And afflict them with poverty and sickness . . .

> . . . And their women shall bring forth
> On my altars, and I will choose the best
> Of them to be thrown back into the sea.

> And that was only on one island.

The God of these poems is not always very nice, but he is less a person than a postulate, or a series of postulates, or the several facets of one postulate. He does not, as yet, 'add up', just as the Jahweh-Shepherd-Servant-Saviour figure of the Bible fails to add up to a recognisable figure encompassable by the human mind. It is not possible that he should. Yet Mr Thomas's myths of God have a certain coherence. They do not present an analogue of Blake's 'old Nobodaddy aloft', but they have certain allegiances to Blake's graphic visions of the Diety, and to Michaelangelo's. Especially, perhaps, in *Frequencies*, God has a cultured background and exists in a landscape. In 'The Gap' God wakes after a nightmare and contemplates man's 'tower' of speech. He 'reclines' on the air like a Roman emperor, he 'measures' the gap with his mind; he considers how he can rest 'on the edge of a chasm a word could bridge'; he 'leans over' from his 'repose' to look at their dictionary. In 'Dialectic' he listens to the equations of his creatures,

> As to a spider spinning its web
> from its entrails, the mind swinging
> to and fro over an abysm
> of blankness

In 'The Woman' he 'quails' before female beauty; in 'The Reception' he withdraws 'to consider, rejuvenating himself at the mind's sources'. The poet has permitted himself to face the same problems as the painter of the ceiling of the Sistine Chapel or the engraver of 'The Ancient of Days'. Blake's God, with his compasses, is strangely akin to Mr Thomas's geometer who 'sits at that strange table of Eddington's'.

The manipulation of created myths demands a strenuous control and strict logic if the result is not to be simple inconsistency. The poet's virtuosity in the pattern of his invention stretches the mind to its limits in a poem like 'The Tool', where there is God, contemplating emptiness, and a face staring, seeking a likeness:

> There was thought
> probing an absence. God
> knew he was naked and
> withdrew himself.

The reversal of the Biblical situation of Adam and Eve creates a Blakean antithesis, yet one realises, on reflection, that there is nothing heterodox about this extension of the 'God' figure to include the feelings proper to his creatures. The revelation may be startling as one reads the poem, but within the terms of the technique it is a perfectly legitimate piece of 'character development'. The same is true in 'God's Story', which begins with a picture of the God who 'burned in the sky as of old' and ends with that same God, guided by 'the cold touch of the machine on his hand' searching for his own identity:

> 'Where are you?'
> he called, seeking himself among
> the dumb cogs and tireless camshafts.

The models and mentors for this kind of religious poetic invention are to be found in the debate between God and Abraham over Sodom (Genesis 18), and in the opening chapters of the Book of Job. Mr Thomas's 'And God said . . .' is the equivalent of Isaiah's 'Thus saith the Lord'.

The created myths create their own sequences of complex images which accrete meaning from poem to poem. Mr Thomas plays a series of variations on the traditional identification of Christ's cross and Adam's tree. The 'green tree' becomes the 'doomed tree', the 'deciduous Cross' becomes an example 'of the power of art to transcend timber'. And so on. But perhaps the most systematic exploration is reserved for the image of the wound in Christ's side (John, 19. 34). The iconography of the water and the blood as the eucharistic water and wine has a long history in mediaeval and Renaissance art, and, occasionally in Mr Thomas's poems, it appears in this form. In 'The Prayer', for example:

> He
> held out his hands, cupped
> as though to receive blood, leaking
> from life's side . . .

But more commonly it has wider reverberations. In 'Rough' it lies behind the startling image of

> God, and in his side like an incurred stitch, Jesus.

It is part of an almost grotesque picture in 'The Interrogation', where Christ in judgement on the financiers

> will feel breaching
> his healed side their terrible
> pencil and the haemorrhage of its figures.

In 'The Woman' God 'put his hand in his side and drew out the thorn for the letting of the ordained blood' (linking the creation of Eve with the soldier's spear), and in 'Roger Bacon' the scientist

> saw the hole
> in God's side that is the wound
> of knowledge and
> thrust his hand in it and believed.

But perhaps the most subtle and evocative use of the image occurs in 'Cain', where Abel's wound and God's argument with Cain lead to God's statement that 'The lamb was torn From my own side' and his preparation for the journey

> To the doomed tree you were at work upon.

What is so impressive and convincing is the cohesion and growth of an image pattern like this through a series of poems in three separate volumes published over a period of six years. Such a development is an index of seriousness and poetic integrity.

Although there are similarities between Brecht's vision in *An Die Nachgeborenen* and Mr Thomas's in his work since 1972, there is one great difference: Brecht is deeply concerned with time, with the moment, and Mr Thomas is not. Such references as there are to matters temporal are casual and lack urgency ('Time running out now, and the soul unfinished'), and this is because Time poses no problems for him; he knows where he stands with it:

> I am a seeker
> in time for that which is
> beyond time . . .   ('Abercuawg', *Frequencies*)

Far more important is Space – a dimension which actively engages the poet's imagination. That time is subservient to space is clear from the reference in 'Dialectic' where God resolves to show his creatures

> space that is bounded
> but without end, time that is where
> they were or will be . . .

Mr Thomas seems to have taken the special theory of Relativity in his stride, but it is the space element which provides his deepest perceptions. To take just one example, the opening poems of *Frequencies* are full of 'space' words: Gap, recede, grew, on a level, measured, wider, nearness, chasm, bridge, the space on the page, at the cell's core, switchboard, interior, looked out, threshold, far down . . . and so on, the list is endless. And it is the spatial metaphor which provides many of the deepest insights in the poet's recent work. In 'Via Negativa' he 'modernises the anachronism' of the Church Fathers to provide a powerful statement about the nature of the Deity:

> . . . God is that great absence
> In our lives, the empty silence
> Within, the place where we go
> Seeking, not in hope to
> Arrive or find. He keeps the interstices
> In our knowledge, the darkness
> Between stars.

'Via Negativa' was published in *H'm* (1972), but the insight is the same, and in the same terms, in a poem like 'Night Sky' in *Frequencies* (1978):

> Godhead
> is the colonisation by mind
>
> of untenanted space . . .

I take 'Night Sky' as one of the key poems, one of the signposts on Mr Thomas's journey ('The best journey to make is inward. It is the interior that calls') towards that Deity he pursues as relentlessly as the Hound of Heaven pursues and preoccupies him. There are others. 'Via Negativa', 'The Island', 'Soliloquy', 'The Moon in Lleyn', 'Abercuawg' and 'Dialectic' mark stages in his progress towards some reconciliation with the *deus absconditus* who loves him and despises him, interferes with him and evades him. A great deal is summed up in one of the last poems in *Frequencies*, 'The Absence', where 'this great absence that is like a presence' compels the poet

> to address it without hope
> of a reply. It is a room I enter
>
> from which someone has just gone . . .

The image is taken up in the volume's concluding poem:

> He is such a fast
> God, always before us and
> leaving as we arrive.

Yet that poem's title is 'Pilgrimages' and the pilgrims are on their
way to Bardsey Island, Ynys Enlli, just over the hill from Aberdaron
and Y Rhiw, the bird sanctuary visited by shy and elusive birds of
passage, where Mr Thomas spends so much of his time.

SOURCE: article, 'Mr Thomas's Present Concerns', in *Poetry Wales*, 14,
no. 4 (Spring 1979), pp. 31–42.

I. R. F. Gordon   The Adult Geometry of the Mind   (1980)

The main features of R. S. Thomas's distinctive quality and power
as a poet from his first published volume, *The Stones of the Field*
(1946), up to *Not That He Brought Flowers* (1968), have been fairly
well defined. ... The terse power of his descriptions of life among
the Welsh hill farmers, the sculptured monosyllabic texture of his
knuckled verse, the paradoxically ruthless compassion and austere
lyricism of his poetry, have become a highly valued and increasingly
familiar part of our literary heritage. ...

But in his poetry of the last decade ... beginning with the
publication of *H'm* (1972), and continuing through *Laboratories of the
Spirit* (1975), *The Way of It* (1977) and *Frequencies* (1978), Thomas
has made clear departures from this earlier line of writing. He has
moved away from the over-riding concern with the Welsh farming
community and national identity. As he says in the opening poem
of *Laboratories of the Spirit*.

> Not as in the old days I pray,
> God. My life is not what it was.   ('Emerging')

... In the recent poetry there is an increasing emphasis on the
pain, loneliness and grief of life. It is not simply an awareness of
age and decay that runs through the poems, although that is present,
but a sense that life is a bitter and painful process. Birth is seen as

a betrayal, and living as hard. 'The bone aches, the blood limps like a cripple about the ruins of one's body', Thomas says in 'Resolution'. These physical pains are themselves reduced to the level of mere irritations beside the memories of one's prevarications and weaknesses, which constitute an even more frightening infirmity. This powerful sense of the grim painfulness of life, both physical and psychological, is strikingly expressed through the allegorical poem called 'Fishing', where the bodies of the fish accumulate and 'the air echoes to their inaudible screaming'.

There is very little joy in the recent poetry. Thomas's view of existence, the future, past and present is frequently apocalyptic in tone:

> Going on, going
> back, standing aside – the alternatives
> are appalling. . . .   ('Travellers')

Past achievements have either been squandered or – discredited. The present must be endured. The future is unimaginable. Like that earlier twentieth-century regional poet, Thomas Hardy, with whom R. S. Thomas has clear pessimistic affinities, there is a constant awareness of time and of the transience of the present. In a startlingly apt image, in a poem called 'Present', Thomas describes the speaker as being 'at the switchboard of the exchanges of the people of all time', receiving their messages whether he will or no. As there is little joy, so there is little light. 'The universe is a large place with more of darkness than light', he says in 'The Listener in the Corner'. Any light in that darkness is merely 'life's decoy' he tells us in 'Almost', and in 'Incense' he describes dawn as 'disingenuous', attracting only to deceive.

And yet running through the poetry is a firm, if resigned and totally unillusioned, belief in God and the consolations of prayer. He does not speak as a poet who is disturbed by God's personal intervention in his life, as Herbert does, nor is he full of wonder at God's creation, as Hopkins is. The dominant attitude is, rather one of resolute acceptance of God's presence and power, and eventual recognition of the impossibility of ever defining the 'mystery at the cell's core' or the 'eternal silence that is the repose of God'. Where Herbert's God makes himself felt in the human world, and Hopkins's God through the natural world, Thomas's God makes his presence felt through abstract concepts and through a twentieth-century

awareness of the complexities of the physical universe: through
the 'unseen power whose sphere is the cell and the electron',
('Adjustments'); through 'that abstruse geometry that proceeds
enternally in the silence beyond right and wrong', ('At It'); through
'the colonisation by mind of untenanted space', and through 'signals
relayed to me from a periphery I comprehend'. ('Night Sky'). The
imagery draws on a vocabulary of advanced scentific knowledge
and of exploration in space.

The machine, which, in earlier poems such as 'Cynddylan on a
Tractor', (1952), had been seen as an ironically bright release from
the drudgery of labour, is seen now as the explicit enemy of mankind
ruthlessly destroying the true human spirit. In the opening poem of
H'm, (1972), Thomas presents a twenieth-century version of the
Fall, in which a modern Adam and Even face a transformed serpent:

> I took your hand
> Remembering you, and together,
> Confederates of the natural day,
> We went forth to meet the Machine.   ('Once')

Satan has found a new guise from which to tempt man. In Thomas's
recent poetry the wheels of the Machine ride roughshod over the
creeds and masterpieces of earlier ages. The new goal of mankind is
production. The poet is left to mourn hopelessly a lost human vision:

> Among the forests
> Of metal the one human
> Sound was the lament of
> The poets for deciduous language.   ('Postscript')

Even God is lost amidst the cold steel of a world ruled by machinery:

> 'Where are you?'
> he called, seeking himself among
> the dumb cogs and tireless camshafts.   ('God's Story')

The dominant tone of the recent poetry is interrogative. Questions
of direction, identity and understanding reverberate: 'Where shall
we go?'; 'Have I been too long on my knees worrying over the
obscurity of a message?'; 'Is there a knowlege not to be known?':
'What does it mean, life?'; 'Is there a place here for the spirit?'; 'Am
I too late?'. The questions are 'vague but formidable':

> We pass our hands
> over their surface like blind

> men, feeling for the mechanism
> that will swing them aside. They
> yield, but only to re-form
> as new problems; and one
> does not even do that
> but towers immovable
> before us.   ('The Answers')

They dominate *Frequencies*, the most recent collection, and indeed the closing lines of the last poem leave us with an unanswered question that echoes in our memory long after we have closed that book:

> Was the pilgrimage
> I made to come to my own
> self, to learn that in times
> like these and for one like me
> God will never be plain and
> out there, but dark rather and
> inexplicable, as though he were in here?   ('Pilgrimages')

Answers are elusive. In 'The Answer' Thomas tells us that faith and prayer offer occasional insight and understanding, but only 'after long on my knees in a cold chancel'. Such consolations are rare, however, and all too often passed by before recognised, as in the sonnet called 'The Bright Field':

> I have seen the sun break through
> to illuminate a small field
> for a while, and gone my way
> and forgotten it. But there was the pearl
> of great price, the one field that had
> the treasure in it. I realize now
> that I must give all that I have
> to possess it. Life is not hurrying
> on to a receding future, nor hankering after
> an imagined past. It is the turning
> aside like Moses to the miracle
> of the lit bush to a brightness
> that seemed as transitory as your youth
> once, but is the eternity that awaits you.

A comparison with Herbert's 'The Pearl' comes to mind. Herbert's poem is a witty and embellished allusion to the gift of God's grace described in Matthew 13. 45–6: Thomas's sonnet is a simple adaptation of three verses from St Matthew:

Again, the kingdom of heaven is like unto treasure hid in a field; the which when a man hath found, he hideth, and for joy thereof goeth and selleth all that he hath, and buyeth that field.

Again, the kingdom of heaven is like unto a merchant man, seeking goodly pearls:

Who, when he had found one pearl of great price, went and sold all that he had, and bought it.   (13. 44–6)

The echoes of this in Thomas's poem are distinct and clear, but it is noticeable how Thomas has subtly conflated the two parables. The rhetorical and measured rhythms of the authorised version have been assimilated and recast in a completely casual and natural tone of voice. The effect is symbolic rather than allegorical; the images speak for themselves rather than spell out a message. Just as the rhythms are simple, and the images pared down to the least explicitly symbolic level possible, so the formal movement from the octave to the sestet is as relaxed and carefree as the attention of the speaker who passed by the 'one field with treasure in it'. Only in the last five lines do the emphases become more pointed as Thomas moves back to the Old Testament and the image of Moses 'turned aside' (Exodus 3.3) to see God in the burning bush. Life, for Thomas, is not a matter of striving after some impossible dream in the future, or of clinging to some fading memory of the past; it is a matter of recognising the all too rare brightness in the present, and of being prepared to 'turn aside' from one's now narrow pathway to see the light existing outside the self. It is the simplicity, directness and depth with which these ideas are presented that makes this poem so striking.

I am reminded of something Thomas said in an interview with John Ormond for the film made for BBC television, broadcast in 1972. He was explaining why he chose to live in the country:

Overtones, those signals from an ever present reality. That's why I've chosen to live in the country because not only from the auditory point of view but also from the visual point of view – one has been blessed with *these sudden glimpses of eternity*. It's Francis Thompson who in his poem 'The Hound of Heaven' says:

> ever and anon a trumpet sounds
> From the hid battlements of Eternity;
> Those shaken mists a space unsettle, then
> Round the half-glimpsed turrets slowly
>   wash again.

The half-glimpsed turrets, the glimpses of this eternal ultimate reality which one gets in Wales when *the sun suddenly strikes through a gap in the clouds and falls on some small field* and the trees around. There is a kind of timeless quality about this, one feels. Well, this is eternity, if one could only lay hold on it. And, of course, then the cloud closes up again and the light fades and the scene's gone. But I firmly believe this, that eternity is not something over there, not something in the future; it is close to us, it is all around us and at any given moment one can pass into it; but there is something about our mortality, the fact that we are time-bound creatures, that makes it somehow difficult if not impossible to dwell, whilst we are in the flesh, to dwell permanently in that, in what I would call the Kingdom of Heaven. But that it is close and that we get these overtones, that we get these glimpses of it, is certainly my most deeply held conviction.

The italics are mine. I do not know whether Thomas gave this interview before or after he wrote 'The Bright Field', which first appeared in book form three years later, but the coincidence of idea and image is clearly more than accidental. That we get 'these sudden glimpses of eternity' is, as he says, his 'most deeply held conviction'.

What the reader feels in R. S. Thomas's poetry of the last decade is the power of his astringent mind and penetrating imagination articulating the soul's struggle to comprehend God's 'abstruse geometry that proceeds enternally in the silence beyond right and wrong, ('At It'). The strained precision of the vocabulary, the metaphysical originality of the imagery, the simple clarity of the symbolism, and the sensitively spare command of syntax and rhythm enforce the feeling that Thomas's recent religious poetry will eventually be as highly valued, and as greatly admired, as his earlier and more established poems about 'Wales and nature'. Thomas's sharp song has emerged from 'the adolescence of nature into the adult geometry of the mind'.

Source: excerpted from article ' "The Adult Geometry of the Mind": The Recent Poetry of R. S. Thomas', in *Little Review*, 6 (Huntington, West Virginia, 1980), pp. 12–14.

Joan F. Adkins R. S. Thomas and 'A Little Point' (1980)

It is man's tragedy that he must formulate patterns, and his glory that he can sometimes – when he needs to – break out of them.

George Whalley, *Poetic Process*

R. S. Thomas is acutely aware of the poet's role at a particular place and point in time. He concerns himself with a modern world progressively dehumanized by war and technology, and with Wales, increasingly dominated by industrial England. Thomas envisions the poet's responsibility as that of curing a sick culture, an attitude which requires that he be intelligible not only to the small coterie of initiates, but even to the uninitiates. 'This is what art could do', he writes, 'Interpreting faith / With serene chisel.'[1] Thomas's poems, rationally structured, strong, spare, and beautifully honed, reflect his ambivalent attitudes toward an indifferent God, a maleficent nature, and an inscrutable mankind. On this tension rests the argument of his poetry.

As W. B. Yeats sought 'an image of the modern mind's discovery of itself', so Thomas finds that image in the anguish of the present, often exacerbating his unitive role of poet-priest as he comes to terms with reality. In 'Temptation of a Poet', he confesses:

> The past calls with the cool smell
> Of autumn leaves, but the mind draws
> Me onward blind with the world's dust,
> Seeking a spring that my heart fumbles.

Thomas neither languishes in pastoral settings of a lost Golden Age nor proffers utopian remedies to the disease of the modern age. Since the priest-artist faces the same world that all other men face, it would be outrageous arrogance for him to assume that his faith provides him with a privileged perspective. Thomas does not suppose that he has been given exclusive charge of the truth about any aspect of human reality. His purpose is to reveal the stark irrevocability of things as they are.

Although his characteristic expression is austere, Thomas can deftly describe sheep with ears like stems of primroses and eyes like

'Two halves of a nut'. He believes in the power of the imagination to draw people together, but the problems of the world are too grave to be couched in flowery phrases – 'waste speech'. Images such as these, he writes, 'are for sheer fancy / To play with' ('Looking at Sheep'). Thomas contemplates himself and his destiny as a spiritual and self-conscious spokesman; and, although he cannot be categorically termed a religious poet – in the sense that Donne and Herbert and Crashaw are religious poets – his poems suggest a final position.

Paradoxically, at the same time Thomas unmasks stereotyped notions and rejects traditional poetic forms, he reveals an affinity with all those who think on the life of the soul-mystics, philosophers, artists. To this degree, R. S. Thomas and Meister Eckhart are kindred spirits, giving back to mankind a viable faith in 'the soul's good form'.[2] Eckhart writes:

The union of the soul with God is far more inward than that of the soul and body. . . . Now, I might ask, how stands it with the soul that is lost in God? Does the soul find herself or not? To this I will answer as it appears to me, that the soul finds herself in the point where every rational being understands itself with itself. Although it sinks in the eternity of the divine essence, yet it can never reach the ground. Therefore God has left a little point wherein the soul turns back upon itself and finds itself, and knows itself to be a creature.[3]

In our relative way of thinking, the finite and the infinite cannot be unified. But in Eckhart's thought, 'a little point' implies integration, not separation. When he says that 'God has left a little point', he reminds us that we are all finite beings, though the term 'rational being' warrants particular emphasis. We are 'creatures', and as such we 'can never reach the ground'; but to sink into 'the eternity of the divine essence' is to be already on the ground. Only when we *see* 'a little point' left by God do we return to ourselves and know that we are creatures. Eckhart's 'little point', then, is the eye: 'My eye and God's eye are one and the same – one in seeing, one in knowing, and one in loving.'[4] The ground is the divine essence, and the sinking is the reaching.

In a similar manner, R. S. Thomas finds, through the writing of poetry, 'a little point', and thus creates from the luminous instant of reality the character of eternity. His poem entitled 'Poetry for Supper' describes the two old men, 'glib with prose', drinking beer at an inn, where they argue the relative merits of poetic inspiration and craftsmanship. Thomas concludes that both qualities are essential:

> Sunlight's a thing that needs a window
> Before it enter a dark room,
> Windows don't happen.

We all share to some degree the capacity to see, to know, and to love. The artist differs, however, in his ability to organize his responses, and to organize them in their primal complexity. Nothing exists in isolation; reality involves relationship which, for human beings, is emotion. In 'Green Categories', Thomas defines reality as a universe of feeling:

> . . . Space and time
> Are not the mathematics that your will
> Imposes, but a green calendar
> Your heart observes; . . .

Vivid apprehension depends upon deep concern and, at the same time, deep concern clarifies and sharpens vision. To *see* with apathetic eyes is to lack the 'feeling' for what we see: it is, in the poet's words, 'Emptiness of the bare mind / Without knowledge, the frost / Of knowledge, where there is no love'.

The special gift of the poet is to find 'a little point' which will touch things into life, even if it demands a penetration into minds fractured by life, including his own. In his poem 'The Mill' Thomas describes a farmer who, 'Lying log heavy', waited nine years for death. While life marched bleakly on, the farmer's wife served him: 'He was one more beast / To be fed and watered / On that hill farm.' From a distance of twenty years, the persona recalls his own priestly duties: 'I read him the psalms, / Said prayers and was still.' The only sounds remaining were mice restling in the drawers and fire crackling in the shallow grate. Was one person's death worth this burden, the poet implicitly asks. Yet the experience creates and recreates the self:

> Had a seed of love,
> Left from the threshing,
> Found a crack in their hearts?

The question is rhetorical. The physical reality deepens the poet's spiritual awareness, as he starkly concludes the poem:

Nine years in that bed
From season to season
The great frame rotted,
While the past's slow stream,
Flowing through his head.
Kept the rusty mill
Of the mind turning –
It was I it ground.

If the poet is to see things as they really are, and be precise about them, he must also be precise about the feelings which attach him to them. The experience of 'The Mill' reveals the awful price man sometimes pays for human sympathy, which leaves at the same time an indelible mark of reality and value. This duality may be what Robert Frost had in mind when he said: 'The right reader of a good poem can tell the moment it strikes him that he has taken an immortal wound and knows that he will never get over it.'[5] Thomas's penchant for truth and incisive expression strikes a sharp blow at staid ideas. Through his persistent refusal to gloss the obvious facts, he establishes 'a little point' of faith. In 'Petition', he writes:

. . . One thing I have asked
Of the disposer of the issues
Of life: that truth should defer
To beauty. It was not granted.

Since Thomas, not unlike 'the disposer' of life's issues, refuses to relinquish truth for beauty, he brings to bear on his peasant figures a wide range of poetic sensibility. He brings compassion to a woman grown old and 'withering to waste', because she was so long neglected by a man whose days were 'lavished upon the land' ('Age'). With a touch of idealism, the poet admires a wife who wears a 'clean apron' and makes 'pastry in the great oven, / Sweetly and surely as hay making / In a June meadow' ('Farm Wife'). Thomas, somewhat in the vein of Wordsworth and the leech gatherer, draws strength from the gardener who continues his work with the land, while a 'corrosive ulcer' gnaws at his life ('The Gardener'). Conversely, the poet portrays a muck farmer who is out of harmony with man and nature, and hence deserves little sympathy: 'A man unfit' to breed sleek herds, his smile is 'rare' and his speech a 'rank garden'. Thomas concludes that it is better to leave him 'crazed and alone', with 'his warped heart' ('The Muck Farmer'). As for the meaning – we may benefit from a note in one of Coleridge's memorandum books: 'And yet what ample materials exist for a true & nobly-minded Psychologist – for in order to make fit use of these materials he must love and honour as well as understand, human nature – rather, he must love in order to understand it.'[6]

   In the haunting figure of Iago Prytherch, Thomas embodies his love for the Welsh hill country and the people who live there. 'Iago Prytherch, forgive my naming you', writes the poet. Because he chose a Welsh farmer as fit subject for poetry ('I took / Your rags for theme'). Thomas counters the world's graceless accusation:

> Fun? Pity? No word can describe
> My true feelings. I passed and saw you
> Labouring there, your dark figure
> Marring the simple geometry
> Of the square fields with its gaunt question.
> My poems were made in its long shadow
> Falling coldly across the page.

Yet even in his love, the poet reveals the 'thought's bareness' of the peasant farmer who, having spent a lifetime toiling on the soil, had no time for science and art, the 'furniture' of the mind ('Iago Prytherch'). In another poem 'Absolution' the poet begins: 'Prytherch, man, can you forgive.' A symbol of permanence in the midst of 'the world's roads', the farmer serves as a foil for the poet who, seeking meaning elsewhere, finds it 'too close for the mind's lenses to see'. Ultimately, it is Prytherch who lends the poet 'a little point', by giving back to life its own value:

> It was you who were right the whole time;
> Right in this that the day's end
> Finds you still in the same field
> In which you started, your soul made strong
> By the earth's incense, the wind's song.

   Through the image of Prytherch, however, emerges the poet's own examen. In his poem 'Servant' Thomas acknowledges his debt: 'You served me well, Prytherch.' The Welsh farmer 'served' to pose questions and doubts, though he did not give 'The whole answer'. Standing apart from the mainstream, 'Where life's flashier illustrations / Were marginal', Prytherch's 'service' was necessarily limited:

> . . . Is truth so bare
> So dark, so dumb, as on your hearth
> And in your company I found it?

Truth, for the poet, may also be found in the 'print of the sky', in 'the mind worked', and in the freedom of choice 'From life's bounty'. Yet the farmer's choice was not his own, and so his heart, 'not rich, nor fertile', yields but one crop. In this insight lies the poet's 'bread of truth'. Thomas's attitude is therefore ambivalent: the farmer's simple goodness untempered by reason is one-dimensional and, by inference, less than 'real' goodness. Although Prytherch's name is not mentioned in the poem 'Truth', most certainly the same image appears. The poet begins:

> He was in the fields, when I set out.
> He was in the fields, when I came back.

The life of centuries beckons the poet. At the same time, he interprets:

> It is the mind
> Calling you, eager to paint
> Its distances; but the truth's here.
> Closer than the world will confess,
> In this bare bone of life that I pick.

Thomas, a poet of autumnal tones, allows the mind's eye to survey the beauty of the last few leaves clinging to boughs of gold, and the image becomes a photograph, 'something to wear / Against the heart in the long cold' ('A Day in Autumn'). Nature is an evanescent painting, 'as slowly the cloud bruises / Are healed by sunlight'. Throughout history the 'great brush' has repeated its masterstrokes of light and distance, colors and forms. Yet the painting remains forever finished, to be observed by 'the tears' lenses' of mankind ('The View from the Window'). The tone of Thomas's poem 'A Blackbird Singing' is reminiscent of Thomas Hardy's 'The Darkling Thrush'. The song of the bird brings a 'sweet disturbance' – a tale of history's aftermath of love, joy and grief. The poet interprets:

> It seems wrong that out of this bird,
> Black, bold, a suggestion of dark
> Places about it, there yet should come
> Such rich music . . .

The blackbird, 'A slow singer', repeats the instinctive message of nature, 'fresh always with new tears'. The earth, Thomas writes, cannot be fully understood by logic, though logic dictates the reality which slumbers in 'Stone, tree and flower'. Even in the 'Constant aggression', there exist moments when man and nature can be at one, sharing their faith over 'a star's blue fire' ('Green Categories').

Thomas reveals a shifting attitude toward nature: the earth provides, to be sure, but not without exacting its toll. The farmer, 'Wresting hourly from the land / The soil's storage of sun', encounters the priest, and their glances meet 'With brute glumness'. Inherent in this vignette is an ironic question: Which of us serves a grateful master? ('Encounter'). Iago Prytherch serves the land for a lifetime, but the return is meagre 'seed sown upon the thin / Soil of a heart' ('Servant'). Always busy sharpening his blade 'On a cloud's edge', the Welsh farmer could never cultivate his mind, 'because of the great / Draught of nature sweeping the skull' ('Iago Prytherch').

At the center of Thomas's stark realism may be found 'a little point': in life's challenge itself lies the faith of man. The poet's finest attempt to reconcile the painful opposites of man and nature may be read in his poem 'The Cry':

> Don't think it was all hate
> That grew there; love grew there, too,
> Climbing by small tendrils where
> The warmth fell from the eyes' blue
> Flame. Don't think even the dirt
> And the brute ugliness reigned
> Unchallenged. Among the fields
> Sometimes the spirit, enchained
> So long by the gross flesh, raised
> Suddenly there its wild note of praise.

R. S. Thomas's prime concern lies in the release of the spirit from the bondage of 'gross flesh'. In tracing the progress of the soul, his poems unfurl 'Beauty, love, misery even, / Which has its seasons in the long growth / From seed to flesh, flesh to spirit' ('The Letter'). The poet shares with many of his contemporaries the conviction that we must cultivate 'those attributes of spirit that make the self worth redeeming once it has been fed and clothed and housed', so aptly expressed by the American scholar, William Mulder.[7]

Thomas believes in the cultivation of the mind, for knowledge is power. But knowledge alone is not enough: 'The nucleus / In the atom awaits / Our bidding' ('No Answer'). Only through the closest kind of human relationship – the relationship of love – can he begin to penetrate the inner nature of life. Spiritual awareness, not material power, is the end of knowledge. Indeed, there is no particular power or worth in knowing facts as facts in an ordinary way. The capacity for a kind of love which becomes progressively sensitive and all-embracing redeems the spirit from abstractions, and thus attaches degrees of value to reality. In his poem 'Composition' Thomas expresses his faith in the power of art to ennoble the soul of man. Before writing a poem, he must measure 'the thought's height / Above the earth', which is itself 'hedged thickly with the heart's cares'. The alternatives represent a fusion of themes: to find 'a little point' in the heart of life is to wound and to heal. The poet concludes:

> He tried truth; but the pen's scalpel tip
> Was too sharp; thinly the blood ran
> From unseen wounds, but too red to dip
> Again in, so back where he began,
> He tried love; slowly the blood congealed
> Like dark flowers saddening a field.

Through the shock of discovery, art can stir and quicken an awareness of realities that impinge upon us from beyond ourselves and it can summon us into the presence of what is apart from, and transcendent to, the human mind.

Thomas seeks to incarnate reality, and he himself becomes the medium through which that reality may pass: if poetry is the sunlight, the poet is the window. He believes, as we have seen, that man remains a diminished being until a higher principle breathes upon him. It is through the poet's search for God, a remote and indifferent God, that the self becomes emptied, annihilated, remade. The persona in 'Making', a poem of the myth of creation, is God. The description of the birth of the world emerges as a pleasant and selfish diversion: God furnished the earth with moss and grass – 'To my taste'; then it seemed proper to create animals – 'To divert me'; next he called forth all the bacteria from the 'primordial' depths. Still 'an absence' disturbed him, and so he slept and dreamed, then fashioned man in his own likeness:

> . . . in love with it
> For itself, giving it freedom
> To love me; risking the disappointment.

In a similar manner, the poem 'Female' represents a reversal of the myth of the Fall. In the traditional version, Satan's words had brought to fruition Eve's own narcissistic daydreams. According to Thomas, man was betrayed by himself, not woman. He (Adam, we may suppose), 'Crazy with the crushed smell / Of her hair', spoke the words of man's own conscience. After the Fall, 'her forked laughter' drove him into shame,

> . . . and his leaves fell
> Silently round him, and he hung there
> On himself, waiting for the God to see.

For Thomas, however, God remains aloof, and the burden of life unexplained. In the poem 'He' the poet, symbolic of man, 'holds out his two / Hands, calloused with the long failure / Of prayer'.

In Thomas's attempt to establish some connection between God and his creation he chooses an appropriate title – 'Echoes'. The poem begins: 'What is this? said God'. But no answer is forthcoming. The creatures' obstinate refusal to answer enrages God, who senses their concession of his absence. When God calls to them – 'Where are you?' – the shapes come forth, 'riding the echo', and comply with his desire to build a kingdom on earth in his honor. The poet concludes:

> . . . On the altars
> They made him the red blood
> Told what he wished to hear.

With still greater harshness is the poet's symbol of the church in his poem 'The Island':

> And God said, I will build a church here
> And cause this people to worship me,
> And afflict them with poverty and sickness
> In return for centuries of hard work
> And patience.

The results are severe: hardened hearts and limited minds and unanswered prayers. Even from those who choose to worship, the best are 'thrown back into the sea'. In the poem 'H'm' Thomas reverses with bitter irony the theme of 'God is love'. The poem begins: 'and one said / speak to us of love'. The preacher utters the word *God*, but it does not fill the void, and so he is asked once more. In the final description, the children with 'big bellies' and 'bow / legs' are too weak from life's burdens and injustices to intuit any association between the words *God* and *Love*.

Concerning the function of poetry, Nathan A. Scott, Jr. makes a valuable statement:

We have long said that poetry's great gift to man is an affair of *katharsis*, and it may well be that that experience involves, fundamentally, the profound relief that is to be had when we succeed in gaining such release from the prison of the mind as enables us simply to contemplate the intractable givenness of reality . . .[8]

R. S. Thomas's poetry is indeed 'an affair of *Katharsis*'. His poem 'Via Negativa' is a metaphorical inversion of an ancient spiritual tradition. In the experience of the mystics, both pagan and Christian, the negative way defines the distance between the Creator and the created. The religious spirit, recognizing the ineffability of God, becomes absorbed and numbed with great admiration. The mystics conclude that God may be known through the obscurity and the clouds, an inaccessible light which no man can see. In this divine ignorance, according to the tradition, lies the true knowledge of God, whose substance is beyond mortal comprehension. Although Thomas recognizes the distance between man and God, he does not perceive it as a result of the mystic experience. He writes:

> Why no! I never thought other than
> That God is that great absence
> In our lives, the empty silence
> Within, the place where we go
> Seeking, not in hope to
> Arrive or find.

For the mystics, God is a 'presence'; for Thomas, he is an 'absence'. We try to see people and places as though God had also looked at them, but we 'miss the reflection'. If man has disappointed God, Thomas implies, it is well to remember that God created man in his own likeness.

With so much negation of traditional spiritual thought, we may ask: Wherein lies 'a little point' of faith? Thomas offers a kind of resolution in his poem 'Invitation'. Two voices of Temptation speak: one holds out the chapel as a means of the soul's salvation; the other tempts with life itself, 'Like an express train running / To time'. Religion or a meaningless existence represent, as Thomas realises, fierce alternatives. He therefore concludes that reality lies in the flame of 'the small soul' fanned to life by one's own breath. 'Does the soul find herself or not?' asks Meister Eckhart. And he answers in the affirmative: '. . . the soul finds herself in the point where every rational being understands itself with itself.'

Reality in its fullest sense is accessible to those who have the greatest depth of awareness. The burden of life itself is a process of discovery: 'Therefore God has left a little point wherein the soul turns back upon itself and finds itself, and knows itself to be a creature.' R. S. Thomas shares with Meister Eckhart that spark of faith which keeps the soul alive. In his attempt to make sense of man, nature, and God, the poet plunges into the raw experience of life, surviving the spiritual upheaval and transmuting baser metals into gold. As Thomas discovers himself in his art, so he reflects both himself and the world. The supreme value of his discovery lies in its communication to others.

SOURCE: article, 'R. S. Thomas and "A Little Point"', in *Little Review*, 6 (Huntington, West Virginia, 1980), pp. 15–19.

NOTES

1. From 'Souillac: Le Sacrifice d'Abraham'. Subsequent poems are identified in context and are taken from three volumes of R. S. Thomas's poetry: *The Bread of Truth* (London, 1964); *Poetry for Supper* (London, 1967); and *H'm* (London, and New York, 1972).

2. The phrase is Thomas's. In the Introduction to *A Choice of George Herbert's Verse* (London, 1967), he commends Herbert's 'relevance for today' in an expression which aptly reflects his own: 'It is reason, not so much tinged with, as warmed by emotion, and solidly based on order and discipline, the soul's good form' (p. 17).

3. Quoted in D. T. Suzuki, *Mysticism: Christian and Buddhist, The Eastern and Western Way* (New York, 1957), p. 61

4. Ibid., p. 63.

5. Quoted in George Whalley, *Poetic Process: An Essay in Poetics* (Cleveland, Ohio, 1967), p. 40.

6. Ibid., p. 38.

7. Dr Mulder's observation, in 'India Revisited: A Brief Report' (University of Utah, March, 1974), seems particularly appropriate: In defence of cloistered studies, he writes: 'The answer must be that we should not add poverty of spirit to the poverty that is all around us' (p. 4). R. S. Thomas certainly supports this thesis.

8. N. A. Scott, Jr, 'Faith and Art in a World Away', in William J. Hardy and Max Westbrook (eds), *Twentieth-Century Criticism* (New York, 1974), p. 433.

> Always the same hills
> Crowd the horizon,
> Remote witnesses
> Of the still scene.
>
> And in the foreground
> The tall Cross,
> Sombre, untenanted,
> Aches for the Body
> That is back in the cradle
> Of a maid's arms   ('Pietà')

'Always the same hills'; R. S. Thomas's poems usually begin in a very distinctive manner. The first line does not appear to be the logical start of a particular thought, or even of a particular experience or event, but to be the moment when some profoundly meditated anguish, or image, forces itself into words. Immense silence of the hills, in the background. History, waiting still longer, for its dead centre. The Virgin, surely not weeping as she receives the Body. A man, brooding on life, and focusing on a brilliant lyrical or dramatic image, or startling statement, as some long notion intensifies and compresses itself towards form. The poem is precipitated, with unusual and brooding power, into the ambience where it then exists: language, submitting after long struggle, to will.

'Always': many of R. S. Thomas's poems home in upon a vivid image which is characteristically in, but not of, time. Some perception, arrested in time and space, acquires tragic or elemental colouring for the reader momentarily before he senses, also, the consolation ('Dear parents, I forgive you my life'; 'Yes: that's how I was'; 'It will always win'; 'I want you to know how it was'). The consolation, coming as it does from some region of consciousness or creation wholly different from the often savage insight, is hard to pin down. Some long-built-up or pent-up force is precipitated, and the poem as a whole seems to be precisely the right weight, and length, to bear it. Only once or twice, as in the beautiful 'The airy tomb', does Thomas take a longer flight, floating more serenely above his sombre tale.

All of Thomas's readers recognise this tone – which one calls Welsh, or laconic, or lacerating, or ironically detached, or bitterly compassionate, or rarely empathetic, or universally human, for all these apparent contraries meet in it – only, it is never despairing, though the word 'despair' sometimes rings out unforgettably. There is pared down linguistic austerity, always reaching towards some apparent simplicity – though when Thomas encounters other people's attempts in this direction, they may wryly amuse him.

> Rose Cottage, because it had
> Roses! If all things were as
> Simple. . . .

Yet this search is also pre-eminently his own, the endlessly sought-after illusion of his kind of art. Kingsley Amis has written of it perceptively in words which, recognising the note of linguistic sparseness, draw attention also to the complex and vivid imagery that accompanies this: 'His imagery, thickly clustered as it frequently is, and made to proliferate and interconnect with great brilliance, is built upon a simple foundation of earth, trees, snow, stars, and wild creatures. To describe the effect of his work it is enough to say that he often moves to tears, and that certain lines of his impress themselves instantly, and perhaps ineradicably on the mind.'

'Pietà' is one of those rare short poems that keeps most of its secrets, look at it though we will. One has to go to 'Western Wind' and one or two of the ballads, to 'The Sick Rose', and Blake's lyrics, to a rather rare species of poetry in fact, to find similar effects. It is precisely the kind of poem that the Imagists wanted to write, but somehow never could; the Imagist theories are fascinating, but where is even one Imagist poem that lives up to them? As Thomas himself has laconically noted, 'It seems that it is always easier for poets to evolve theories of language than to stick to them.' In 'Pietà' it seems that all the human emotions are transferred to objects apparently inanimate, and the real emotion, the grief beyond expression, to the Cross. The hills 'Crowd the horizon', suddenly very much present, yet still 'Remote' as they watch; and the scene remains 'still'. And then, as is Thomas's way, the strange note enters – an effect encountered also, though in a very different mood and with more conscious theological point, in the famous Good

Friday hymn: *Crux fidelis, inter omnes / Arbor una nobilis: / Nulla silva talem profert, / Fronde, flore, germine. . . . / Dulce lignum, dulce clavos, / Dulce pondus sustinet.*

The instrument of death and torture has, as instrument of salvation, its own ineffable moment, and its own dereliction. For thirty years or so the Virgin has 'ached' with Christ, perhaps never more than at the foot of the Cross; for three hours his body has ached on the Cross, to the point of death. But it is not the Virgin, or Christ, who aches in this poem: it is the Cross itself, 'Sombre, untenanted' (marvellous word), which grieves, its purpose fulfilled now (*consummatum est*) and the tree, which went to make it, good now only for superstition, or decay, or burning, like any other wood in the world. It is not as if Thomas is telling us that human torturers suffer with their victims, but something far more elusive, more totally and inexorably Christian. If this weird and eerie paradox means anything, it means salvation ('salvation acquired by an increased guilt', as he writes in a later poem). *Rex tremendae majestatis*: and should the Cross which, in its destined moment, has been the death of the King, not ache in bereavement as the Body leaves it – for what created thing could fulfil such a role, and not take on something of the consciousness and pain? In this short poem, life passes into death; the Christ is dead, his voice which raised others will not raise himself; Easter morning is an infinity away. So, at the end, Christ returns to the beginning, to the arms of the maid. She has lost him in life, through the normal processes of adulthood, and perhaps in a way special also to herself in its pain ('Woman, what have I to do with you?' – John 2:4; 'Then one said to him, behold, your mother and your brethren stand outside desiring to speak with you. But he answered and said, Who is my mother? and who are my brethren? And he stretched his hand towards his disciples, and said, Behold, my mother and my brethren' – Matthew 12:47–50; . . . 'And if any man come to me and hate not his father, and mother, and wife, and children, and brethren, and sisters, yes and his own life also, he cannot be my disciple' – Luke 14:26). Again, she has lost him now in death. Her own paps no longer give milk, and if they could it would be useless. At the moment of *pietà*, the beginning comes full circle, and is *really* the end. It is the moment when Christ is totally human, and totally dead. All he has said and suffers remains now in the balance, in vacuum. Only the Cross feels and 'Aches' since it, at least, has had its moment and its grief, and is now finished with, whatever other end there might be.

'Pietà' is a poem which contains as many subtle intimations as does Michelangelo's carving. Everything that is not present in both – the incredible absences – contributes to the effect. ('There were days', Thomas writes in a later poem about the Holy Spirit, 'so beautiful the emptiness / it might have filled, / its absence / was as its presence.') Could the tone be described as neutral? Only, I would say, in the most *literal* sense. . . .

. . . 'Here' (from *Tares*, 1961) . . . discovers . . . multiple questions lurking under an apparently simple surface, and . . . seemingly two wholly different interpretations contained in the one artefact. If the images are taken as metaphor – and it seems that for most readers, this is the first natural response – you have a poem about 'man' coming to evolutionary, or possibly to adult, self-consciousness:

> I am a man now.
> Pass your hand over my brow:
> You can feel the place where the brains grow.

The 'brain' is the new feature, allowing the unnamed speaker to look back, seeing 'The footprints that led up to me'; and the rest of the imagery, powerfully organic and elemental, could be interpreted either as the human race coming to consciousness of itself (something more than animal) or as an individual becoming aware of himself as unique being (something more than child). But knowledge is suffering: the poem records strong perversities in the knowledge, hands that 'will not do as I say', prayers unanswered, inner will violated. Perhaps the head might have been (or might be) the original flaw – yet 'here', the place of the poem's title, ends with the strange, and apparently opposed assertion:

> It is too late to start
> For destinations not of the heart.
> I must stay here, with my hurt.

The 'destinations' of 'the heart', perhaps too late discovered or rediscovered, or perhaps recognised now as a possible evolutionary path which has not viably been taken, appear in conflict with the head and the 'brains'. Has the evolution of higher intelligence, of more sensitive awareness, brought to man only an increased awareness of the meaningless of his life?

Taken in this way, the poem might seem to affirm not religious belief, but bitter atheism; at the very least, an unhealed experience of the absence of God. It is undeniable that the major religious poems which have been written later can, and do, strike some readers in this light. . . . But, if we look again at 'Here', allowing something like an optical illusion to happen, it offers back a startlingly different report. If the images are taken literally and not metaphorically, surely we have a poem about one particular man, in one place? The mysterious image including 'swift satellites' and the assertion 'the clock of my whole being is slow' could intimate darkness over the face of the earth. If so, the claim for special purity in the third stanza would be explained by virgin birth; the unmoving hands in stanza four by actual nails (never far from Thomas's imagination) . . . the cry 'Does no God hear when I pray?' as the special anguish of '*Eloi, Eloi, lama sabachthani?*', and the final stanza as the *consummatum est*: a destiny now accepted to the ultimate point of no return. On this reading, the opening stanzas turn inside out. 'I am a man now' means not, 'I am a man, no longer an animal or a child' but 'I am a man now, no longer God': the witness of the 'brains' meaning Incarnation. In fact, 'brains' are not really a distinguishing mark between man and the brutes, or between grown man and child (though the position and importance ascribed to them may be); certainly for Christ, the brains would be full awareness of the Word made *flesh*. The 'hurt' discovered 'here' is no longer a special anguish of our modern dilemma, but the mysterious task of salvation, foreseen before the creation itself. We have, in fact, a poem about Christ, at the moment when his death is upon him, and God appears to be absent from God.

To see this is to become aware that 'ambivalence' is at best a weak word to describe the poem, which is bifocal in a specially radical way. I do not think the effect can possibly be accidental (though this is not to say that it was necessarily 'intended', by the poet, in any crude sense). If images, differently interpreted, produce what at first seems to be a wholly different poem, the phenomenon cannot be ascribed to a mere trick in the use of language, or in the nature of words. Rather, the images do *in fact* work as they do, for readers who have any knowledge of Christian theology – almost as if witnessing to the Cross on their own. Is there something *in* the Cross ('the original fork / in existence', as it is called in 'Amen') which by its actual nature bypasses theology and, at the level of language and image, testifies to itself? 'I am a man now': the image

of evolved man, alone in a creation where God is dead, is held in
exact silhouette against the other image of Christ on the Cross,
when God is absent. If the Christian religion has this paradox at its
heart, perhaps it is not irrelevant to modern doubt after all, but
simply an anticipation of it by 2000 years. And, if the revelation of
love is 'Here', where the title directs us, then Christian faith and
love have perhaps always been odder than naïve belief, or unbelief,
would like to suppose. Such a vision is closer to Greek tragedy, to
Hindu mythology, to agnostic doubt, even to atheism, than it is to
middle-class churchgoing; it may well prove closer to the original
New Testament documents, stripped of their deceptive familiarity,
as well.

Thomas's own churches are often empty of worshippers, and this
is no unmixed blessing, since when they come, as in 'Service', they
may be merely the Cross for a private crucifixion of the priest:

> We stand looking at
> Each other. I take the word 'prayer'
> And present it to them. I wait idly,
> Wondering what their lips will
> Make of it. But they hand back
> Such presents. I am left alone
> With no echoes to the amen
> I dreamed of. I am saved by music
> From the emptiness of this place
> Of despair. As the melody rises
> From nothing, their mouths take up the tune,
> And the roof listens. I call on God
> In the after silence, and my shadow
> Wrestles with him upon a wall
> Of plaster, that has all the nation's
> Hardness in it. They see me thrown
> Without movement of their oblique eyes.

We are to hear much, from now on, of the priest alone on his knees,
praying without certainty and almost without hope, as the silence
closes in, and only one sound remains:

> There is no other sound
> In the darkness but the sound of a man
> Breathing, testing his faith
> On emptiness, nailing his questions
> One by one to an untenanted cross.   ('In Church')

If we had Thomas's poetry to this point alone, he would still rank

among the truly important moderns. But it is the three volumes of
the 1970s (*H'm* appeared in 1972) which take him into a still rarer
class of excellence. As the religious quest comes to the fore, and the
dialectic between poem and poem reaches new complexity, he takes
his place . . . among the very greatest creators of this century. . . .

. . . Increasingly, Thomas sets up echoes between his poems, as Yeats
did, mutually enriching and elusive, to an almost equal degree. Does he
believe, does he not believe? – as in Yeats, so in Thomas, these very
questions seem futile – something left over from childhood, or innocence,
left far behind. . . . First, 'The Kingdom', from *H'm* (1972):

> It's a long way off but inside it
> There are quite different things going on:
> Festivals at which the poor man
> Is king and the consumptive is
> Healed; mirrors in which the blind look
> At themselves and love looks at them
> Back; and industry is for mending
> The bent bones and the minds fractured
> By life. It's a long way off, but to get
> There takes no time and admission
> Is free, if you will purge yourself
> Of desire, and present yourself with
> Your need only and the simple offering
> Of your faith, green as a leaf.

'The Kingdom' has something of the rare economy of Yeats's 'An
Irish Airman Foresees His Death'. There are powerful contrasts
which might signify mutual cancellation, or a strange fulfilment,
since the driving emotion is at once apparent, and hard to pin down.
'It's a long way off': the opening phrase, later repeated, demands
teasing clarity of utterance, though whether wistfulness, bitterness
or mockery predominate, who is to say? Sufficient, no doubt, that
the poem's first half rehearses the essence of the kingdom as Christ
proclaimed it, in some ways enhancing its fairy-tale charm and
uncancelled allure. That this vision resembles neither the Church
of Christ in any of its visible branches nor any perceptible realities
in the world that we know is likewise apparent, with a poignancy
impossible to miss. Is the poem's indictment chiefly of the Church,
or of Christ's original vision? A real question – yet, if the kingdom
is impossible, how comes its power to haunt unnumbered lives
(including Thomas's own)?

In the second part, the price of admission is again impeccably

scriptural, though posed with a simple (or artful) directness that
staggers the mind. Sunday by Sunday, such sentiments resound in
hymns, ring out in scripture, are expounded in sermons: day by day
they mock, or are mocked by, the Church. Note the extraordinary
neutrality of the last lines, actively defying us – since, if we read
them aloud, we have somehow to declare ourselves, like it or not:
'. . . your faith, green as a leaf', 'the simple offering' – simple as
curing the blind, mending the world, loving mankind. . . . The sting
of this poem is surely its appearance of innocence, as its unanswered
questions (savage indictment? – betrayed salvation? – pure
nonsense?) tug at the mind. I am reminded of Dostoevsky's Grand
Inquisitor, indicting the returned Christ from his own worldly
wisdom: how dared Christ imagine that his terrible 'gifts' (love,
freedom, healing) would remain in the Church, or meet real human
needs? In the parable, Christ is dumb before his accuser, as in the
original story: at the end, he kisses the old man's cheek. The kiss
burns there, and the old man releases him from a second immolation;
but the old man does not change his views.

   At this moment precisely, the poem turns inside out, a perfect
optical illusion (like 'Here' before it), so that for a moment one
wonders how one could doubt the kingdom at all? The lost paradise,
the promised eternity – are these not perpetual archetypes; and is
not 'mending / The bent bones and the minds fractured / By life'
a major reality – among surgeons, psychotherapists, day-to-day
exercises of generosity and friendship – despite the mockery cast
round it by the self-styled 'churches' of Christ? One recalls that
Christ called his kingdom a leaven, not a political formula; and that
leaven is hidden, has to be looked for, but does have its effect. Christ
himself said that not all who say 'Lord, Lord' to him enter the
kingdom; he pointed to children, casualities, outcasts when asked
for a clue. Perhaps Wordsworth's 'Tintern Abbey' will also be
recalled, and allied poems: notably Wordsworth's ascent, from
admitted sublimity, to the yet greater reality: 'that best portion of
a good man's life; / His little, nameless, unremembered acts / Of
kindness and of love'. From here, a return to Thomas's poem is
simple, and to the particular scriptural image that clearly lurks.
Christ, confronted by a blind suppliant (Luke 18:41), asks a simple
question, 'What would you have me to do?' The reply, 'Lord, that
I might have my sight', is granted; and the first image the blind
man sees is Love looking back at him.

Like other optical illusions, this poem can turn back on itself a few moments later, leaving us staring bleakly, again, at the 'to get / There' clause. A poem of faith, a poem of doubt, or something more elusive? – for readers of Yeats, the problem is familiar enough, if not in this guise.

I start from this poem since it may be a clue to the volume, where alternations of view seem often carefully placed. From man's disappointment, through necessary complexity, to God's disappointment: we can make the journey backwards, or forwards, or shuttle to and from. In 'Petition' we face this:

> Seeking the poem
> In the pain, I have learned
> Silence is best, paying for it
> With my conscience, I am eyes
> Merely, witnessing virtue's
> Defeat; seeing the young born
> Fair, knowing the cancer
> Awaits them. One thing I have asked
> Of the disposer of the issues
> Of life: that truth should defer
> To beauty. It was not granted. . . .

But 'Via Negativa', though almost as bleak, at least embodies traditional spirituality:

> His are the echoes
> We follow, the footprints he has just
> Left. We put our hands in
> His side hoping to find
> It warm. We look at people
> And places as though he had looked
> At them, too; but miss the reflection

– and this is followed, as if in counterpoint, by one of God's soliloquies, in which the Creator laments the desertion, of himself, by the being made in his likeness:

> I slept and dreamed
> Of a likeness, fashioning it,
> When I woke, to a slow
> Music; in love with it
> For itself, giving it freedom
> To love me; risking the disappointment.   ('Making')

Looking at the volume, one can see a group of three poems together, clustered near the centre, all of which – but with mounting savagery –

record God's terrible and inexplicable curse on man ('Ruins', 'The Island' and 'He'). More spread out, there are groups that could spell out man's disappointment with God, and God's disappointment with man. Between these, there are new themes appearing – notably, two poems of ironic intent concerning the Church obliquely ('Acting' and 'All Right'), and one concerning it very directly (the title poem, 'H'm'), and poems in which 'The Machine' appears almost as Frankenstein: a creation made perhaps to punish man, but now running out of control of God Himself ('Once' and 'Other'). The older theme of the Cross is less evident, though at least two poems ('Cain' and 'The Coming') add yet further perspectives to Thomas's long fascination with this great symbol joining present and past.

But maybe it is the new savagery which dominates *H'm*, which makes it Thomas's most memorable and most terrible volume to date. The opening of 'Soliloquy' fuses Jehovah and Zeus, in images of apocalypse:

> And God thought: Pray away,
> Creatures; I'm going to destroy
> It. The mistake's mine,
> If you like. I have blundered
> Before

while the closing poem is a rare mingling of violence, cynicism and finally controlled laughter and compassion, in the image of an idiot riding a bumper-car at a fair:

> This is mankind
> Being taken for a ride by a rich
> Relation. The responses are fixed:
> Bump, smile; bump, smile. And the current
>
> Is generated by the smooth flow
> Of the shillings. This is an orchestra
> Of steel with the constant percussion
> Of laughter. But where he should be laughing
> Too, his features are split open, and look!
> Out of the cracks come warm, human tears.

So, as men's machines kill Prytherch, Prytherch becomes still more evidently, at least by implication, man's image. But Thomas, as the 1970s progress, has new things to add.

In *Laboratories of the Spirit* (1975) certain themes, perceptible earlier, emerge far more clearly – the limitations of language; the positive absence (or perversity) of God; flaws or apparent flaws in the very nature of creation, and salvation; the indissoluble union of God and Jesus, in a manner unknown to previous theology. This faith – if such it is – is not in any normal sense incarnational; even poems where the beauty of nature is acknowledged contain details which seem to forbid any direct leap to revelation. In 'The Flower', the 'riches' of 'the earth, the sea, / the immensity / of the broad sky' are acknowledged as both asked for, and granted; yet the poet turns away to another, invisible universe 'whose roots were not / in the soil, nor its petals the colour / of the wide sea', where his own lonelier and different battle for understanding is fought out:

> its own species with its own
> sky over it, shot
> with the rainbow of your coming and going.

And even in 'Good', the final poem, the old man who recalls life with contentment is surrounded by ambiguity of detail: a 'chill in the flesh', and a nature where 'The kestrel goes by with fresh prey / In its claws'.

'Sea-watching' presents a lovely image of the Holy Spirit, watched for through a lifetime, and wonderfully elusive:

> Ah, but a rare bird is
> rare. It is when one is not looking,
> at times one is not there
>   that it comes.

Thomas is not a poet of transfiguration, of the coming of the Spirit and the witness of holiness, in any obvious sense; his poems have few saints, though . . . the anguish and brokenness of the Welsh peasants is indeed a witness to the divine, if one has eyes to see in the great darkness of life. No: Thomas is now, as always, a poet of the Cross; and the Cross without the exegesis or piety of the ages to help it – more than ever facing us with its own starkness, as God's side of the dialogue. 'Poste Restante' opens with the possibility that the Cross itself might grind 'into dust / under men's wheels', just as it might shine 'brightly as a monument to a new era', and with this huge possibility open, his poem is a bleak record of the anguish of a priest *now*, compressed between its first line, 'I want you to know how it was,' and its last, 'you, friend, who will know what happened'. Many poems, such as 'Emerging', 'The Hand' and 'The Combat',

conduct a kind of imaginary dialogue with God – in which are faced
such possibilities as God's own surprise at, and challenge by,
'the machine'; God's possible impotence or unwillingness as the
explanation of unanswered prayer: God's dismay at his creation, or
almost demonic laughter in the face of it. This technique, which we
have encountered earlier, and which developed in *H'm*, is now
central. The image of Wrestling Jacob is used more than once,
always with ironic inversions. In 'The Hand', we are confronted
with a silent battle between God and the hand he has made – the
hand pleading its own need to be blessed, pleading God's own need
for the works it will do:

> But God, feeling the nails
> in his side, the unnerving warmth
> of the contact, fought on in
> silence. This was the long war with himself
> always foreseen, the question not
> to be answered. What is the hand
> for? The immaculate conception
> preceding the delivery
> of the first tool? 'I let you go',
> he said, 'but without blessing.
> Messenger to the mixed things
> of your making, tell them I am.'

. . . There are two poems in *Laboratories of the Spirit* which stand out,
. . . 'Rough' and 'Amen' . . . whether they turn out to be new
departures, or a final summing up of the old. First, 'Rough':

> God looked at the eagle that looked at
> the wolf that watched the jack-rabbit
> cropping the grass, green and curling
> as God's beard. He stepped back;
> it was perfect, a self-regulating machine
> of blood and faeces. One thing was missing:
> he skimmed off a faint reflection of himself
> in sea-water; breathed air into it,
> and set the red corpuscles whirling. It was not long
> before the creature had the eagle, the wolf and
> the jack-rabbit squealing for mercy. Only the grass
> resisted. It used it to warm its imagination
> by. God took a handful of small germs
> sowing them in the smooth flesh. It was curious,
> the harvest: the limbs modelled an obscene
> question, the head swelled, out of the eyes came
> tears of pus. There was the sound

> of thunder, the loud, uncontrollable laughter of
> God, and in his side like an incurred stitch, Jesus.

I think we must accept that there is in this volume an element of experiment, of playing with notions, which has been a characteristic from the first, but only now fully declares itself. If I am right, each poem is a tentative whole, an autonomous creation, but the full effect depends upon dialogue. The result is not unlike that familiar in Yeats, as I have already hinted, though the two poets differ greatly in their religious vision.

Readers of Yeats are teased continually by poems which appear to work out a perfect if internally intricate statement of a theme or themes, but which then give place to other poems where different yet equally authoritiative effects are achieved. A tone of almost prophetic assurance overlays highly shifting and tentative explorations; no single poem can be paraphrased, and often a criss-cross of echoes and references seems the best approach to interpretation. In the growing body of art, we then become aware of coherence, individuality, a highly distinctive approach to life, which must in some sense correspond to the 'poet's' explorations . . . .

Thomas's recurring themes are naturally different, but the best comment on his poems is often, in the same way, an interplay of echoes. The play of opposites moves between great tenderness and savage, yet always somehow unexpected, violence. The tone, though frequently an instrument to underline the violence rather than a check upon it, has also a deliberate extravagance that acts as warning. Clearly, any single poem is not the last word: and, if it were, the others would be impoverished rather than enriched. But, equally clearly, a poem such as 'Rough' could be the last word: no doubt, some men might discover in it a lucid, sufficient statement of the universe, as they know it.

What sort of God do we find in 'Rough'? He could be a monster, if moral judgements were made. But the moral judgements would have to be imported from outside, and where then would they come from? The God could be scientist experimenting, making a creation of horror. 'It was perfect': the notion of perfection is aesthetic; and perhaps an intellectual 'self-regulating machine' of some kind – perpetual motion? – is one of the oldest desires of ever-hopeful men, offended by transience. 'One thing was missing': this ironic comment, of obscure direction, falls into the poem. God inserts into creation the image of himself, made not of earth and air but of water and air –

the water capturing the notion of reflection, but also distortion, in the last creature made. The 'one thing missing' proves to be the greatest killing-machine of them all. Note the word 'mercy' in this unpropitious context – presumably, squealing to be let off death, or, alternatively, to be killed painlessly. The scene seems fitter for a Hobbesian universe, where God is non-existent, and life a mere play of blind forces, than for a universe made by a monster. Perhaps the truly disconcerting factor is that God's response to the squeal, if that's what it is (though the parenthesis about the grass allows us to disconnect the two if we wish), is finally to throw in 'germs', which, presumably, bring a horrible death by physical disintegration – to whom? It is indisputable that in our own lifetime man threw a handful of germs into a world of unwanted rabbits, and produced symptoms akin to those described in this poem. If man treats the creation over which he has godlike powers in this way, might this be after all more the God that man makes in his image than the other way round? But at least there is a sign, thunder: followed by a strange conclusion. The God of the poem ceases to be the intellectual maker of a 'perfect, a self-regulating machine' and becomes himself instinctual, uncontrollable. The laughter of God may be purely demonic, but the consequence is apparent – not perfect mechanism after all, but a flaw, fatal to God: 'And in his side like an incurred stitch, Jesus'. 'Incur' is defined usually as 'a risk run' – often with the added suggestion of recklessness, or deliberate criminality. But it does have the secondary meaning of 'running up against': a consequence not to be evaded, given the course or direction; the courage needed for a difficult and dangerous undertaking. Whatever we make of God here and in the other poems, Jesus goes with him; and with Jesus go the nails, the Cross, the pain.

The only thing that seems remotely detached from disaster is the grass – 'green and curling as God's beard' (a deliberately unusual anthropomorphic variant) warming its imagination (what does grass imagine?) at man's cruelty. Grass is important to most of Thomas's people ('And the world will grow to a few lean acres of grass'). The peasants tear their living from reluctant, infertile soil, and the grass is there always, a consolation and a beauty so usual as to fade beyond the border of consciousness, perhaps because men who now 'operate on the earth's body' with their machines, for produce, still find the grass useless for food.

'Rough' would seem to suggest a creation flawed not accidentally, but in its inception. It is not a random but a planned artefact, but the creator is schizoid, or at least an amoral perfectionist whose energies have run out of control. The 'perfection' envisaged is of blood and faeces: man the image of God, or, possibly, God the image of man; and, at the heart, the inescapable God–man 'incurred'.

Now let us turn to 'Amen':

> It was all arranged:
> the virgin with child, the birth
> in Bethlehem, the arid journey uphill
> to Jerusalem. The prophets foretold
> it, the scriptures conditioned him
> to accept it. Judas went to his work
> with his sour kiss; what else
> could he do?
>   A wise old age,
> the honours awarded for lasting,
> are not for a saviour. He had
> to be killed: salvation acquired
> by an increased guilt. The tree,
> with its roots in the mind's dark,
> was divinely planted, the original fork
> in existence. There is no meaning in life,
> unless men can be found to reject
> love. God needs his martyrdom.
> The mild eyes stare from the Cross
> in perverse triumph. What does he care
> that the people's offerings are so small?

A flawed creation; a flawed salvation? The two are linked: 'The tree, / with its roots in the mind's dark, / was divinely planted.' So, Jesus and the Cross again, as a constant: and this poem as far from the sadness, piety and immense tragic meditation of thousands of Good Friday sermons as 'Rough' was from the feast of the Nativity and joyous welcome to God-made-man at Christmas.

The tone seems to signal something; but what? If we take the poem at face value, I suppose there are two kinds of men who might accept it as a near total and final statement about reality – just as there is one kind of man who might so accept 'Rough'. Such men would normally be simple in their deepest responses to life and possibly fanatical – doubtless, far less complex than such real-life men as Schopenhauer, Hardy and Conrad. I suppose that in 'Amen' a total sceptic might find room to say 'yes': someone determined, let us say, to find in the Christian witness such a mixture of contradiction and horror or both that he could lacerate believers (and more secretly perhaps himself) with a QED demonstration of its impossibility, or its evil. (I am tempted to wonder what poet or sceptic could write a more effective anti-Christian poem, if he wanted to). Or, if 'Amen' is not a deliberate mockery of the whole story (and to read it aloud is to experience the difficulty of keeping the *tone* appropriate to such an interpretation – though a certain bitter anger, if not a hint of perverse satisfaction, seems equally difficult to keep out of the reading voice), then might it not be seen, rather, as the actual faith of a Calvinist or Jansenist – the perfection of the theology of divine predestination and total depravity, which manages to co-exist somehow for some 'Christians' with a belief in God as Love rather than as a monstrosity, and which manages somehow to worship God, not entirely through fear? It might be possible to interpret the whole of history as a film made by God before time started, with predestination to damnation as much a feature for some men in the divine drama, as it is for the 'villains' of an unsubtle human melodrama. The Judas of this poem might be recognised as authentic, and not pitied, by some calling themselves Christian; perhaps the terrible insight about the 'meaning of life' would also give gloomy satisfaction to some, and not appal? Even so, I suppose that even Calvinist readers might be thrown from their assent by the end of the poem. If they get that far, will they further accept Jesus as made in *their* image ('mild', 'perverse'), and will they accept the final stroke, that even the word's neglect may please Christ, since it leaves all the more of the suffering to him?

The poem cannot possibly (I would assert; but how do I set about demonstrating?) be anything of these kinds; so what is it? Another trial exploration, I suggest, on the very edges and outer boundaries of faith. 'It was all arranged': there is, in fact, that 'side' to the gospel; and, given that, perhaps the story cannot help coming out like this, if warped one way? Classic Christian theology had had to distinguish between God's 'foreknowledge' and 'predestination', between his power to bring good out of evil through the Cross, and his unconditional gift of free-will to the creature made in his own image; between a man tortured to death in Jerusalem in comparatively recent history and a God of infinite love who is to be apprehended in the same image. Perhaps R. S. Thomas is reminding us that theology does not remove the mystery; or perhaps he is reminding others that the mystery cannot, after all, be exhausted in *this* mode, though on the surface 'Amen' may seem simple and obvious. 'What else / could he do?' The question appears rhetorical, but in fact it simply hangs there – like the poem, which is an extension of it. The paradox of 'salvation acquired / by an increased guilt' pushes relentlessly towards the yet more excruciating paradox: 'There is no meaning in life / unless men can be found to reject / love'.

I am not sure that Thomas does not offer this poem as a temptation to the fashionable reviewers who still ignore his work, but might swallow this? It sounds profound, it sounds true; in fact, no doubt it is profound and true. But Christian prayer has trodden in anguish through such mysteries. Does the poet whose destiny is to 'kneel on' (see 'Moon in Lleyn') endorse such views, on his knees in the empty church? The destiny of priest and poet are inseparable, and no doubt he is forcing us to see the shocking implications in Christianity, partly because without these, we might not take it seriously? I think perhaps he shows that the shocking implications are the starting place for faith and devotion – the only starting-place, because a divide; on one side of which stand, perhaps, the respectable churchgoers (in church when fashionable, otherwise not so), along with the establishment as we know it; and on the other side of which are all of humanity's victims, all of its Christs? And between the two, at the dead centre, are the doubtful and tormented; wondering whether there is, in this strange religion, something that can only be mocked, only be shuddered at; or, rather, whether there is, in the Cross, a dark key, which happens to fit the dark mystery and exposure of human experience?

'Amen' seems to me a poem poised at cross-roads. Either you do not come to it, preferring a view of life which bypasses the territory; or you go past it, to join those who kneel in prayer. But you cannot stop here: not unless you think the poem merely a smart joke (updated Shaw in verse, perhaps); or unless you feel that it is in fact the end: the way things irrevocably are.

But either of these views seems untrue to the poem, if one looks at it as it nakedly is. The prophets may have 'foretold', but they had no understanding of their message; they were as much in the dark as Caiaphas himself. And, of course, Judas did *not* have to betray Christ; the sour kiss might have come from any of the other twelve. Christ did not have to accept his destiny – just as he did not accept as it stood much that was 'written' in the Old Testament. And, naturally, the eyes were not 'mild' on the Cross, they could only be tortured; mild eyes belong to the parody crucifixes in

comfortable, uncaring churches. The word 'perverse triumph' are
mere shorthand for Good Friday meditation, which must bypass
such words if salvation is at all to be reached. I would suggest that
'Amen', along with all these poems, should be read as an artefact;
and the 'meaning' searched in, and through, the volume as a whole.

> After Christ, what? The molecules
> Are without redemption. . . .   ('Pre-Cambrian')

H'm was a volume chiefly bitter in tone; *Laboratories of the Spirit*
charted new, and growing philosophical, directions. Both pion-
eered strange dialogues of God with himself, which become one
of the features of *Frequencies* (1978). This latest volume abounds in
'anthropomorphisms of the fancy' (a phrase taken from it), yet
'fancy' is surely chosen with tongue-in-cheek. The vision of a deity
more akin to Zeus than to Jehovah or Christ grows, even in poems
when the Christian scriptures are invoked. As in the previous
volumes, we encounter a God who may shrink from his creation,
fearing it; or one who laughs demonically at the sufferings he chooses
to cause. Flawed creation, flawed redemption, flawed religious
traditions: and the suffering people afflicted further – with germs,
fire or poverty – for the lot he has caused them to bear. . . .
    . . . The poet of *Frequencies* exists between 'faith and doubt' (his
own placing), needing now 'a faith to enable me to out-stare / the
grinning inmates of its asylum, / the failed experiments God put
away'. Yet his question – 'Why, then, do I kneel still / striking my
prayers on a stone / heart?' – is far from rhetorical, invoking anguish,
which has belonged with faith, throughout history, as well as with
doubt.
    The dialectic, still resisting synthesis, becomes in this later phase
as teasing as religion, itself. Though Thomas's earlier ambivalences
yield to new ones, in appearance more sombre, we can never say
'here we have him', any more than the poet can say this of God the
Spirit – or even of himself:

> All my life I tried to believe
> in the importance of what Thomas
> should say now, do next. . . .

Ironically, the poem which these words open ('In Context') discusses
his former belief that he and 'destiny' were together working on
some plan, however mysterious – destiny working on 'a big / loom',

> I with a small needle,
>
>   drawing the thread
>   through my mind, colouring it
>   with my own thought.

That belief is now swept away – in this poem, at least – with verbal precision that denies any appeal:

>   Impossible dreamer!
>   All those years the demolition
>   of the identity proceeded.
>   Fast as the cells constituted
>   themselves, they were replaced. It was not
>   I who lived, but life rather
>   that lived me. There was no developing
>   structure. There were only the changes
>   in the metabolism of a body
>   greater than mine, and the dismantling
>   by the self of a self it
>   could not reassemble.

What we have here is no solipsism of the feelings, however. Repeatedly in these later poems, R. S. Thomas strives to renounce 'the heart' for 'the mind'. The ambiguous balance he has always kept between the two, and the occasional swing from one to the other in quest of the least unreliable oracle, is a further link with Yeats. In *Frequencies* we are assured that the mind, too, has its solipsisms, even if – on the surface, at least – it is just now in the ascendant:

>   Well, I said, better to wait
>   for him on some peninsula
>   of the spirit. Surely for one
>   with patience he will happen by
>   once in a while. It was the heart
>   spoke. The mind, sceptical as always
>   of the anthropomorphisms
>   of the fancy, knew he must be put together
>   like a poem or a composition
>   in music, that what he conforms to
>   is art. A promontory is a bare
>   place; no God leans down
>   out of the air to take the hand
>   extended to him. The generations have
>   watched there
>   in vain.   ('Emerging')

Thomas's 'mind' signifies no classicism or neo-classicism, reaching

for universals, but the mediating of those dissolving insights of
Hume, Kierkegaard, Eddington which our new science confirm.
Maybe the mathematician is our hope, with his habit of using the
impossible? Yet Thomas's God remains on guard, against all
assaults. In 'The Gap', the first poem in *Frequencies*, God wakes, as
if from sleep, but 'the nightmare did not recede'. He is haunted by
the fear that man's language, a new Babel reaching insidiously
upwards towards him, may one day jump the narrowing gap, and
destroy his peace. But:

> He leaned
> over and looked in the dictionary
> they used. There was the blank still
> by his name of the same
> order as the territory
> between them, the verbal hunger
> for the thing in itself.

So God's decree for the gap 'No, no, no / wider than that!' is fulfilled
still, leaving him safe in the eternal silence which equally is his
repose, and man's unquenchable torment. Note the word 'they' at
the start of l. 3 above, with its hint of rooted distaste as well as
resolute distancing. What can this be, if not a slap in the face for
incarnational hope? Far from the 'Word' coming down, made flesh
to reveal God's glory, we find men's own words monitored and
blocked in their persistent upward assault upon God's inscrutable
ways. On our side, the unending pain, love, bereavement, sacrifice,
longing for knowledge and comfort; on God's side, the unending
mockery of silence (and fear).

When the poet speculates, he knows that the material world is as
strange as the spiritual, and as little likely to satisfy that ache for
understanding which is part of our doom:

> I think he sits at that strange table
> of Eddington's, that is not a table
> at all, but nodes and molecules
> pushing against molecules
> and nodes; and he writes there
> in invisible handwriting the instructions
> the genes follow.

In this poem ('At It'), the poet says that, if he could, he would
storm at the god 'as Job stormed, with the eloquence / of the abused
heart'. But there will be no judgement, by man at least, in man's
language: there will be no judgement at all, only

> The verdict
> of his calculations, that abstruse
> geometry that proceeds eternally
> in the silence beyond right and wrong

In the same vein, 'Play' underlines the folly of any hope that God's mind will meet man's in any perceptible commerce . . . . The almost throwaway words . . . 'As though one can sit at table / with God!' glance back at the upper room, and maybe the poet priest's lifetime of Eucharists; yet are 'the pawns' really less than other pieces (were they entirely so, even in Prytherch days?). This image of play occurs again in 'The Game', which identifies God now with a shadow-show: 'It is the play of a being / who is not serious in / his conclusions.' This poem (one of the most characteristic) proceeds to consider further riddles that defeat human intellect as 'we are forced / into the game, reluctant / contestants', and ends with a more humanly pessimistic conclusion:

> But the rewards
> Are there even so, and history
> festers with the numbers of the recipients
> of them, the handsome, the fortunate,
> the well-fed; those who cheated this
> being when he was not looking.

All those quotations come from the dark side of *Frequencies*, but the pattern always has two sides (maybe the enigmatic back of a tapestry will show, to practised eyes, more than the face?). Even 'Emerging', a poem whose opening, already quoted here, offers little positive, moves to a conclusion where other perspectives, in counterpoint, come into sight:

> We are beginning to see
> now it is matter is the scaffolding
> of spirit; that the poem emerges
> from morphemes and phonemes; that
> as form in sculpture is the prisoner
> of the hard rock, so in everyday life
> it is the plain facts and natural happenings
> that conceal God and reveal him to us
> little by little under the mind's tooling.

And, looking again through *Frequencies*, we notice that, if the assertions of God's absence seem as lucid as Wallace Stevens's, though far angrier, there is a parallel possibility (perhaps the anger is always its tribute?) of converse truths. Possibly 'The Porch' is one of the strongest images, in the strand I have so far explored; and I want to quote it, not simply as yet one further example of Thomas's extreme beauty and economy, but for the multivalence unobtrusively built in. The thrust of the apparent meaning needs little exposition; but note that the first line at least implies *human* interest; that 'driven' does not explain itself and is not necessarily inwardly motivated; that the first line of the second half does not say there *was* no prayer, or anything like it; and that 'kept his place / there for an hour' has more of dignity than absurdism, in this place 'neither outside nor in':

> Do you want to know his name?
> It is forgotten. Would you learn
> what he was like? He was like
> anyone else, a man with ears
> and eyes. Be it sufficient
> that in a church porch on an evening
> in winter, the moon rising, the frost
> sharp, he was driven
> to his knees and for no reason
> he knew. The cold came at him;
> his breath was carved angularly
> as the tombstones; an owl screamed.
>
> He had no power to pray.
> His back turned on the interior
> he looked out on a universe
> that was without knowledge
> of him and kept his place
> there for an hour on that lean
> threshold, neither outside nor in.

Does this brief poem turn inside-out, like certain others, conforming to the effect of optical illusion remarked on before? If we toy with the possibility that 'A universe / that was without knowledge / of him' is the man's consciousness, not the universe's (as why should we not?), then maybe the 'forgotten' name is God's name for us all; and God might still be betrayed by men, not the other way round. So, against the bitter statements in 'Bravo!', 'Fishing', 'Pre-Cambrian' and maybe the majority of these poems, we can place hints more positive in kind. In 'Adjustments', there is the hope that God might yet be found obliquely, despite all the problems:

> We never catch
> Him at work, but can only say,
> coming suddenly upon an amendment,
> that here he has been.

. . . In 'Epiphany' we are faced with the possibility that Christ, 'Far / off from his cross in the wrong season' still 'sits at table / with us' ('Play' notwithstanding) – even though the royal presents are gone, and it is 'the fool's cap of our paper money' that we force him to wear. 'The White Tiger' . . . envisages that God may be as much our victim, after all, as other wild animals, forced into smallness, emptiness, perhaps even silence, by man's grossest affronts. The words 'you can imagine' keep open, as always, ambiguity: but their inclusion allows every indictment of God to be turned back upon man – and very particularly here, upon the man in the pew:

> you can imagine that
> God breathes within the confines
> of our definitions of him, agonising
> over immensities that will not return

With this in mind, it is interesting to note that two or three times in *Frequencies* Thomas returns to old ground, always with some suggestion of hubris in his own former self. 'Gone?' is positively the last Prytherch poem: but, whereas earlier the contrasts were chiefly between the peasant's coarseness and the poet priest's 'refinement', along with complex uncertainties about which was humanly finer, and more fitted or likely to endure, this poem is on another track. Now Wales has been captured by the machine, the tractor, the global village of television and the universal idiocy of greed – so Prytherch, at last a memory for elegy, becomes definitive symbol of a better, if bleaker, lost world . . . . The final poem in the collection, 'Pilgrimages', does something to heal, if not to resolve, much that has gone before it, in its images. The poet prays on still, . . . as he always has done:

> Was the pilgrimage
> I made to come to my own
> self, to learn that in times
> like these and for one like me
> God will never be plain and
> out there, but dark rather and
> inexplicable, as though he were in here?   . . .

SOURCE: excerpted from section 3, 'The Poetry of R. S. Thomas: What

Resource?', in *Yeats, Eliot and R. S. Thomas: Riding the Echo* (London and Basingstoke, 1981), pp. 285–8, 302–3, 303–5, 306–8, 308–12, 312–13, 314–18, 319–22, 322–4, 325, 326.

SELECT BIBLIOGRAPHY

A great body of work now exists, on these poets, much of it excellent; to mention individual books and articles – even among those which I had reluctantly to exclude for reasons of space – would be invidious. Students would be well advised to consult the full book, or context, of the extracts which are included here: especially, since a number of critics have written on contemporary poetry at length, and have excellent chapters on two or all of these poets, only one of which I could choose. My main concern has been to choose writing which reaches a perceptible standard of critical insight, and then to attempt to cover the main debates, and positive approaches, to Thom Gunn, Ted Hughes and R. S. Thomas until 1982. Further, I have attempted to include material on all their major volumes – the material upon which their reputation was built, and is firmly established; and to chart – by arranging the essays in order of their chronological concern, where possible – the general development of their art and vision.

As I have stressed in my Introduction, they are all poets engaged on a lifetime quest, in matters of religion, psychology and consciousness which affect their own, and our, humanity. In addition, they are masters of their craft, and poets of vision; possibly, our nearest approach in the poetry written in English in the second half of this century, to prophets. I trust that students studying their work for examination purposes will find sufficient material and guidance here to help them; and that they will come to feel the quality of greatness in the work itself. For those already committed to these poets, the fullest possible critical exploration alone will satisfy.

Fortunately, there are excellent complete bibliographies of all three, in the period covered here; so I will list these first:

THOM GUNN: *A Bibliography 1940–1978*: compiled by Jack W. C. Hagstrom and George Bixby, with an Introductory Biographical Essay by Thom Gunn, Bertram Rota, London, 1979.

TED HUGHES: *A Bibliography 1946–1980*: by Keith Sagar and Stephen Tabar, Mansell Publishing Limited, 1983.

R. S. THOMAS: *A Bibliography 1946–1980*: included in her doctoral thesis by Sarah Anstey, for the University of Wales; and to be published, in an expanded form.

These three poets have given various interviews, in Britain, the USA and elsewhere, and all these are worth tracking down. The brief extracts included in this volume can be followed up; fuller research will start with the bibliographies mentioned above.

Three collections by the poets themselves – selected prose from Gunn and Thomas, and a critical book by Hughes, are invaluable. These are:

THOM GUNN: *The Occasions of Poetry: Essays in Criticism and Autobiography*, Clive Wilmer (ed.), Faber & Faber, 1982.

TED HUGHES: *Poetry In The Making*, Faber & Faber, 1967.

R. S. THOMAS: *Selected Prose*, Dandra Anstey (ed.), Poetry Wales Press, 1983. (N.B. includes further bibliographical details of Thomas's prose, and of Anstey's bibliographical research, listed above.)

One more recent book on R. S. Thomas, by a philosopher, might be of use – since it approaches the poet from an unusual perspective. This is:

R. S. THOMAS: *Poet of the Hidden God* (Meaning and Meditation in the poetry) by D. Z. Phillips, Professor of Philosophy, University College of Swansea (Macmillan, 1986).

Unfortunately, there is as yet *no* interim *Collected Works* of these three poets available, as at the time of this publication. For students, this is a great inconvenience. When the volumes are published (one hopes, not for some while yet, if they are to be posthumous) they will be among the outstanding works of the century, and major landmarks in the annals of English poetry. This lack may be the responsibility of their publishers – along with the current market problems for any outstanding art, and (in the case of R. S. Thomas) the complex copyright problems caused by his earlier publisher being now in other hands. I have a suspicion that Thom Gunn and R. S. Thomas (certainly), and Ted Hughes (probably) are not anxious to precipitate interim Collections – of the kind which Eliot, Auden, and many lesser modern poets enjoyed in their lifetimes – and that their future editors might have a major, scholarly task to perform, tracking down occasional poems which they have not since reprinted.

Meanwhile, the volumes published by their major publishers are readily available in libraries and bookshops – though there are periods when some are out of print. Gunn and Hughes have been published by Faber & Faber; R. S. Thomas first by Rupert Hart-Davis, latterly by Macmillan, London. In addition, there are early, and private, and limited editions – often of early work – which are collectors' items. These contain some extremely fine poems, which can scarcely be said to be in the public domain.

For the time being, most students have to depend on Selections – authorised by the poets themselves. These include some, but by no means all, of the poems discussed in this Casebook. In my own judgment, they exclude more than half of the very best work, and are wholly insufficient for the needs even of sixth-form students; for the casual reader, they are better than nothing.

THOM GUNN: *Selected Poems 1950–1975*, Faber & Faber, 1979 (and subsequent reprints). Includes poems from *Fighting Terms*, *The Sense of Movement*, *My Sad Captains*, *Touch*, *Moly*, and *Jack Straw's Castle*.

TED HUGHES: *Selected Poems 1957–1981*, Faber & Faber, 1982 (and subsequent reprints). Includes poems from *The Hawk in the Rain*, *Lupercal*, *Wodwo*, *Crow*, *Cave Birds*, *Season-Songs*, *Under the North Star*, *Gaudete*, *Remains of Elmet*, *Moortown*.

These are paperback volumes. R. S. Thomas has two *Selections*, one of early, one of later poems: both published in hardback only, and by different publishing houses. They are:

R. S. THOMAS: *Selected Poems 1946–1968*, St. Martin's Press, N.Y., 1974 (and subsequent reprints). Includes poems from *Song At The Year's Turning*, *Poetry for Supper*, *Tares*, *The Bread of Truth*, *Pietà* and *Not That He Brought Flowers*.

R. S. THOMAS: *Later Poems 1972–1982*, Macmillan, London, 1983 (and subsequent reprints). Includes poems from *H'm*, *Young and Old*, *What Is A Welshman?*, *Laboratories of the Spirit*, *The Way of It*, *Frequencies*, *Between Here And Now* – along with a section called *New Poems*, not elsewhere collected.

NOTES ON CONTRIBUTORS

JOAN F. ADKINS: Professor of English in Marshall University, Huntington, West Virginia.

CALVIN BEDIENT: Professor of English in the University of California at Los Angeles.

MERLE E. BROWN: Professor of English in the University of Iowa, and editor of the *Iowa Review*.

ANTONY CONRAN: poet and critic, he has for many years been closely associated with the teaching of literature in the University College of North Wales at Bangor.

MARTIN DODSWORTH: critic and reviewer, he lectures in English at Royal Holloway College, in the University of London, and is also closely associated with teaching at Birkbeck College.

A. E. DYSON: general editor of the Casebook series, he taught for twenty years in the School of English and American Studies, University of East Anglia, where he is now Honorary Fellow.

TERRY EAGLETON: well-known as a critic in the Marxist tradition, he is Fellow of Wadham College, Oxford, and university lecturer in English.

EKBERT FAAS: Professor of English in York University, Ontario; well known critic, especially prominent in Ted Hughes studies.

COLIN FALCK: poet and editor, he has since 1965 lectured in Humanities at Chelsea College in the University of London; he was associate editor of the *Review*, and now contributes regularly to the *New Review* and other journals.

G. S. FRASER (1915–80): poet and critic, he was for many years a distinguished member of the English Department in the University of Leicester; a former literary editor of the *New Statesman*, he was one of the best-known and influential literary journalists.

TERRY GIFFORD: Senior Lecturer in Bretton Hall College of Higher Education, Wakefield. Recent books include *Teaching A Level English* (with John Brown) Routledge, 1989. Organizes annual festival of *Mountaineering Literature*.

I. R. F. GORDON: lecturer in English in the Cambridgeshire College of Arts and Technology.

STUART HIRSCHBERG: academic and critic, now living in New Jersey.

JOHN MOLE: poet and critic, and formerly teaching English in schools in Hertfordshire, he is now editor at the Mandeville Press, Hitchin and contributor to *New Poetry*, *New Review* and other literary periodicals.

BRIAN MORRIS: formerly Professor of English in the University of Sheffield, he is now Principal of St David's University College at Lampeter; a well-known editor and critic of 17th century poets and dramatists, he is General Editor of the 'New Mermaid' series of drama texts.

KEVIN NICHOLS: The Rt. Rev. Monseigneur Kevin Nichols, a Roman theologian who contributed this piece on R. S. Thomas to *Clergy Review*.

NEIL ROBERTS: Senior Lecturer in English, University of Sheffield. Author of *George Eliot: her beliefs and her art* (1975); with a special interest in contemporary poetry.

M. L. ROSENTHAL: critic and poet, and for many years Professor of English in New York University and Poetry Editor of *Present Tense*; his many publications on British and American literature include *Poetry and the Common Life* (1974) and *Sailing into the Unknown: Yeats, Pound and Eliot* (1978).

KEITH SAGAR: a well-known critic, with particular interest in D. H. Lawrence and Ted Hughes, he is Senior Staff Tutor in Literature of the Extra-Mural Department in the University of Manchester.

PATRICK SWINDEN: Senior Lecturer in English, University of Manchester, his publications include studies on the Novel and on Shakespearean Comedy, and the Casebooks on Shelley and on George Eliot's *Middlemarch*.

GEOFFREY THURLEY: Lecturer in Literature in the University of Essex, having previously taught in the University of Adelaide; his publications include *The Ironic Harvest* and *The American Moment: American Poetry in the Mid-Century*.

CLIVE WILMER: Freelance writer, lecturer and broadcaster. A poet himself: edited Gunn's *Occasions of Poetry*, and a recent Festschrift 'Thom Gunn at 60' in *P. N. Review*.

YVOR WINTERS (1900–68): for many years Professor of English in Stanford University, California. One of the best known and most astringent of American critics and poets, he was friend and mentor to Thom Gunn, who has called one of his poems 'Yvor Winters'.

ACKNOWLEDGEMENTS

The editors and publisher wish to thank the following who have kindly given permission for the use of copyright material: Joan F. Adkins, article, 'R. S. Thomas and "A Little Point"', *The Little Review*, vol. 6 (1980), by permission of *The Little Review*; Calvin Bedient, extracts from *Eight Contemporary Poets* (1974), by permission of Oxford University Press; Merle E. Brown, extracts from 'A Critical Performance of Thom Gunn's "Misanthropos"', *The Iona Review*, 4 (1973), by permission of *The Iona Review*; Anthony Conran, extracts from 'R. S. Thomas as a Mystical Poet', *Poetry Wales*, vol. 14, no. 4 (Spring 1979), by permission of Poetry Wales Press Ltd.; Martin Dodsworth, extracts from 'Thom Gunn: Poetry as Action and Submission' from *The Survival of Poetry* (1970), by permission of Faber & Faber; A. E. Dyson, extracts from *Yeats, Eliot and R. S. Thomas* (1981), by permission of Macmillan; and from 'Ted Hughes: "Hawk in the Rain"', *Critical Quarterly*, vol. I, no. 3 (1959) by permission of the author; Terry Eagleton, extracts from 'Myth and History in Recent Poetry' in Michael Schmidt and Grevel Lindop, (eds), *British Poetry Since 1960* (1974), Carcanet, by permission of the author; Ekbert Faas, extract from *Ted Hughes: An Unaccommodated Universe* (1980), by permission of Black Sparrow Press; Colin Falck, extracts from 'Uncertain Violence', *New Review*, Nov. (1976) by permission of the author; G. S. Thomas, extracts from 'On the Move', *Critical Quarterly*, vol. 3, no. 4 (1961), by permission of Eileen Fraser; Terry Gifford and Neil Roberts, extracts from *Ted Hughes: A Critical Study* (1981), by permission of Faber & Faber; I. R. F. Gordon, extract from '"The Adult Geometry of the Mind": The Recent Poetry of R. S. Thomas', *The Little Review*, vol. 6 (1980), by permission of *The Little Review*; Thom Gunn, extract from *The Occasions of Poetry: Essays in Criticism and Autobiography* (1982), by permission of Faber & Faber; extracts from poems from *Fighting Terms, My Sad Captains, The Sense of Movement, Touch* and *Passages of Joy*, by permission of Faber and Faber; Stuart Hirchberg, 'Conclusion' from *Myth in the Poetry of Ted Hughes: A Guide to the Poems* (1981), by permission of Wolfhound Press; Ted Hughes, for unpublished material on *Crow*, by permission of the author; extracts from poems in *The Hawk in the Rain, Lupercal, Crow, Cave Birds* and *Moortown*, by permission of Faber & Faber; Brian Morris, extracts from 'Mr Thomas's Present Concerns', *Poetry Wales*, vol. 14, no. 4 (Spring 1979), by permission of Poetry Wales Press Ltd.; John Mole, extracts from 'On the Recent Poetry of R. S. Thomas', *New Poetry*, no. 43 (1978), by permission of *New Poetry*; Kevin Nichols, extract from 'Untenanted Cross: The Poetry of R. S. Thomas', *The Clergy Review*, vol. 63 (1978), by permission of *The Clergy Review*; M. L. Rosenthal, extracts from *The New Poets* (1967), Oxford University Press, Inc. Copyright © 1967 by M. L. Rosenthal, by permission of the author; Keith Sagar, extracts from *The Art of Ted Hughes* (1975), by permission of Cambridge University Press; Patrick Swinden, extracts from

ACKNOWLEDGEMENTS   289

'Thom Gunn's Castle', *Critical Quarterly*, vol. 19, no. 3 (Autumn 1977), by
permission of the author; R. S. Thomas, extracts from Sandra Anstey, (ed.),
R. S. Thomas: Selected Prose, (1983), Poetry Wales Press Ltd., by permission
of the author; extracts from poems in *Laboratories of the Spirit*, *Frequencies*,
Between Here and Now and *H'm* Macmillan, and *Song at the Years Turning*,
Selected Poems 1946–68 and *Pietà*, Collins, by permission of the author;
Geoffrey Thurley, extracts from *The Ironic Harvest: English Poetry in the
Twentieth Century* (1974), by permission of Edward Arnold; Clive Wilmer,
extracts from 'Definition and Flow: A Personal Reading of Thom Gunn',
PN Review, vol. 5, no. 3 (1978), by permission of the author; Ivor Winters,
extracts from 'Early Gunn' in *Forms of Discovery* (1967), by permission of
Janet Lewes Winters.

Every effort has been made to trace all the copyright holders but if any
have been inadvertently overlooked the publishers will be pleased to make
the necessary arrangement at the first opportunity.

INDEX

Themes such as 'Art', 'Consciousness', 'Creativity', 'Culture', 'Influence', 'Intention', 'Modern', 'Natural', 'Psychological', 'Religious', 'Romantic', 'Sexual', 'Symbolic' – the entire human and literary spectrum, in short – occur throughout, and are not listed.

This index includes significant references to other important, but less pervasive themes (entries in italics); and to persons mentioned (entries in capitals).

To save space, particular poems and works of art will be found subsumed under the entry for their creators.

For Thom Gunn, Ted Hughes and R. S. Thomas, however, poems mentioned more than once or discussed in detail are listed in alphabetical order, under the entry for the poet.